COVER-UP:

The Army's
Secret Investigation
of the Massacre
at My Lai 4

COVER-UP

Seymour M. Hersh

Random House 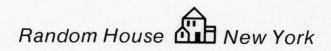 *New York*

Library of Congress Cataloging in Publication Data

Hersh, Seymour M.
Cover-up.

Bibliography: p.
1. My lai (4), Vietnam—Massacre, 1968. 2. Vietnamese Conflict, 1961–   —Atrocities. I. Title.
DS557.A67H467   959.7'04342   79–37048
ISBN 0–394–47460–0

A portion of this book appeared
originally in *The New Yorker*.

Manufactured in the United States of America
by The Colonial Press Inc., Clinton, Mass.

9 8 7 6 5 4 3 2

First Edition

For
Elizabeth,
Matthew
and
Melissa

Contents

Preface

*T*his book is based primarily on the official transcripts and documents of an extended military investigation into the cover-up of My Lai 4. I also added additional information from a variety of other sources and made judgments about some critical points of dispute based on my own personal investigations.

Although it would be impossible not to draw some conclusions—good or bad—about the individuals described herein who were connected with the My Lai 4 investigations, the real focus of this book is elsewhere: in the Army as an institution, which, I believe, made so much of My Lai 4 inevitable.

Most of the officers and enlisted men mentioned are identified by their rank and position at the time of My Lai 4 or the subsequent investigations of it. Since then, of course, many have received promotions or left the service.

I wish to thank Philip M. Stern and James Boyd of the Fund for Investigative Journalism for their support of my initial research into the tragedy. *The New Yorker* magazine also generously aided my work, and its editor, William Shawn, was especially generous in his understanding, from the beginning, of my purpose in writing this book. Robert Loomis, my editor at Random House, provided his usual invaluable guidance and advice; as did Bertha Krantz, also of Random House. I received professional help and cooperation from the officers assigned to the information offices at the Department of Defense and the Army.

Finally, I am greatly indebted to those officers and civilians who aided me anonymously, in the hope that this book would help force some desperately needed changes.

Seymour M. Hersh
Washington, D.C.

December 17, 1971

COVER-UP:

The Army's Secret Investigation of the Massacre at My Lai 4

Three Hundred Forty-Seven

Early on March 16, 1968, a company of Americal
Division soldiers was dropped in by helicopter for
an assault against a hamlet known as My Lai 4, located in the bitterly contested province of Quang
Ngai, on the northeastern coast of South Vietnam.
The one hundred GIs and officers stormed the
hamlet in military-textbook style, advancing by
platoons; the men expected to engage the 48th Viet
Cong Battalion there, one of the enemy's most successful units, but instead, found women, children,
and old men—many of them still cooking their
breakfast rice over outdoor fires. During the next
few hours the civilians were ruthlessly murdered.
Many were rounded up in small groups and shot;
others were flung into a drainage ditch at one edge
of the hamlet and shot; and many more were shot
at random in and about their homes. Some of the
younger women and girls were raped, and then
murdered. After the shootings the GIs systemati-

cally burned each home, destroyed livestock and food, and fouled the area's drinking supplies.

None of this was officially told by the company—Charlie Company—to its task force headquarters; instead, a claim that 128 Viet Cong were killed and three weapons were captured eventually emerged and worked its way up to the highest American headquarters in Saigon, where it was released to the world's press as a significant victory.

The GIs kept what they had done largely to themselves, but there were other witnesses to the atrocity. The first investigations which followed erroneously concluded that twenty civilians had inadvertently been killed by artillery and heavy crossfire between American and Viet Cong units during the battle. The investigation involved all the immediate elements of the chain of command: the company was attached to Task Force Barker, which in turn reported to the 11th Light Infantry Brigade, which was one of three such units making up the Americal Division.

Task Force Barker's victory remained just another statistic until April, 1969, when an ex-GI named Ronald L. Ridenhour wrote letters to the Pentagon, the White House, other government offices, and twenty-four Congressmen describing the murders at My Lai 4. Ridenhour had not participated in the attack on the hamlet but he had discussed the operation with a few of the GIs who did. Within four months many details of the atrocity had been uncovered by Army investigators, and in September, 1969, a young lieutenant named William L. Calley, Jr., was charged with the murder of 109 Vietnamese civilians. No significant facts about the Calley investigation were made public at the time; instead, the Army released an inaccurate and misleading statement that gave no hint of the number of murders involved in the case. But the facts gradually did emerge, and in mid-November a series of newspaper stories was published partially revealing the extent of the massacre. Subsequent stories told enough about My Lai 4 to create a world-wide outcry. A few weeks after the first newspaper accounts, the Army announced that it had set up a panel to determine what had kept the initial investigations in the spring of 1968 from learning of the atrocity. The panel was officially called "The Department of the Army Review of the Preliminary Investigations into the My Lai Incident," unofficially known as the Peers Inquiry, after its director, Lieutenant General William R. Peers. The three-star general, then fifty-six, had spent more than thirty months as a troop commander in Vietnam.

Peers and his team of assistants, which included two New York lawyers, quickly determined that they could not adequately explore the cover-up of the atrocity without finding out more about what had, in fact, happened on the day the troops were at My Lai 4. On December 2, 1969, the investigating team began interrogating officers and enlisted men of the units involved—Charlie Company, Task Force Barker, the 11th Brigade, and the American Division. Four hundred and one witnesses were interrogated—about fifty in South Vietnam, and the rest in a special operations room in the basement of the Pentagon before Peers himself and a panel of military officers and civilians that varied in size between three and eight men. The interrogations inevitably produced much self-serving testimony. To get at the truth, the Peers Panel recalled many witnesses for subsequent interviews and confronted them with conflicting testimony. Only six witnesses before the Panel refused to testify, although all legally could have remained silent; few career military men can appear to be hiding something before a three-star general.

By mid-March the Peers Panel had compiled enough evidence to recommend that charges be placed against fifteen officers; a high-level review subsequently concluded that fourteen of them should be charged, including Major General Samuel W. Koster, who was commanding general of the Americal Division at the time of My Lai 4. By 1970 Koster was superintendent of West Point, the military academy, and the filing of cover-up charges against him stunned the Army. One other general was charged, along with two colonels, two lieutenant colonels, four majors, two captains, and two first lieutenants.

Army officials told newsmen that the Peers Panel accumulated more than twenty thousand pages of testimony and five hundred documents during its fifteen weeks of operation. The resource material alone, it was said, included thirty-two books of direct testimony, six books of supplemental documents and affidavits, plus volumes of maps, charts, exhibits, and internal documents. It was carefully explained that none of this material could be released to the public, to avoid damaging pre-trial publicity, until the legal proceedings against the accused men were completed; a process, officials acknowledged, that might take years. In addition, it was explained that upon release, the materials would have to be carefully censored to ensure that no material damaging to America's foreign policies or national security was made available. In May, 1971, fourteen months after the initial report, officials were still quoted as saying that "It might be years" before the investigation was made public. By then, charges against thirteen of the fourteen initial defendants had been dismissed without a court-martial.

Early in the spring of 1971 I was provided with a complete set of more than thirty volumes of the testimony, documents, and other materials of the Peers Panel. What follows is based largely on those papers, although I supplemented them with documents from different sources, in-

cluding the Army's Criminal Investigation Division
(C.I.D.), which had the main responsibility for conducting
the initial investigations into both the My Lai 4 massacre
and its cover-up. I further interviewed scores of military
and civilian officials, including men who had been witnesses
before the Peers Panel, and some who should have been but
were not called to testify or refused to do so. I also discussed some of my findings with former members of the
Army who were directly connected with the Panel.

There is no question that a serious concern for the rights
of possible court-martial defendants does exist at all levels
of the Army, but a careful examination of the accumulated
testimony and documents makes equally clear the fact that
it is the Army itself that is most adversely affected by the
material. Many documents indicate that military officials
have deliberately withheld from the public important, but
embarrassing, factual information about My Lai 4. For
example, the Army has steadfastly refused to reveal how
many civilians were, in fact, killed by Charlie Company on
March 16, a decision that no longer has anything to do with
pre-trial publicity. Its spokesmen have told many newsmen
that the information is not available. Yet in February, 1970,
a census of civilian casualties in My Lai 4 was secretly un-
dertaken at the request of the Peers Panel by the Criminal
Investigation Division. After an analysis of existing data,
the C.I.D. concluded in a memorandum to General Peers
that Charlie Company had slain 347 Vietnamese men,
women, and children in My Lai 4 on March 16, 1968, a
total twice as great as had been publicly acknowledged. In
addition, the Peers Panel subsequently learned that Lieutenant Calley's first platoon, one of three which made the
attack upon My Lai 4, was responsible for ninety to one
hundred and thirty murders during the operation—roughly
one-third of the casualties. The second platoon was deter-

mined to have murdered as many as a hundred civilians, with the rest of the deaths attributed to the third platoon and the helicopter gunships.

Even more striking, however, than the detailed evidence of widespread murder and cover-up in connection with My Lai 4, was the revelation during the hearings that all of the Army's command and control and reporting systems were inadequate, at least in the Americal Division as of 1968. The officers at the top were shown to have little understanding of the problems and activities of men in the platoons and companies below. Atrocities could be committed almost at will throughout the operating area of the Americal Division, with no means for even detecting them at higher headquarters.

Thus, the Peers Panel discovered that the attack on My Lai 4 was not the only massacre by American troops in Quang Ngai Province that morning. Three infantry companies, the Army investigators learned, had been committed to the "Pinkville" operation by Task Force Barker headquarters. Alpha Company had moved into a blocking position above My Lai 4, where it theoretically would be able to trap the Viet Cong as they fled from the American assault. Bravo Company, the third unit in the task force, was ordered to attack a possible Viet Cong headquarters area at My Lai 1, about one and a half miles east of My Lai 4. Its men, too, were told to prepare for a major battle with an experienced Viet Cong unit. But there were no Viet Cong at My Lai 1.

2

The Other Massacre

*B*ravo Company was told about the planned assault on My Lai 1 at a briefing the night before. The tense men of Task Force Barker were called together on March 15 by their officers and told, as one GI recalled, "This is what you've been waiting for, search and destroy, and you got it." Moments earlier, Captain Earl R. Michles, the company commander, had carefully outlined the mission and its objective to his platoon leaders and sergeants. The key target was My Lai 1, a small, often-attacked hamlet that was considered to be the headquarters and hospital area of the 48th Viet Cong Battalion. Most of the Americans serving with the task force believed that the citizens in the target area—Quang Ngai Province—were either Viet Cong or Viet Cong sympathizers. Army maps showed that My Lai 1 and the neighboring hamlets of My Lai 2, My Lai 3, and My Lai 4, were part of the village of Son My, a heavily populated geographical area, embracing dozens of hamlets, that was known to the GIs as "Pinkville." The name derived from the fact that Son My's high population density caused it to appear in red on Army maps, but to the men who operated in the area, "Pinkville" meant Viet Cong guerrillas and booby traps. More than ninety percent of the Americal Division's combat injuries and deaths early in 1968 resulted from booby traps and land mines that were put in place by a frustrating and unseen enemy. Bravo Company would be helicopted into the area, engage the Viet Cong at My Lai 1, and then move to the south into other "Viet Cong" hamlets along the South China Sea. Precisely what information Michles gave his men is impossible to determine, but his briefing, as did a similar briefing by Captain Ernest L. Medina at another Task Force Barker fire base a few miles away, left the soldiers with the impression that everyone they would see on March 16 was a Viet Cong cadre or sympathizer.

Michles' radio operator, Lawrence L. Congleton of Evansville, Indiana, recalled that after the briefing, "There was a general conception that we were going to destroy everything." Donald R. Hooton of Jackson, Michigan, an infantryman, remembered that Michles "didn't say to level that village; he more or less told us that we'd have a real good fight." But Hooton said the message was clear: "We all knew what he meant." Lieutenant Kenneth W. Boatman was assigned to Bravo Company as a forward artillery observer; he would coordinate any artillery attacks the next day. "We were informed to go down there and clean the damn place out," Boatman told the Panel. "He said that we were going to take care of them, get rid of them . . . I think everybody was enthusiastic about going down there in that respect. We were going to get rid of it—clean the place out . . ."

Only a few of more than forty former B Company GIs interviewed by me or questioned by members of the Peers
Panel recalled hearing a specific order to kill civilians.*
Larry G. Holmes of Peru, Indiana, summed up many GIs'
recollections when he testified: ". . . We had three hamlets
that we had to search and destroy. They told us they . . .
had dropped leaflets and stuff and everybody was supposed
to be gone. Nobody was supposed to be there. If anybody is
there, shoot them." There were no specific instructions
given about civilians and prisoners, the men reported. "We
were to leave nothing standing because we were pretty sure
that this was a confirmed VC village," recalled Homer C.
Hall of Jonesboro, Georgia. Mario Fernandez of Miami,
Florida, when asked what instructions Michles gave them
for handling civilians, said, "I'm not sure, but I think they
said to kill them, you know? And that's what they did, but
I'm not sure about it." One ex-GI, Barry P. Marshall of
Rochester, New York, told the Panel of overhearing a conversation between Lieutenant Colonel Frank A. Barker, Jr.,
the commander of the task force, and Michles. "I don't
want to give the idea that Colonel Barker wanted us to kill
every blankety-blank person in there," Marshall said.
"They were just talking . . . Colonel Barker was just saying
that he wished that he could get in here and get rid of the
VC . . . I know Captain Michles' own personal feeling was
that he wanted to take every civilian out of there and move
them out of the area to a secure place, and then go in and
fight the VC. It's so hard when you've got all these people
milling around in there to really conduct an operation of
any significance."

Nine troop transport helicopters and two gunships from

---

* All of the quoted testimony, unless otherwise identified, was given to
the Peers Panel.

the 174th Aviation Company and the 71st Aviation Company, combat units attached to the Americal Division, flew from 11th Brigade headquarters at Duc Pho fifteen miles north and began ferrying the men of Charlie Company from their assembly point at Landing Zone Dotti, the task force headquarters, to their target area just outside My Lai 4. The helicopters completed that task by 7:47 in the morning, according to the official task force journal for that day, and then flew a few miles north to Bravo Company's landing zone to begin shuttling those men for the second stage of the assault. It's not clear why Charlie Company's assault took place first. Large numbers of Viet Cong were expected to be at both locations and, according to the official rationale for the mission, surprise was a key factor. As it was, the first elements of Bravo Company did not reach their target area until 8:15, and it took an additional twelve minutes for the full company to assemble. The men, of course, were apprehensive, and nothing at their landing zone near My Lai 1 soothed them. As they jumped off the aircraft, rifles at the ready, they heard gunfire in the distance.

The shots were coming from My Lai 4 one and a half miles to the west, where, by this time, Charlie Company was in the midst of massacre. A third platoon machine gunner, Ronald J. Esterling of Barbarton, Ohio, testified that "when we landed we had to take cover . . . because we thought we were getting shot at. We found out later, well, about fifteen minutes or so, it was Charlie Company from over in the other direction. Some of their bullets were coming in our direction unintentionally . . ." Although the sounds were frightening, there was no immediate threat to Bravo Company. The landing zone was "cold"; no enemy shots were fired at the GIs during the vulnerable moment as they deplaned from the helicopters. The men milled around a few moments, and then began to move out.

The first platoon, headed by Lieutenant Thomas K. Willingham of Allenhurst, New Jersey, marched a few hundred yards south. Its mission was to cross a narrow bridge to a small peninsula—really just a spit of land with the small hamlet of My Khe 4 on it—on the South China Sea. The second platoon, headed by First Lieutenant Roy B. Cochran, was to search My Lai 1 and destroy it. But My Lai 1 was screened by a thick hedge and heavily guarded by booby traps. Within minutes one of the mines hidden in the hedge line was tripped and the men of Bravo Company heard screams. Lieutenant Cochran was killed and four GIs seriously injured in the explosion. Helicopters were called in to evacuate the men; the second platoon was hastily reorganized with a sergeant in command and ordered to continue its mission. Another booby trap was tripped; once more there were screams and smoke. This time three second platoon GIs were injured and the unit was in disarray. The surviving GIs insisted they were not going to continue the mission, and said as much to Captain Michles. Colonel Barker flew in himself to see to the evacuation of the wounded, and then made an amazing decision: rather than call on the first or third platoon to complete the mission, he simply canceled Bravo Company's order to search and destroy My Lai 1. "He told them not even [to] try to go in there," Larry Congleton recalled. "Just sort of forget about that part of the operation." The order was relayed to Captain Michles via radio; Barker did not get off his helicopter. The second platoon, relieved at not having to enter My Lai 1, began a rather aimless and half-hearted movement through huts and hamlets to the south, across the water from My Khe 4 and the first platoon.

The booby traps, perhaps, served as a literal trigger for the by now thoroughly frightened men of the first platoon. "When Cochran got killed, I sort of giggled," Terry Reid of

Milwaukee, Wisconsin, recalled, "but other guys started to cry. This was just before we crossed a bridge [to My Khe 4]. Then the word came that we're going to go down and wipe them out."

My Khe 4 was a scraggly, much-harassed collection of straw and mud houses. Its population was perhaps a hundred women, children, and old men. After carefully crossing the bridge, some of the GIs could see the unsuspecting villagers through the heavy brush and trees. "They might have been doing some washing or something, just their household chores," one GI recalled. Willingham, according to many witnesses, ordered two machine gunners in his platoon to set up their weapons outside the hamlet. And then, inexplicably, they began to systematically spray bullets into My Khe, shooting at the people and their homes.

A few GIs later testified that a hand grenade had been thrown at them; others said that some sniper shots had been fired. But no one was shot and none of the GIs said they ever actually saw the grenade; they only "heard about it." Homer Hall tried to explain to the Peers Panel why it happened: "They said one [grenade] was thrown. That was good enough . . . The movements that were going on in the village, we just perceived that it was a VC village. There seemed to be different types of tracks. Like I said, when you're over there awhile you feel like you develop an ability to read a VC footprint or something like that. They always seemed to wear a type of tennis shoe or something. It just looked like a VC village to us . . . the way that we could see it." By now it was about 9:30, and the men in the rear of the first platoon were ordered to pass forward extra belts of machine-gun ammunition and hand grenades.

The platoon, led by four point-men (GIs who serve as advance scouts), walked into the hamlet when the machine guns stopped, and began firing directly at Vietnamese civil-

ians and into Vietnamese homes. One of the machine gunners moved forward, firing his weapon from the hip, cow-
boy-movie style. A Peers panelist had this later exchange
with a participant:

Q. "Tell us what happened . . . ?"

A. "We started shooting."

Q. "Everybody in the platoon?"

A. "I'd say everybody. Everybody was shooting, and [Vi-
etnamese] people were on top of this hill and running
around like crazy people."

Another GI who participated in the shooting told what
happened to those Vietnamese who ran: ". . . The village
wasn't so big, but there were trees, shrubbery, hootches.
Maybe if one would run to another or something like that,
you couldn't tell if it was a man or a woman. And, of
course, we engaged upon them whenever they would run
like that."

One of the participants later told me details that, he said,
he didn't provide the Panel during his testimony. "We were
out there . . . having a good time," the ex-GI said. "It was
sort of like being in a shooting gallery." He told of a machine gunner who with a blaze of bullets methodically tore
one woman in half at the waist. And he told of a tiny infant,
barely of crawling age, who became the object of a marks-
manship contest. A rifleman had taken careful aim at the
infant with a .45-caliber pistol. "I remember that the baby
was about from here to the tape recorder [a distance of
about ten feet in the ex-GI's living room], and he fired at it
with a .45. He missed. We all laughed. He got up three or
four feet closer and missed again. We laughed. Then he got
up right on top of him and plugged him." Retelling the
story prompted the ex-soldier to begin laughing again. I
waited. "I don't know what it was and what possessed him
to do it," the youth said after a short pause, "but it really

doesn't matter. It really wasn't funny at all—I mean he was just going to shoot the baby—until he began missing." By this point, the ex-soldier said, "the word was out. You know, like you more or less can do anything you like. The Vietnamese were running around. Most of them squatted on down. That really made a tough target. Some of them came out [as the troops raced into the village after the machine-gun barrage] and just sort of stood around." The GI kept on talking. "Captain Michles—he'd tell us about treating the people right. 'Now remember they're human,' he'd say—and then he'd sort of snicker."

The gunfire was intense. Terry Reid recalled that he was standing a few hundred feet below the hamlet when it began. He knew civilians were being shot. "As soon as they started opening up, it hit me that it was insanity. I walked to the rear. Pandemonium broke loose. It sounded insane—machine guns, grenades. One of the guys walked back, and I remember him saying, 'We got sixty women, kids, and some old men.'" At one point during the shooting, Lieutenant Willingham apparently moved closer to My Khe 4, enabling the men with him to see what was taking place. One of his radio operators told a Peers panelist what happened when he asked the lieutenant's permission to move into the hamlet: "He told me to shut up and stay where I was at. I wanted to go up and help a little bit, you know." The panelist asked, "Were there women and children up there that might need some help?" "It wasn't that kind of help," the ex-soldier replied.

A few of the GIs from the first platoon stayed back by the bridge they had just crossed. They began firing, too, after hearing the commotion in the hamlet. Their targets, they later testified, were a cluster of ducks in the water below. They were careful, they said, to avoid hitting the birds, but instead tried to aim a few inches away to make them fly.

After the shootings in My Khe 4, a few of the first platoon GIs began systematically blowing up every bunker and tunnel. A helicopter loaded with extra supplies of dynamite and other explosives was flown to the men, apparently at Willingham's request. At some point that morning, according to some members of the first platoon, word was passed to stop the killing, and many of the surviving members of the village were allowed to flee to the nearby beach. They would live to tell about the massacre. Others remained huddled in the family shelters inside their homes. They were not spared.

Larry Holmes described it best: "A chopper brought in TNT, a hundred sticks of it . . . and it was thrown in bunkers and stuff, and blowing everything up and burning." Homer Hall recalled that "we just flattened that village, and that was it." Some Vietnamese attempted to flee the bunkers before the explosives were thrown in. They were shot. "Try to shoot them as they come out," one member of the first platoon was instructed. Another ex-GI told me what happened to those who stayed in the bunkers: "You didn't know for sure there were people in them until you threw in the TNT—and then you'd hear scurrying around in there." The youth laughed nervously, and added, "There wasn't much place for them to go." Others told me and the Panel about making a game with the explosives: "We were more or less having a contest to see which one could get the shortest fuse on the TNT." About twenty to thirty houses were blown up, one ex-GI said, utilizing more than one hundred and fifty pounds of TNT. The operation lasted through lunch.

Mrs. Nguyen Dhi Bay, one of the survivors of the massacre, told C.I.D. investigators that the American soldiers slaughtered ninety of the one hundred residents of My Khe 4. Mrs. Bay said she and three other women, along with four children, had fled in terror into a bunker when the GIs began shooting. A few minutes later, she said, she left the bunker and watched the Americans blow up homes and kill women, children, and old men. Mrs. Bay's official C.I.D. statement, transcribed on December 17, 1969, in South Vietnam, told what happened next: "After that, two other colored soldiers entered the hootch . . . started to take off their pants, and instructed the women to lay on the floor so they could have sexual intercourse with them . . . The women refused, and one of the colored soldiers struck the women with the butt of his rifle . . . At this time they did not bother the women any more. A short while later the women related to the soldiers that the children needed some food. One of the soldiers took two rounds of ammunition and told them that this was food for the children. The same soldier hit the women a few more times with the butt of his rifle. After this the two soldiers raped Bay. She does not remember how many times, but she was told by the other women she was raped by both of the soldiers." Later the women and children were taken to another home near the South China Sea. Mrs. Bay said that she was two months pregnant at the time of the incident; she lost her baby the next day.

Precisely how many residents of My Khe 4 were murdered will never be known. The Army later charged Lieutenant Willingham with involvement in the death of twenty civilians, but the charges were never pressed. Some survivors told military investigators in early 1970 that at least ninety to a hundred women, children, and old men were slain. One ex-GI who kept a count said he knew of 155 deaths; other estimates ranged from sixty to ninety.

There was some immediate concern over the shootings, at least among the commanders of Bravo Company. Donald Hooton recalled that at one point "somebody flew over in a helicopter and undoubtedly saw all kinds of bodies. He must have said something because Michles said he didn't want any more killing." Later, the ex-GI told me, "Lieutenant Willingham came around and said, 'We'd better do something about the bodies.' We threw some straw on them, but didn't really cover them up."

The few wounded survivors of My Khe 4 received scant medical attention. One of the company medics had explained to a number of his fellow GIs that "I won't patch them gooks up." Marvin G. B. Jones of Detroit, Michigan, told the Peers Panel about one little boy whose arm had been shot off at the shoulder during the morning assault. The medic "put a pad on him," Jones related, "but he didn't wrap it, talking about 'I don't have enough for you all. I haven't got enough.' He put a gauze or something on it, but he didn't wrap it." The child, not crying, silently took the gauze in the hand he had left and pressed it to his shoulder socket.

The official Task Force Barker log for March 16 shows that Bravo Company claimed an enemy kill of thirty-eight in three separate messages to the task force during the day. At 9:55 A.M. it reported killing twelve Viet Cong; at 10:25 it claimed another eighteen; and eight more were claimed at 2:20 in the afternoon, more than two hours after the massacre. At 3:55 P.M. it reported further that none of its victims were women or children.

The 11th Infantry Brigade had established an SOP (Standard Operating Procedure) for determining body counts in early 1968, requiring an on-site identification of a dead enemy soldier before it could be reported. All of the Task Force Barker officers interviewed by the Panel indicated an awareness of this regulation and claimed that it was adhered to in the task force.

Yet an ex-GI, one of the four point-men who entered My

Khe 4 first, gave me this version of how the totals of twelve and eighteen were arrived at: "I had this little notebook that I used to mark down the kills of the point-men in. This day—well, this was a red-letter day. Seems like for about fifteen or twenty minutes there, all I was doing was recording kills. Willingham got on the radio [by then he had moved to the rear] asking how many kills we got. Old Jug [the nickname for one of the point-men who was later killed in Vietnam] said he got twelve and we called in what we had. He [Willingham] checked with us a couple times in the early part of the day."

Another ex-GI testified that some of his fellow soldiers counted thirty-nine bodies in parts of the village and then told Willingham that "the biggest part of them was women and children."

Willingham's reports were relayed by Michles without challenge to the task force headquarters, although Congleton, his radioman, told me: "When they [the first platoon] started turning in kill counts, I figured they were destroying everything over there. At the time I didn't think that it was anything exceptional—maybe just a little more killing than usual." Michles had stationed his command post across the water from the My Khe 4 peninsula.

Asked by a panelist if it was "common practice to report a body count if there was, in fact, not a body count," Congleton replied, "Maybe not common, but it was done . . . You can't really take too much stock in what was put on the log or something like that, because it seemed like sometimes the commanding officers were like trying to write a movie script and make it read a little more juicy for the people that were going to read it." (At the end of the day, when an official after-action report had to be filed by Bravo Company to task force headquarters, Congleton said Captain Michles "told me to make it look good." The GI thus radioed that the company had discovered twenty booby traps, three enemy hand grenades, "and stuff like that.")

Another member that morning of the command post, Richard F. Silva of Ludlow, Massachusetts, later told the Peers Panel that it never mattered to him what was reported over the radios: "They could say two thousand were dead, you know. I could care less . . . as long as none of my men were hurt. They can say whatever they want over their radios and everything else because from past experiences I knew it was a bunch of bull anyway."

The first platoon spent the night in the field near My Khe 4, but the rest of Bravo Company rendezvoused with Charlie Company to set up a joint defense near a cemetery along the South China Sea. A few men from the companies exchanged war stories. In the morning Bravo Company reunited and spent the next twelve hours marching south along the coast to the Tra Khuc River, burning every hamlet along the way. Again there was an element of revenge. A popular member of the first platoon had lost a foot early in the morning while probing for a mine along the bridge leading from the My Khe 4 peninsula to the mainland.

The Peers Panel subsequently determined that the platoon had failed to post guards on the bridge overnight, although it provided the only access to the peninsula. A few men testified that the wounded GI was, in fact, recklessly attempting to defuse the booby trap with his bayonet when it went off, wounding him. But most of the GIs saw it as another example of treacherous enemy tactics, which renewed their anger at anyone Vietnamese. As the men marched south, the destruction was complete. By then Task Force Barker had provided a special team of demolition experts who blew up bunkers and other remains after the hamlets were set ablaze. Clouds of smoke from the operation could be seen for miles.

The hamlets destroyed were identified on American maps as Co Lay 1, Co Lay 2, and Co Lay 3. One of the GIs involved remembered the area as "the prettiest place I've seen since I've been over there. There were a lot of sailboats on the water, different colors, real pretty . . ." Another ex-GI said that there "was not a lot of excitement" on the second day of the operation: "We did burn more hootches that day, and they were bigger and more nicer-type villages than the ones we just left out of [My Khe 4] . . . These people done fishing and stuff like that."

The techniques used in destroying the houses along the coast apparently amazed the panelists. One GI testified that it was not his responsibility as a demolition man, but that of the infantry, to make sure no civilians were inside any of the bunkers he destroyed. He would generally drop two or three pounds of TNT into each bunker, he said, without checking for inhabitants. Another demolition "expert" told how he used as much as thirty pounds of dynamite to destroy each bunker, also without inspecting inside: "The bunkers were searched before I ever got to them, sir. That was the infantry's job."

Again, it is impossible to determine how many Vietnamese citizens were killed while huddling inside their bunkers during Bravo Company's march to the south. The GIs burned and destroyed every home they came to, often using cigarette butts to touch off the fires. Terry Reid, already considered a malcontent because of his often-voiced criticism of Bravo Company's killing tactics, recalled that he almost broke into tears during the march: "We'd go through these village areas and just burn. You'd see a good Vietnamese home—made with bricks or hard mud, and filled with six or seven grandmothers, four or five old men, and little kids—just burned. You'd see these old people watching their homes." The Army's concept of destroying bunkers and tunnels after burning the homes always left him in the dark anyway: "They call them bunkers and tunnels but you know what they are—basements. Just basements."

On the second day of the operation Donald Hooton remembered seeing large volumes of smoke to the west, where Charlie Company was operating inland. "We had this big contest to see who had the biggest fire," he told me. "We saw them across the river with a fire and said, 'Goddamn, we got to get a bigger one.'" Then word was suddenly passed down from Captain Michles to stop the burning.

Morris G. Michener of Charleston, West Virginia, told the Panel that by this time "there was a rumor going around the entire company. They wondered why we suddenly stopped burning hootches and they said, 'Somebody is all fired up about it and they are having some sort of an investigation or something.'" After that, Michener said, "Captain Michles was real careful. Up to the time that he got killed [in a helicopter crash June 13, 1968, along with Lieutenant Colonel Barker], we didn't burn any more hootches unless he received orders from higher up himself."

On March 18, the third day, Bravo Company's mission suddenly changed. Task Force Barker called in medical evacuation units and the men were ordered to round up the citizens for baths, examinations, and, in some cases, interrogation by intelligence officials. Between five hundred and a thousand civilians were treated for diseases or given food and clothing by the GIs. According to Larry Congleton, "it seemed like we just changed our policy altogether that day. We went from a search and destroy to a pacification, because we went to this village and we washed all the kids. Maybe somebody had a guilty feeling or something like that." Talking about it a year after his testimony, Congleton remarked that "we reversed the whole plan just like we were going to redeem ourselves." Morris Michener thought

"most of the people were a little ashamed of themselves—
and I was very ashamed of even being a part of the group."
James L. Sweeney of Marietta, Ohio, also was upset about
that day, but he wasn't so sure that the Vietnamese themselves minded: "I don't know, the villagers over there—
death is just something everyday to them and they don't
pay as much attention to it as we would. I think our outfit
was more upset than what the villagers were themselves,
really."

Not everyone experienced remorse, however. One of the
point-men had appropriated, in effect, Mrs. Nguyen Dhi
Bay, after the assault on My Khe 4, and forced her to serve
as a human probe for booby traps. Such treatment of civilians was common among the frightened infantrymen in
South Vietnam, but this GI went a step further. He tied a
heavy rope around Mrs. Bay's neck and drove her, as one
would a horse, ahead of him for the next twelve hours.

On March 19 Bravo Company was lifted by helicopter
from the peninsula and flew back to its regular landing
zone. A few of the soldiers later heard about the excesses
committed by Charlie Company and the impending investigations there, but somehow there was never any concern
about the atrocities they had committed. Only one GI considered reporting the My Khe 4 massacre to his superiors,
but as he later testified, he quickly dropped the idea. "I
guess I just let it go when I shouldn't have," Ronald Esterling explained. "I thought the company commander knew
these things were going on . . . It was all general knowledge
through the whole company and I didn't see any sense in
talking it over with the company . . . I just didn't tell anybody about it."

By the time news of the Army's mass murder charges
against Lieutenant Calley became known in the United
States, most of the men of Bravo Company were back in the

United States, out of the Army. Only a few connected their activities with Bravo Company of March 16 to the operation Calley was alleged to have participated in. Terry Reid, for one, walked into a Wisconsin newspaper office a few days after the Calley story broke in November, 1969, and gave an interview about the atrocities he had observed while serving with the 11th Brigade in South Vietnam. He told of one operation in which, after some GIs had been wounded by a booby trap, his company responded by killing sixty women, children, and old men. He didn't realize until months later, Reid told me in mid-1971, that what had happened to his outfit was directly connected to Task Force Barker's mission: "I used to think my company was a bad-ass one until I started seeing others. Sometimes you thought it was just my platoon, my company, that was committing atrocious acts, and what bad luck it was to get in it. But what we were doing was being done all over."

The men of Bravo Company were silent about My Khe 4 until investigators from the Peers Panel and, later, from the Army's Criminal Investigating Division began interviewing them in early 1970. And when the investigation was completed, it was the Army's turn to forget.

The incident at My Khe 4 would perhaps be just another Vietnam atrocity story if it weren't for four facts: its vital connection to the My Lai 4 tragedy; the total ignorance of the American public about it; the total and detailed knowledge of it by the Peers Panel, the Department of the Army, and higher Pentagon officials; and the failure of any of those agencies to prosecute fully those involved.

3

A Division
at War

On March 16, 1968, Major General Samuel W. Koster was near the peak of a brilliant Army career. At the age of forty-eight, he was a young two-star general whose next assignment, he thought correctly, would be as superintendent of the military academy at West Point. After that would come a third star, perhaps as a corps commander in Germany or even again in South Vietnam. Another promotion, to the rank of full general, would quickly follow along with an assignment possibly as commander of one of the overseas United States Armies. By the middle or late 1970s he would be among a group of ambitious, competent generals seeking Presidential appointment as Army Chief of Staff. Like most future candidates for the job of Chief of Staff, Koster had been earmarked as a "comer" by his fellow officers from his days at West Point. In 1949 he had served as a highly prestigious tactical officer at the Point, assigned to a cadet company as the man responsible for their training. By 1960 he had served in the sensitive operations office at both the Far East Command in Tokyo and at the Supreme Headquarters of the Allied Powers, Europe (SHAPE), in Paris. His career was patterned after that of his chief benefactor and supporter, General William C. Westmoreland, who by 1968 was the head of all military operations in South Vietnam. Westmoreland and Koster had served together in the Pentagon during the mid-1950s, both in key staff jobs. Westmoreland later became Superintendent of West Point.

Koster's assignment in the fall of 1967 as commanding general of the Americal Division could be underestimated at first by outsiders: the Americal, a hastily thrown together conglomerate of independent infantry units, was far from an elite outfit. But the job was extremely important to the young two-star general, as the Peers investigation learned: he had been hand-picked by Westmoreland after a sharp debate inside military headquarters in Saigon. As initially set up, the Americal was composed of three separate 5,000-man infantry brigades, each with its own support units such as artillery and cavalry. The concept had been effectively utilized by General Douglas MacArthur in World War II. Lieutenant General Bruce Palmer, then deputy commander of the U. S. forces in Vietnam, explained it this way to the Peers Panel: "In the earlier days [in South Vietnam], where there were fewer troops, the separate brigade was quite useful because you could send it to a new area. It was self-sustaining, complete. You didn't have to tear up a division to pull a brigade-sized force out of the division. General Westmoreland very much liked the idea of the independent brigades in the early days. Then when we had enough troops where they didn't have to do this fire brigade business— some units were like a yo-yo, going up and down the coast of Vietnam, he conceived the idea of pulling three brigades together . . . The division headquarters and so-called division base was an ad hoc thing to start with."

In later months the Americal would be restructured to make it more conventional and provide more centralized control, a factor that Palmer and others thought highly desirable. But when Koster took over, it was a new kind of fighting unit highly endorsed by Westmoreland; the pressure on the new commander was inevitable.

Adding to the pressure was the low caliber of officers initially assigned to the Americal by other units. Lieutenant Colonel Cecil E. Granger, Jr., who served briefly in the important operations office (known as G3 in the military) of the new division in late 1967, testified about his personnel problems: "In the G3 section, the quality of the personnel was not what one would ask in a division, to be perfectly honest. Among the field grade officers [major and above] there was only one major in the entire section who graduated from Leavenworth [the Army Command and Staff School in Kansas], and of all of them, there were only two who had not been passed over for promotion to lieutenant colonel. That would indicate that in some cases not the highest caliber of people were being provided . . ."

Koster responded to the staff problems by running a virtual one-man show. He trusted no one to make decisions on the operations and maneuvers of the division. Every military engagement or tactic had to be personally approved by him, including such details as the allotment of helicopters for combat assaults. He filled the two most important positions in his headquarters, chief of staff and head of G3 operations, with artillery officers, highly unusual positions for such men in a combat infantry division. Colonel Nels A. Parson, Jr., the chief of staff, was one of the two West Pointers in a key headquarters slot, but his inexperience in infantry tactics inhibited him: he spent much of his time, according to testimony, ensuring that fences were painted and grass was kept closely cropped. The other West Pointer, Lieutenant Colonel Jesmond D. Balmer, the operations officer, was more ambitious than Parson, but ended up more frustrated. He testified: "I was not a textbook G3, either as taught at Leavenworth or throughout the Army or practiced at any other divisions. The commanding general was in fact his own G3 . . . I was not operating that division. I was doing certain planning and trying to keep the TOC [tactical operations center] going . . . I can't visualize that any staff officer there would visualize Balmer, even now, as being a key mover in that division. I was far from it." Balmer thought, however, that Colonel Parson had even a worse relationship with the general: "It was very evident to all concerned that General Koster had no confidence or did not trust much responsibility, except answering the telephone in the headquarters and doing the normal headquarters chief of staff job, to Colonel Parson, and to a similar degree this went down to the staff . . . It was the most unhappy group of staff officers and unhappy headquarters that I have ever had any contact with and certainly ever heard tell of."

Koster's relationship with Brigadier General George H. Young, Jr., his deputy division commander, was less frosty but far from warm. Young, then two years older than his superior, had graduated from the Citadel Military Academy in Charleston, South Carolina. He, too, was restricted in the degree of command authority he could exercise, although he had been placed in administrative control of the aviation and supply sections of the division. He could recommend decisions but not implement them. Most of the other headquarters officers were either "non-ring-knockers," men who either had begun their careers as enlisted men or graduates of college ROTC programs, or graduates of private military schools such as the Citadel, which are considered second-rate by many West Pointers.

For most of the officers and men, the commanding general was an aloof and cold figure who compelled respect—with a touch of fear. "General Koster was so smart, he was too smart for the rest of us," recalled retired Lieutenant Colonel Charles Anistranski, who served as the Americal Division G5 (in charge of pacification and civil affairs) in early 1968. Anistranski particularly remembered the general's crisp method of barking orders: "Koster would say, 'I don't like that and I want you to do *this* and *that*.' " The general wouldn't join the after-dinner drinking bouts at the division officers' club, the former colonel said, choosing instead to return to his quarters. James R. Ritchie III worked as an Americal Division headquarters clerk in 1967–8 and remembered Koster during an interview with me as being "very cold: I worked near him in that office for over five months and I was never introduced to him. I passed notes to him, but really, I never knew the man. They were all afraid," Ritchie said of the headquarters staff. "They were all afraid of Koster." Most of the general's contact with his staff came during the two daily briefings that were a fixture in the headquarters routine. In the morning he met with his top leadership, including the two deputy division commanders, his chief of staff, and the heads of personnel (G1), intelligence (G2), operations (G3), supplies (G4), and civil affairs (G5).

In the evening about thirty to forty officers assembled to get an up-to-date summary of combat actions during the day. "It was quite formal," Chief of Staff Parson told the Panel. "The general walking in, everyone at attention, and sitting down and hearing the briefing. Then he would walk out."

If life was sometimes strained at headquarters, there were many amenities. High-ranking Army officers traditionally pride themselves on the quality of the meals served at headquarters. For "comers" such as Koster, maintaining an impeccable generals' mess was important for no other reason than to serve a memorable meal to visiting dignitaries. Nothing was spared to make General Koster's mess an excellent one. Ritchie recalled that dinner was an elaborate affair, served by uniformed GIs wearing white waiter's coats. There was wine, engraved china with the Americal Division emblem, a well-stocked bar, and excellent French food on occasion. Steak and lobster were often served. Up to fifteen officers would attend, including Koster, his deputy commanding generals, the key headquarters staff, and occasional guests—very often Red Cross nurses. After dinner the dining hall was darkened and those officers who chose to stay were treated to private screenings of movies.

Koster was perfectly at ease as commanding general of the Americal Division, but he showed signs of tension whenever General Westmoreland visited. "I think they were all afraid. Everyone seemed to be afraid of Koster, and Koster, whenever Westy [Westmoreland] would come to visit, he'd be jumping," Ritchie told me. The former clerk said that along with even more elaborate meals, the whole headquarters staff, led by Colonel Parson, would conduct lengthy rehearsals of the scheduled briefings for Westmoreland.

The normal work schedule of General Koster and his key aides, like that of their social life, seemed to have little relationship to the realities of the guerrilla war going on a few miles away. Koster lived in an air-conditioned four-room house on a hill at division headquarters in Chu Lai; he was served by a full-time enlisted aide and a young officer. A few yards away was a fortified bunker with full communications in case of attack. Most of his workday was spent in a helicopter visiting the brigades and battalions under his command. Every morning he would give a short speech to the inevitable batch of new soldiers who were arriving at the division replacement center. Generally he tried, his aides testified, to be where the action was—to monitor his troops in combat. For Koster, just like a young company commander, was being judged largely on the basis of how many enemy soldiers his men claimed to have killed. But by early 1968 the Vietnam war had become a focal point in the campaign for the Democratic Presidential nomination being waged by Senator Eugene J. McCarthy, Minnesota Democrat, and the overt emphasis on killing the enemy was being muted.

Major John D. Beasley, III, the division's assistant chief of staff, told the Peers Panel about a potentially significant change concerning the concept of search-and-destroy missions: ". . . we received some additional guidance on that, through messages . . . This got to be a pretty big thing about that time, sometime in the spring. I think this was pretty important that we stop saying this kill, kill, kill, destroy, destroy, destroy, and working with the people . . . Working with the Vietnamese became a little bit bigger about this time. There was a new word—pacification, I think was the word I got on my first tour [in Vietnam] in 1965, and we later started—somebody came up with some new words that meant work with the Vietnamese and pacify the hell out of things . . ." Despite the new emphasis, when Koster left Vietnam he was praised enthusiastically by his superior, Lieutenant General Robert E. Cushman, commanding general of the Third Marine Amphibious Force (III MAF) in South Vietnam, for the high number of enemy kills recorded by the Americal Division; it was the only praise that mattered.

Koster's arrival by helicopter at local units would create as much of a flurry—and as much fear—as a visit from Westmoreland to division headquarters, although certain battalions and brigades were visited more often at lunchtime because they had better messes.

Even with these visits, the general was far removed from the problems and fears of the "grunts," the ground soldiers assigned to squads, in platoons of companies attached to battalions in one of the three brigades under his command. When problems and complaints did arise, they often would be deliberately withheld from the general by his aides. James Ritchie, assigned as one of the chief administrative clerks in division headquarters, and working directly for Colonel Parson, recalled that he was ordered to screen all of the mail personally addressed to Koster: "Parson wanted to know anything that was on Koster's desk other than routine stuff. A lot of stuff I know never got to Koster," but was instead handled by Parson.

Most of the senior staff officers at headquarters knew of the practice but did not complain, even when a letter they addressed to Koster would be returned with a response from Colonel Parson. The reason: Parson was their rating officer, and for an ambitious lieutenant colonel who had not attended West Point, one bad rating could be the end of a career. This kind of reasoning went up the chain of command: in May, 1968, a Special Forces camp in the Americal Division's area of operations was overrun, with heavy losses to one of the Americal battalions that attempted to relieve the camp. Koster ordered an investigation, but as the Peers Panel was told, never filed it with higher headquarters "because it made the division look bad."*

* The assertion was made by Colonel Jack L. Treadwell, who served as chief of staff of the Americal Division from September, 1968, until

The net effect of such practices was a form of self-imposed ignorance: few things were ever "officially" learned or reported. By March, 1968, for example, murder, rape, and arson were common throughout many combat units of the American Division—particularly the 11th Brigade, which operated in hostile Quang Ngai Province—without any "official" reports of them at the higher levels. Most of the infantry companies had gone so far as to informally set up "zippo" squads, groups of men whose sole mission was to follow the combat troops through hamlets and set them on fire. Yet Koster, during one of his lengthy appearances before the Panel, calmly reported that "we had, I thought, a very strong policy against burning and pillaging in villages. Granted, during an action where the enemy was in there, there would be some destruction. But I had spoken to brigade commanders frequently, both as a group and personally, about the fact that this type of thing would not be tolerated. I'm sure that in our rules of engagement it . . . [was] emphasized very strongly." The rules of engagement was a formal seven-page codification of the division's "criteria for the employment of firepower in support of combat operations." It provided stringent restrictions on the use of fire-

March, 1969. Treadwell told Peers that sometime late in 1968 the division historian had discovered a report dealing with the heavy losses at the Kham Duc Special Forces camp, near the Laotian border in Quang Tin Province, on the western edge of the American Division's area of responsibility. Total casualties, most of them South Vietnamese, were nearly eight hundred during the three-day siege of the camp by North Vietnamese troops. Enemy losses were reported at 345. "The historian," Treadwell said, ". . . wanted to know what disposition we should make of it because the word that was passed on to me, General Koster did not want this report forwarded to USARV [United States Army headquarters, South Vietnam] because it made the division look bad." Treadwell said he took the document to Major General Charles M. Gettys, then the commanding general of the division, and recommended that it be forwarded up the chain of command.

power and called for clearance before firing on any civilian areas. The rules, unfortunately for the Vietnamese, had little to do with the way the war was being fought.*

Ironically, their publication allowed commanders to treat brutalities such as murder, rape, and arson as mere violations of rules, and in any event, such serious crimes were rarely reported officially. Lieutenant Colonel Warren J. Lucas, the Americal Division provost marshal (chief law enforcement officer), testified that most of the war crime investigations conducted by his unit involved the theft of goods or money from civilians or, occasionally, a charge that GIs had raped a prisoner of war at an interrogation center. The concept of murder during a combat operation simply wasn't raised. Sometimes, Lucas said, he or his men would hear rumors or reports of serious incidents in the field, but "if it was declared a combat action, I did not move into it at all with my investigators." Of course, the men who could declare such incidents as being combat-related were the officers in charge; in effect, their choice was between a higher body count or a war crime investigation. Murder and similar combat violations of international law were never "reported through military police channels," Colonel Lucas said. If they were, he could still not begin an

---

* Although the Americal was organized in September, 1967, publication of the rules did not come until March 16, 1968 (coincidentally the day of the My Lai assault). Each brigade headquarters also was expected to publish its own version of the rules, using the division document as a basic source of policy. For Koster and the brigade commanders beneath him, the mere publication and discussion of the rules seemed to meet all of the responsibilities of enforcing them. Asked a second time about his rules of engagement by General Peers, Koster replied that his March 16 memorandum had been published in draft form months earlier and also transmitted verbally many times. "I know personally at one meeting where I had all commanders in," Koster explained, "I made quite a point of the burning of buildings based upon the burning of a building or two in another area."

investigation of such incidents without express approval of
Chief of Staff Parson or General Koster.

Lucas apparently never conducted such an investigation
while serving with the Americal. He expressed grave
doubts, anyway, about the feasibility of such an effort: "If
you try to get investigators out to a village that's in the middle of the combat action—it was almost impossible at times,
and then you might wait a week to get hold of the witnesses
. . . and then they may be dead in the meantime because of
combat action. It's very difficult." What happened, in effect,
is that after promulgation of the rules, the military honor
system went into effect. Under this system, as it was applied
in the Americal Division, violations of the rules of engagement simply did not take place.

Lieutenant Colonel Anistranski, the former civil affairs
officer for the division, explained how it worked in an interview with me in mid-1971: "Every time a hamlet would
burn, it was reported to me. If it was in a friendly area, we'd
go back and rebuild it. Sometimes it would come up at the
nightly briefing [the fact that some Americal units had
burned a hamlet without clearance]. General Koster would
come up to me and say, 'Check it out.' I'd get the S5 [the
lower-ranking officer in charge of civil affairs of the unit in
question] and say, 'You'd better get on it; the old man
wants to know what happened out there.' They'd come
back after a little while and say it was set on fire during a
fire fight. I'd go and tell the old man that."

During the hearings, Lieutenant Colonel Balmer was
asked, "In general, you relied on integrity, and the system,
and the reports that came through channels, to learn what
was going on?" "Yes, sir," Balmer replied. "The normal reporting procedures—whether it be by radio, whether it be in
writing, whether it be reports coming back from members

of the division staff or command group who had
—were our means of getting information."

Koster could, of course, have court-martialed s[
tors of international law for their crimes. This might have
limited the number of such violations, but it also would
have signaled to higher headquarters that such infractions
of law did occur. Koster's efficacy as a commander would
have been questioned and the name of the division sullied
by the inevitable press reports. That this difficult situation
exists is well known to officers throughout the Army, but
the theme rarely emerges in public. One occasion when it
did was during a television interview in June, 1971, with
Lieutenant Colonel Anthony B. Herbert, a much-decorated
Vietnam veteran who broke ranks in 1971 by filing charges
against his superior officers in connection with alleged war
crimes. Herbert compared the filing of formal war crime
charges by an officer in Vietnam to ". . . one of the gunmen calling up the head of the Mafia and saying, 'Hey, tomorrow let's all go to the police,' or, 'I'd like to go to the police and talk.' How long do you think that fellow's going to
last . . . I mean, really."

Such talk wasn't heard at the American Division headquarters. The men there took their jobs at face value. Father
Carl E. Creswell served as an Episcopal chaplain at Chu
Lai; he resigned soon after his tour with the division. He
testified: "I became absolutely convinced that as far as the
United States Army was concerned, there was no such thing
as murder of a Vietnamese civilian. I'm sorry, maybe it's a
little bit cynical. I'm sure it is, but that's the way the system
works." During a later interview at his parish in Emporia,
Kansas, Father Creswell bitterly complained about his fellow officers: "The whole thing reminded me of World War
I. The commanders would fly at day, watch the troops get

killed, and then come back to a hot shower, the officers' club, or a flick." The priest told of an exchange he had in late 1967 with a senior colonel who was in charge of a troop voyage from Hawaii to one of the American Division brigades. The colonel, irritated at the ship's slow progress due to heavy rains, was complaining about the weather with a group of fellow officers, including Creswell. "Hey, Father," the colonel called out, "why don't you ask our boss to do something about this?" The officers chuckled. The priest replied, "I'm not sure God is in that much of a hurry for us to get to Vietnam to kill people." There was silence. That evening, Father Creswell recalled, his dining place was removed from the colonel's table.

The emphasis on killing with impunity inevitably led to a widespread lack of concern for the civilians of South Vietnam, particularly those living in such contested areas of South Vietnam as Quang Ngai Province, which had been declared in large part a free-fire zone. "A free-fire zone," III MAF Commander Cushman testified, ". . . this was such hostile territory that you were allowed to fire. The people were supposed to get out of there, if they did not want to be subjected to this. They were supposed to move out." Before such attacks, even in free-fire zones, the civilians were to be warned by propaganda leaflets and loudspeaker announcements to clear the area. Lieutenant Colonel Stanley E. Holtom, the chief psychological warfare officer (PSYOP) for the American Division, explained why—at least in early 1968— this rarely happened: "I believe I'd be honest in saying that . . . PSYOP was—if I can try and get the impression across to you, sir, that PSYOP was like the bastard child at that time. They were left out in the cold, and this was one thing that I was very concerned about when I first got there . . . Prior to about June of 1968, there was no liaison, no coordinated effort made to ensure that these things [loudspeaker broadcasts, etc.] were . . . planned prior to an operation . . ."

The result of such poor planning was the inadvertent murder of many civilians in violation of international law and the division rules of engagement. The statistics tell the story: a consistent problem for the military throughout the war has been the great disparity between the number of Viet Cong soldiers reported to have been killed and the number of weapons that were captured. Although the obvious answer seemed to be that Viet Cong in fact were not the only victims of American gunfire, artillery, and gunship strikes, high-ranking officers at the top headquarters commands simply could not—or would not—accept that fact. Thus, commanding officers in the Americal Division were always urging their troops to "close with the enemy" and not to rely on helicopter or artillery support, thereby increasing their chances of capturing enemy weapons.

Often the rationale for the statistical imbalance was strained. Brigadier General Carl W. Hoffman of the Marine Corps, who served as chief operations officer of III MAF in early 1968, agreed with General Peers that the March 16 report by Task Force Barker of 128 Viet Cong deaths and three captured weapons represented "a ratio that we would not normally like to see. However, we had experienced other reports in which we later found that the attacking troops had found a graveyard with fresh graves, and they determined then that these deaths had occurred on previous days because of artillery fire or gunship fire. Therefore, the total on a given day could be quite high and the weapons invariably would be very low . . . We did see other instances in which we had very few weapons captured and quite a number of enemy bodies counted. This is true in Marine operations and Army organizations throughout III MAF."

"It's like a game," Lieutenant Colonel Anistranski remarked during my interview with him. "Everybody come
on, we're going to have a bonfire. The way Koster used to
look at me—he knew they [the brigades] were lying. He
tried to stop it, but there's so much going . . . so much
going on." Anistranski remembered that on occasion Koster would storm out of the nightly briefing, obviously angered, after hearing reports of large numbers of Viet Cong
killed by his troops, with no captured weapons. "He'd get
mad," Anistranski said of the general, "but me? I used to
look at it and laugh. 'There's another battalion commander
who's pushing the full colonel list,' I'd say." He could laugh,
the retired officer added, but the general was trapped by his
position: "Koster's got bird colonels working for him; he's
got to accept their word."

Great masses of credible testimony were developed by
various Vietnam veterans groups during 1970 and 1971, indicating that there were serious abuses in the treatment and
interrogation of Vietnamese prisoners. The use of torture by
intelligence officers in the Americal Division was common.
Yet Koster, during a discussion with General Peers about
the training of troops on the rules of land warfare and the
Geneva Convention, could only brag about his daily talk to
new arrivals to the division: "I personally talked to them for
the first half-hour or so. I stressed the importance of relations with the Vietnamese; the fact that we were not only
allies but that we were really guests in their country; that
they had certain laws and rights and we should very definitely respect them; that they were people that needed all of
the help and consideration that we could give them . . . I
was followed . . . by an hour's instruction by a JAG [judge
advocate general—a military lawyer] officer who went into
the rules of land warfare, the details of the handling, treating of combatants, noncombatants, PWs [prisoners of war],

et cetera . . . I would say that I addressed ninety-eight percent of all replacements that came into the division . . ."

A similar disparity over talk and action existed at all levels. Lieutenant Colonel Patrick H. Dionne, chief information officer for the Americal Division, was asked about the
division rules for destruction of civilian property. "There
was a specific order out that it would not be done," Dionne
replied. Asked if the order was understood by troops
throughout the division, the officer said, "I don't know; it
was understood at the headquarters. General Koster had issued a letter about abuse of civilian property in January,
and commanders were required to bring this to the attention of all their personnel."

The reliance on directives, rather than investigation and
prosecution, wasn't confined to the Americal Division.
There was concern about reports of prisoner mistreatment
even in the Pentagon, but the result—as in the Americal—
was to issue further directives and increase troop training
rather than order more courts-martial. In May, 1968, General Harold K. Johnson, the Army Chief of Staff, complained in a private letter to the American command in Saigon about the mistreatment of prisoners. His letter followed
a wave of news stories and photographs depicting the brutal
mistreatment of Vietnamese prisoners; the articles apparently were the Pentagon's first inkling of the scope of the
problem. General Palmer's response from Saigon on June
15 acknowledged that "something more needs to be done."
He went on to note that "a review of records . . . reveals
that most incidents of detainee maltreatment occur in forward combat areas, too frequently with the knowledge of
senior noncommissioned and company grade officers present. It is at the point of capture and during the period of
evacuation that our training occasionally fails."

Given the scope of the problem, General Palmer prom-

ised that his command would attack it with "reinforced individual and troop training . . ." One possible reason for
the large number of lapses, he suggested, was: "Instruction
in the Geneva Conventions has tended to be abstract and
academic, rather than concrete and practical." Palmer recommended increased troop training on prisoner treatment,
more press attention to "stories which illustrate the payoffs
derived from proper PW handling," and the production of
an Army motion picture "describing and emphasizing
proper handling of PWs at point of capture through evacuation from the battle area." An additional benefit of such a
movie, the general added, would be its "dual purpose of
teaching the soldier and reassuring the public of Army concern for humane treatment of the captive." As it happened,
none of the recommendations stemmed the growing number of prisoner abuses by Americans in South Vietnam.
And the one solution that the Army seemed unable to risk
was to begin prosecution of offenders.

4

The 11th Brigade

The American Division consisted of three combat infantry brigades in early 1968. One of them, the 11th, was commanded by Colonel Oran K. Henderson. Henderson had been in the Army twenty-five years by early 1968, and like all colonels, wanted very much to become a general—an ambition seemingly at odds with his frustrating assignment with the 11th Brigade. A non-West Pointer, he had failed during a tour of Vietnam in 1963–64 to get the command assignments necessary for promotion; later he spent more than two years in subordinate roles with the 11th Brigade. On March 15, 1968, the Army gave him a chance: on that day he formally took command of the brigade's four infantry battalions and 3,500 men. During formal ceremonies at the Duc Pho headquarters area in southern Quang Ngai Province, Henderson accepted the unit's colors from the outgoing commander, Brigadier General Andy A. Lipscomb, who was retiring from the service. Lipscomb had recommended Henderson for the job, and was delighted when Major General Koster approved the choice. Henderson "was completely loyal to me," Lipscomb explained to the Peers Panel. "When I left, and I made out an efficiency report on Colonel Henderson, I recommended him for promotion to brigadier general, which I didn't do to too many colonels along the way." But Koster had at least one major reservation about giving Henderson the commander's job, as he testified: "I knew him to be a brave individual and I thought a fairly strong leader. I wasn't sure that he was necessarily the most intelligent of the people I had commanding the brigades."

Henderson himself admitted he had seen little combat in Vietnam. He said that the Task Force Barker attack on My Lai 4 "was the first combat action I had been involved in or observed. As the brigade executive officer up to this point and time, I was pretty well limited to Duc Pho. Occasionally I could get an H-23 [observation helicopter] and get out on the periphery or something, but as a general rule, I was stuck at Duc Pho. I had not participated in a CA [combat assault] nor had I observed any combat action except that at the Duc Pho Province." Henderson was referring to the occasional Viet Cong mortar attacks at his brigade headquarters area. There was even some question raised about the dangers of those attacks. According to Lieutenant Colonel Richard K. Blackledge, the brigade intelligence (S2) officer, his experience in Vietnam was "the first time I was ever in any kind of a situation where I was shot at in my life . . . We had a few mortar attacks during the time I was there, but . . . those mortar attacks always ran right down the runway, so I was able to stand outside my tent and watch them and never felt in any danger."

Upon taking over the top job in the brigade, Henderson immediately began acting like every other commander in Vietnam. Every day he would assemble a few personal aides and fly throughout his area of responsibility, observing the infantry battalions in action. Joseph W. Walsh, one of the brigade's senior sergeants who spent many hours flying with General Lipscomb, told the Panel how he began flying with his new boss: "I went with Colonel Henderson a lot, but it was simply a case of a carry-over from my previous commander's policy. I never asked him, and he never questioned me. He never said I couldn't."

The new commander was formal and crisp with his staff; he had what the military calls "command presence." He rarely smiled; and a few of the younger officers and clerks around headquarters called him "the Cortisone King"—but behind his back. In other officers, he inspired nothing less than fear. "I'm scared to death of Colonel Henderson," Captain Donald J. Keshel, the brigade civil affairs (S5) officer, testified. "I walked out of that brigade after eighteen months; I was scared to death of Colonel Henderson . . . He's just got to be the hardest man I've ever worked for." But Henderson, too, had at least one man he feared—Major General Koster, whose rating of him as a brigade commander would make, or break, his chances of becoming a general. Koster's doubts about his intellectual ability were known to the colonel. He got along easily with General George H. Young, Koster's deputy, but his relations with the division commander seemed to be tense. "You could always distinguish rank when they were talking," recalled Michael C. Adcock, a GI who served as one of the colonel's radio operators.

Henderson, and Lipscomb before him, also followed the usual commander's practice of emphasizing body count, and competition for enemy kills was constant among the battalions and companies of the 11th Brigade. John Waldeck, who served as a clerk in the operations center of the 11th Brigade, recalled during an interview with me that Henderson would immediately ask, "What's the body count?" after radioing from his helicopter and being told some of his units were in contact with the enemy. There were three-day passes for the individuals who achieved high body counts; sometimes whole units would be rewarded. The brigade was operating in Viet Cong territory, yet rarely had any stand-up fights with the enemy. Instead, there were the inevitable booby traps and the inevitable hatred of all Vietnamese.

Murder of civilians was common throughout all battalions of the brigade. "We killed people just for the sake of killing," said William Bezanson, now of Detroit, who served in the brigade at the time of My Lai. "Guys would come out waving a pass and we'd just waste them." Sometimes "I'd kill a bunch of people here, thinking that maybe the guy next to me was killing enemy with guns. But the guy next to me was killing people, thinking I was getting the enemy."

At one point Henderson personally ordered a program set up offering helicopter pilots three- to five-day passes for bringing in military-age males for questioning; the program was initiated because the brigade was unable to develop reliable intelligence information on the Viet Cong. It was known informally among 11th Brigade air units as "Operation Body Snatch." Within weeks the operation had degenerated and the pilots, instead of "snatching" civilians, were deliberately killing them sometimes by running them down with their helicopter skids. Other pilots devised even more macabre forms of murder, including a process in which a lasso was used to stop a Vietnamese peasant attempting to flee. Helicopter crewmen would then jump out, strip the victim, and replace the rope around his neck. The helicopter then would begin to move at low speed with the Vietnamese running along. After a few minutes the victim could no longer keep up; he would fall, snapping his neck.

Yet Sergeant Major Robert K. Gerberding, one of the brigade's senior noncommissioned officers who spent most of his workdays monitoring troop progress in the unit's tactical operations center (TOC), told the Peers Panel: "I have never had one innocent civilian reported to me as killed. You will have to realize the area we were operating under— entirely Viet Cong dominated . . . These people [in Quang Ngai] were not sympathizers, they were active supporters. Anybody. If you say innocent civilians killed, nobody could determine if he was an innocent civilian, because nine out of ten cases he was an active hamlet village guerrilla. A farmer in the daytime, and at night he carried his rifle. So you cannot use the term in this area saying he was an innocent civilian, because the VC ran this area and everybody was a VC. Men, women, children . . . I cannot recall that any reports have come in of innocent civilians, women or small children being killed, inadvertently or accidentally."

There is evidence that some instances of serious mistreatment were known to Henderson. For example, an official closely connected with the My Lai 4 investigation told me Henderson had said that he was forced to cancel "Operation Body Snatch" after learning of its excesses. But the colonel and his battalion commanders had no qualms about engaging "military-age" males with rifles or hand grenades from their helicopters. The rules of combat in free-fire zones permitted helicopter pilots and door gunners to fire on such men if they began to run from the path of the aircraft in prohibited areas. The act of running from the helicopter was called "evading" by the Americans. Henderson himself was wounded in the leg in late March while engaging a Viet Cong suspect with a hand grenade from his helicopter.

Of course, there were inevitable abuses with such wide discretion; many battalion commanders in Vietnam became well known for "gook-hunting" from the air. Dr. Brian Schoolfield of Flint, Michigan, served as flight surgeon for the 174th Aviation Company in 1968. He recalled during a mid-1971 interview that many of the pilots in his unit "didn't like flying for the [lieutenant] colonels in the 11th Brigade. The officers used to make low-level passes at water buffalo and do a lot of gook-hunting." Many lieutenant colonels, he said, "would shoot carbines at gooks" from the doorways of the command and control helicopters, although Army regulation specifically forbade such action. Some pilots in the 174th eventually became so disgusted with the officers' action, Schoolfield said, that "they put notices on the back of their chairs saying that 'firing carbines or automatic weapons from this helicopter is illegal.' Then if a colonel gave a direct order to do it, the pilot could report him." The Vietnamese killed by such actions would be reported as Viet Cong.

Some of the problems concerning control of the troops and officers in the brigade were apparently well known, at least according to General Lipscomb, who said that he had "never stopped questioning any body count that would be reported to my headquarters. I think there were many, many estimations on these body counts. A lot . . . were estimated from the air." Asked by a Peers panelist if he had suspicion that some of those counted as Viet Cong might have been women and children, Lipscomb replied dryly, "Had a suspicion? Yes, I'd say I had a suspicion. I think that the general feeling over there was that anything that was shot was a VC. I'm speaking bluntly here now, but I think that generally was the accepted *modus operandi* over there . . . I don't think that they went to a great deal of trouble to distinguish between men and women."

Despite his knowledge of the situation, General Lipscomb made no attempt to change the procedures in his brigades. Many witnesses before the Panel told of having received no training whatsoever on the Geneva Convention or the proper treatment of prisoners of war during training in Hawaii or in South Vietnam. The official history of the 11th Brigade for 1967, the year in which it was in training for Vietnam duty, makes no mention of any classes at all on international law or the law of land warfare. "In Hawaii, the emphasis was on tactical combat operations throughout," James E. Ford, a public information clerk for the brigade, testified. "I think perhaps during that time . . . they might have said something about pacification and about the S5's function, civil affairs. But I don't think it was an active part of the tactical training, though."

The brigade S5 was only a captain, although Army manuals state that the position should be filled by a major. The Army is loath to say so in public, but the job of division G5 or brigade S5 is considered a lowly one in the military—one to avoid if rapid promotion is desired.* Donald Keshel, as S5, was in charge of making cash payments to Vietnamese victims of accidental American shootings. He had made about thirty such solatium payments (at the time about $33, or 4,000 piasters, for each adult and half as much for children fifteen and under) during an eight-month period ending in September, 1968. The total seemed high to him, and he mentioned his concern to Colonel Henderson. Henderson, in turn, "mentioned it to the battalion commanders at

---

* Lieutenant Colonel William O. Glaff, who served in March, 1968, as G5 adviser for the 2nd South Vietnamese Division operating in Quang Ngai, told the Peers Panel: "Sir, a G5 adviser is as far as I'm concerned next to nothing. I felt like it was for me, from the experience I had in the past in the Army, it was probably the least lucrative, the lowest position that I have held in the Army in years."

one of his briefings. And all of the battalion commanders, boy, they really got down on me. Now they said, 'Well, you know we got lieutenants out there with the platoon, or rifle company commanders out there with the companies, he'd get fire from a village, he's got to return fire to protect his command, and when this happens, perhaps a civilian will get shot.' "

The concept of a battlefield war crime did not exist in the 11th Brigade. Major John L. Pittman, provost marshal of the unit, testified that he could not recall giving the military policemen under his command any instructions or training about their obligations to report war crimes. On two or three occasions, Pittman said, he did report instances of prisoner mistreatment to both Lipscomb and Henderson. They responded predictably, not by ordering an investigation, but by putting out specific instructions against such practices at the next staff meeting.

There was specific testimony presented, however, that Lipscomb had ordered at least one village burned or destroyed in response to sniper fire from it. The information was supplied by Ronald Ridenhour, the ex-GI whose letter had triggered the initial investigation. Ridenhour, quoting —as he did in his My Lai 4 letter—from the statements of others, told of a helicopter door gunner for Lipscomb's command-and-control helicopter who returned to the barracks "day after day . . . and repeat[ed] stories to me of how General Lipscomb had referred to the Vietnamese as 'dinks' and 'gooks' and how he had been very callous in his command direction of his troops in the villages, especially as far as having almost utter disregard for the crops and homes of Vietnamese civilians . . . This young man told me [that] somebody called up and said we received a couple of rounds of sniper fire from a village, and [Lipscomb] said, 'Burn it. Wipe them out.' This is a direct quote . . . It's secondhand and, therefore, you have to judge with a grain of salt, but the thing that sticks firmly in my mind is that he came back with stories of this sort so often, and then I knew the guy very well, and he is not a bull-shitter."

There is no dispute that official brigade policy ruled out indiscriminate burning, but many GIs and some staff officers did not know it. Arthur J. Dunn, a lieutenant who served as brigade press officer, told the Peers Panel that he had reviewed photographs showing Charlie Company GIs burning My Lai 4. He didn't find what was shown to be that unusual, but was surprised that the infantrymen would act so freely in front of a cameraman. "I'm not sure I ever really considered brigade or division policy . . ." Dunn said. "But I don't believe this kind of action was uncommon . . . that it would call for any kind of action to be taken right at the time. They [senior officers] might well have told them not to do this again."

Even if Henderson—and some of his brigade staff officers—remained largely ignorant about the war taking place a few miles from their headquarters,* he met the other basic requirements of a Vietnam commander: he had a su-

---

* The ignorance of some brigade staff officers about the war was considerable. For example: Blackledge, the brigade intelligence officer, told the Peers Panel that brigade personnel had instructed the Vietnamese in its area of operations to not run from helicopters during combat operations. Asked why, Blackledge replied, "We had many, many cases where the VC were attempting to get right in the middle of the civilians . . . so we attempted to get these civilians to not run, told them 'don't run.' " A moment later this exchange was held between a Peers investigator and the intelligence officer:
Q. "How do you say halt in Vietnamese?"
A. "I believe we trained them to say 'dung lai,' or something."
Q. "Did the troops in Task Force Barker know this?"
A. "This is pretty common among troops, especially the ones that are out there doing the shooting. We had little cards that were passed out to troops that had little phrases which included this. There was another way of saying halt in addition to 'dung lai,' but I've forgot this now."

perior mess hall and a rebuilt officers' club. There was considerable emphasis on the social side of being an officer and a gentleman: many GIs who served in the 11th Brigade talked to me with bitterness about the life style of the senior officers. "They had a fantastic mess hall," Jay A. Roberts, who worked in the public information office near headquarters, recalled. "The officers would have cocktail hour for an hour every night before dinner." Others talked about the ice cream, shrimp, and steak that were often on hand for the officers. Also frequently noted was the fact that Henderson utilized the headquarters' allotment of air conditioners for his mess hall and his personal quarters. Plans, perhaps only half serious, constantly were being developed by the headquarters clerks to blow up the mess hall. Other GIs boasted of being able to appropriate bottles of whiskey and cold beer from the officers' walk-in cooler. Frank D. Beardslee served as driver for Lieutenant Colonel Frank Barker and would often take him to the Duc Pho officers' club in time for the "5:30 happy hour. It was just like they were in Washington," Beardslee said of the officers. "They would talk about promotions and all that stuff—just like a cocktail party back in the world."

The brigade commanders, even if they couldn't match the four-room house of the division commander, did their utmost to live comfortably. Jay Roberts recalled the night in February, 1968, when General Lipscomb "used up a month's worth of flares to light up the road between the port [on the South China Sea fourteen miles south of Duc Pho] and headquarters area to bring up his house trailer." The trailer had been shipped from Hawaii. The flares were used to help troops, and accompanying helicopters, guard the highway, which was considered insecure against Viet Cong attack. "We really were short of flares [for combat operations] after that," Roberts said. "It made everybody mad."

Shortly before Lipscomb, a West Pointer, retired, the brigade public information office presented him with a scrapbook of photographs and news clippings highlighting his service with the 11th Brigade. Similar scrapbooks were made up for most senior officers who left the unit. Such work didn't upset Ronald L. Haeberle, a photographer for the brigade, at the time. But later, when the cameraman was criticized by the Peers Panel for not turning over his photographs of the My Lai 4 massacre to higher authorities, he explained why he never considered such a step: "You know something? . . . If a general is smiling wrong in a photograph, I have learned to destroy it . . . My experience as a GI over there is that if something doesn't look right, a general smiling the wrong way . . . I stopped and destroyed the negative."

Task Force Barker

*F*or a non-West Pointer, Lieutenant Colonel Frank A. Barker, Jr., had everything going for him. In January 1968, he had been pulled from his job as operations officer of the 11th Brigade and given command of a three-company task force of five hundred men that had been grouped together to find and destroy the enemy in the Batangan Peninsula area of eastern Quang Ngai Province. The peninsula was "Indian country," as far as American and South Vietnamese soldiers were concerned. Few operations had ever been mounted in Son My village, which was widely considered to be the staging and headquarters area for the main force of the 48th Viet Cong Battalion, one of the strongest units in Quang Ngai.

The area was heavily booby-trapped and the men of Task Force Barker—the lieutenant colonel followed a custom by naming the unit after himself—suffered. About fifteen GIs in the three companies were killed and eighty-five wounded by March 15, a high percentage of casualties—but one that did not necessarily reflect much direct confrontation with the enemy. For example, Charlie Company had four of its men killed and thirty-eight wounded in that time span, but the Peers Panel determined that only three of the casualties, including one death, resulted from direct enemy contact. But "Barker's Bastards," as the unit was quickly dubbed by the brigade public information office, seemingly was able to do what no other unit in the brigade could—find and destroy the enemy. In February the brigade reported two heavy engagements with the 48th Viet Cong Battalion in Son My village near the hamlets of My Lai 1 and 4. The 48th was an old nemesis to the South Vietnamese troops from the 2nd ARVN (Army of the Republic of South Vietnam), headquartered in nearby Quang Ngai City. During a three-day operation beginning February 12, the task force, led by Bravo Company under Captain Michles' command, reported the death of eighty Viet Cong. No one in the brigade or task force headquarters raised any questions about the fact that no enemy weapons were captured during the operation. On February 23–24, seventy-five Viet Cong were reported killed, and six weapons captured.

"We devoted quite a bit of coverage to Task Force Barker," James Ford, the brigade information office clerk, testified. "Up until Task Force Barker deployed, we hadn't been seeing too much action. As a result, our public information coverage was kind of slim . . . They were getting good contact and we were getting good copy out of it." Michael Adcock, who served both Lipscomb and Henderson as an aide, recalled that "it seems as though the people put together for Task Force Barker seemed to do a little better. They accomplished a little more . . . This started the ball rolling, so to speak." Barker's men had the highest body

count by far of any unit in the 11th Brigade; other officers
would speak admiringly of the commander's "luck" in getting solid contact. Donald Hooton, who served with Bravo
Company, had a different point of view about Barker, expressed during a mid-1971 interview: "Everybody said
'He's got the most phenomenal luck'; what they meant is
we'd go out and gun down a lot of people."

But the GIs, even Hooton, admired Barker. He wasn't
afraid to land his helicopter during a battle and often he
would join in the fray, firing his .45-caliber pistol at Vietnamese from a low-flying helicopter. He made sure that the
troops received at least one hot meal a day when in the
field. There were other reasons, too, for the widespread ad-
miration for Barker: he was "lean and mean," in military
tradition; handsome, with neatly chiseled features; friendly
to the "grunts," always accessible and always making it
clear that he understood their problems. Beardslee, Barker's
driver, will never forget how he got his job. He had been
routinely assigned to give the lieutenant colonel a ride while
the 11th Brigade was still in Hawaii, training to go to Vietnam. "How good are you?" Barker suddenly asked his
young driver. "Can you drive and keep your mouth shut?"
Told yes, Barker wanted him to "prove it." The next few
minutes were spent in a wild driving demonstration;
Beardslee won the job and the colonel won a loyal aide.

Barker's flash had attracted the attention of Major General Koster, who personally selected him to head the task
force. "Barker, in my estimation, seemed to have his finger
in and was pretty well in tune with what was going on . . ."
the general told the Panel.

Barker's responsibilities as a commander inside his assigned area of operations were total; he was in charge of the
intelligence, planning, and initiation of all task force operations, always with the approval of his superiors. "His opera-

tions, overall, I thought were successful in that area," Koster said. "He, I thought, was accomplishing the mission. Based on his performance there, I thought he should have a battalion when a battalion was freed up." Barker's promotion by Koster to the task force left a crucial administrative gap in the brigade headquarters, one that Henderson, then acting as assistant brigade commander, tried to fill. But when Henderson assumed control of the brigade on March 15, he was not assigned a new administrative aide and was forced to do his paperwork alone at night.

Another reason, perhaps, for Henderson's anxieties over the task force was the Barker–Koster relationship. There were 15,000 lieutenant colonels in the Army in 1968 and fewer than three hundred battalions to command. Without such command experience in Vietnam, a young lieutenant colonel could not expect promotion. The pressure for the jobs was so intense that the Army limited battalion commander tours to six months. Normally, Henderson could expect to have a powerful hold over Barker, who would need his approval before commanding a battalion; the bargaining and negotiating for such jobs goes on daily in the Pentagon and elsewhere. But General Koster had already promised the next battalion command to Barker by the time Henderson took over the brigade. In effect, Henderson's potential patronage—an important part of a commander's job—was diminished, and a protégé, if he had one, would have to wait longer for a battalion commander's spot.

There was no fancy officers' club at the task force headquarters located at Landing Zone (LZ) Dotti a few miles from Quang Ngai City, the provincial capital. (The landing zone was named after Barker's wife, Dotti.) Barker, like all commanders, spent most of his working days in a helicopter and tried to catch up on the paperwork with his aides at night. The administration of the task force fell to the opera-

tions officer, Major Charles C. Calhoun, a Southerner who
was serving his second tour in Vietnam. The task force
headquarters was severely understaffed; it had only one
typewriter assigned to it and one clerk to operate it.

As a result, it was loosely run. There was no time, and no
staff, to prepare the required task force version of the rules
of engagement or provide instructions for the troops on the
Geneva Convention. Captain Ernest Medina testified that
his men had not been given the pocket-sized cards outlining
some of the rules of land warfare that the military command provided for each GI in Vietnam. Even if the cards or
similar materials had been available, there is little reason to
believe that the attitude of Bravo and Charlie Companies
would have changed. Murder, rape, and arson were part of
the war. The unofficial task force rule seemed to be not to
commit such actions directly in front of the commanding
officer. "If it's not done right in front of him," Larry Congleton said, speaking of Captain Earl Michles of Bravo
Company, "he'd try to ignore it. But if he ever caught you
smoking pot, he'd have gone wild." Michles wasn't as strict
about killing innocent civilians. Congleton, who served as
the captain's radio operator, recalled that the officer
"wanted kills. By the first time we actually killed anybody
who was a Viet Cong with a weapon, we had reported
twenty or thirty confirmed kills, and I said, 'Hey, we just got
our first kill.' He really got mad. The captain was straight
military. He didn't have any honest compassion for the people. If he thought being good to the Vietnamese would have
enhanced his career, he would have done it."

Sergeant Lones R. Warren, who was commander of the
military police unit assigned to Task Force Barker, told the
Peers Panel that he and his men had never received any
training on the reporting of war crimes or of atrocities.
"There's no way in hell you can police a company in the

field," Warren said. "It's got to be left up to the unit commander, and then if there is some discrepancy [over an inci-
dent], he has got two ways he can go. He can go to the military police or he can go to his immediate commander [to
report it]." Asked if he had ever reported a serious crime to
his superiors at the task force or at the brigade, Warren
said, "No, sir, because none was reported [to him]."

Those who objected to the methods of Task Force Barker
simply kept their mouth shut and waited for a chance to
transfer out of the unit. Major Patrick M. Trinkle, a young
West Pointer who later taught tactics at the military academy, served with the task force for one month as commander of Alpha Company. At that time the three task force
companies were operating independently of one another,
two on duty at separate fire bases and one on patrol in the
field. The pattern pleased Trinkle. "I did not like the way B
Company or C Company, either one, operated, so I always
pulled strings so that A Company did not get involved with
operations with the other two companies any more than we
absolutely had to," the major testified. "I felt that Michles
and Medina, neither one, understood what kind of problems we were faced with . . . I felt Michles' biggest problem
was gross exaggeration. If he saw two or three people running, he would shoot at them and report them as VC . . .
Medina's biggest problem, I think, was discipline. From his
radio transmissions and his reports to task force, it is my
personal opinion that his company shot and asked questions later."

Trinkle also told the Panelists that Barker, in his opinion,
"was a weak commander . . . Barker, from the time the
task force was formed, gave me the impression that he did
not really know what he wanted to do or how he wanted to
do it. He seldom talked to us [company commanders] as far
as sitting down and discussing the operations or how we

should do them. Most of my operations . . . were things which really Major Calhoun and I more or less got together and sat down, and tried to figure out where the VC were and how we could sneak up on them . . . I cannot remember Colonel Barker ever sitting down and really talking to me about what the area of operation was like."

Barker, Medina, and Michles were all respected by their men as officers who "took care of their troops." Trinkle, who did not let his men rape women and indiscriminately burn civilian homes, had a price on his head. Frank Beardslee recalled that "the kids wanted him. He [Trinkle] was a real uptight guy. For one thing, he didn't look after his people. He was a superbrain but he didn't have it out in the field." Trinkle was shot in the back with a rifle bullet while leading his company into action north of My Lai 4 on February 23, during the first day of a two-day operation that was to net a body count of eighty. Some GIs were convinced his own men had shot him. Michael Adcock, then working for General Lipscomb at brigade headquarters, recalled in an interview that "there was a stink about it, that he had been shot in the back."

Trinkle was evacuated to a hospital and given a medal, and Alpha Company got a new commander. The policies of this replacement were more in line with what seemed to be the normal practices of Task Force Barker. Lieutenant Donald R. Coker, who served as a platoon leader under Trinkle and his successor, told the Panel how the company began to burn and kill: "I was generally unhappy with the way he [the new company commander] was conducting the war, because blowing up a house with rice in it doesn't do anything but scatter rice. Burning hootches that you don't get fire from just hacks off the people that were maybe neutral—or maybe they were on the VC side because the VC happened to control the area. But this was his policy . . . and it really bothered me at that time."

Task Force Barker's two February missions into Son My village were officially described as unqualified successes, although the disparity between total Viet Cong kills and captured weapons—155 to six—was extreme. Even the Panel's analysis of the operations assumed that the task force had been in heavy contact with the enemy. Discussing the first operation that began February 12, it said: "As B Company approached My Lai 4, heavy fire was received from the enemy occupying prepared positions . . . A platoon of B Company attempted to flank the enemy position and was pinned down. A platoon of armored personnel carriers was committed and, by using heavy suppressive fires, extracted the platoon." Most of the action revolved about Bravo Company, and its men received a number of medals, including a Silver Star for Captain Michles and Bronze Stars for some of the infantrymen.

Larry Congleton, the radioman for Michles, remembered a much different operation, which he described to me in mid-1971: "Everybody said we were in contact with a VC battalion. Well, there *might* have been thirty in there—but those VC really had their shit together. I still had all these feelings then that Americans never retreated; they always go on the attack. It was ridiculous. We had three platoons spread out. One of them got fired on by some VC, and then the VC ran. The second platoon took off running and shooting after them, but got led into rice paddies and got pinned down there." It was then, Congleton said, that Michles called the armored personnel carriers (APCs) for help in getting the men out of the area. It was an overcast day and aircraft were of no use. "Michles was in a panic," the ex-GI said. "He was using both radios and got their

cords all tangled . . . The biggest thing Michles wanted to
do was to get everybody out of there."

Congleton did not recall any attempt to flank the Viet
Cong position. The captain and others in the command post
ran behind the APCs and went into the area to help evacuate the troops. By this time, according to Congleton, the
Viet Cong were long gone: "We fired more than eight hundred rounds of 105-millimeter shells—all we had. The body
count [of seventy-eight for that phase of the operation] was
personally determined by Barker, but I didn't see any dead
Viet Cong that day." Adding to everyone's fears and miser-
ies, the radioman said, was the fact that the APCs got lost
and eventually were rerouted while attempting to lead the
men out of danger; at one point they were driven into a
stream too deep to ford.

Terry Reid also recalled the mission, Bravo Company's
first big operation. "Michles was in the rear directing his
platoons and we were all running around in circles, running
into each other. We retreated behind tracks and ran around
for half an hour before finally getting back," he told me.
"Our lieutenant told us that we could get six or twelve
Bronze Stars out of this—and then told us the story they
were going to give Division." One machine gunner was
given a Bronze Star for his activity under enemy fire although his weapon had jammed early in the day and was in-
operable, Reid claimed.

The operation that day was staged in a section of Son My
that technically was the responsibility of the ARVN, and
many of the task force GIs understandably castigated the
Vietnamese soldiers for not coming to their aid. The Vietnamese inaction prompted General Lipscomb, then the brigade commander, to personally complain to ARVN headquarters. Then, as Colonel Carl C. Ulsaker, at the time the
senior American adviser to the Vietnamese Army at Quang

Ngai, testified: "I reminded the general that you didn't cross somebody else's boundary unless they asked you to, and I had personally called Colonel Barker on the radio and asked him. I said, 'We know you got an engagement going. Do you need help?' He said, 'No, the company's doing fine.'"

According to the official final enemy body count for that day of the operation—seventy-eight Viet Cong killed, with one American fatality—there would have been little reason for Colonel Barker to request the aid of South Vietnamese troops. The suspicion exists that Barker did not want any other unit to detract from his "success"; particularly since the South Vietnamese also were quick to claim miraculously high enemy body counts.

Alpha Company bore the brunt of the enemy fire on the next operation, which began February 23. Summarizing that engagement uncritically, the Peers report noted that "heavy enemy fire was received, including mortars, recoilless rifles, rockets, and automatic weapons. Artillery and air strikes were quickly called in and the APCs swept toward the enemy outpost line . . . By late afternoon the enemy broke contact and was able to escape by intermingling with civilians . . . and by using the complex tunnel system honeycombing the sector." Bravo Company's role in this operation was minor, but Congleton again was left with the impression that the reports of large enemy forces firing at them were exaggerated. "We were walking through some rice field trying to relieve a platoon and the guys were laying in the fields shouting, 'Get down. Get down. They're shooting at us.' We just walked through," Congleton told me. Donald Coker, who was commanding an Alpha Company platoon during the assault, said in a mid-1971 interview that he was convinced his men had faced an organized enemy attack. Coker acknowledged, however, that he only "saw four or five enemy bodies—that's about all." He added, "I think we did get a couple [of Viet Cong]." And at least one of his casualties, he said, was the result of careless fire from the APCs.

There is no question that the task force was in contact with at least some Viet Cong troops during the February operations, unlike the operation in My Lai 4 on March 16, when there was no organized opposition. Yet that vast disparity did exist between the high enemy body count and the extremely low weapons count. To notice this, however, would have called for some kind of an investigation or inquiry, and thus would have violated all of the operating procedures at Division and Brigade. Such inquiries were initiated only by complaints from below, not at the top.*

Instead, Lieutenant Colonel Barker was able to tell his superiors, in a glowing after-action report on his own mission: "This operation was well planned, well executed, and successful. Friendly casualties were light and the enemy suffered a hard blow. However, many enemy soldiers were able to escape with their weapons and the weapons of the enemy dead. This was caused by several factors . . . Although the air strikes were timely and effective . . . time was lost waiting for aircraft . . . Air evacuation of wounded was a contributing factor in allowing the enemy time to escape, since supporting fires had to be stopped each time the medevac helicopter was brought in. The ground units were not as aggressive later in the battle as they were earlier . . . Aggressiveness increased again at the insistence of the task force commander [Frank Barker], but during the lull several VC had escaped with weapons."

* As of December 4, 1971, the official Pentagon enemy death count, including both Viet Cong and North Vietnamese troops, was 785,572. The tabulations began on January 1, 1961.

Barker's after-action report was written March 24, one month after the operation, but only eight days after the My Lai 4 and My Khe 4 massacres. Perhaps that is why he concluded with the following paragraph: "Although control of noncombatants posed no particular problem . . . operations of this type should provide for the establishment of a civilian collecting point and a medical evacuation plan."

6

Planning the
Mission

*I*t was inevitable that Barker decided to conduct
another operation in Son My. He talked about it
sometime early in March with General Lipscomb,
and got his approval. "Barker said to me on one or
two occasions that he was going back into Pinkville," Lipscomb told the Panel. "This 48th [Viet
Cong] Battalion was a thorn in his side there, and
he was going to go back in there . . . It just was
something that had to be done before the area
would be under control." Before committing
troops, Barker had unsuccessfully sought permission to clear the Son My area with Rome plows,
monstrous 2,500-pound bulldozers capable of lev-
eling hundreds of acres per day. Cecil D. Hall, who
served as communications sergeant for the task
force, told me during an interview of Barker's failure to convince brigade officials of the need for the
plows. "I heard him mention many times," Hall
said, "that it'd sure be nice if we could get some

bulldozers and clear that place once and for all."

Theoretically, Son My was not within Task Force Barker's prescribed area of operations (AO) but was the responsibility of the 2nd ARVN Division headquartered less than ten miles away at Quang Ngai City. But Barker and his men had only contempt for their allies, stemming largely from the ARVN's failure to support the task force during its operations in Son My in February. "The 2nd ARVN Division would never do anything," Captain Eugene M. Kotouc, the task force intelligence officer, told General Peers. "Sir, they wouldn't fight, and they would not even protect themselves very well, sir. Colonel Barker was a good commander and Colonel Barker wanted to relieve the pressure on the Quang Ngai area and also on our area. The VC were in that area. They were not in our AO and we knew where they were, down in that area. Colonel Barker wanted to go down in there and fight them . . ."

Contempt for the Vietnamese Army was not confined to the men of the task force. American province officials routinely approved Barker's request for permission to operate in the Son My village area, but no details of the task force plans were revealed in advance to 2nd ARVN officers. Lieutenant Colonel William D. Guinn, Jr., deputy adviser for military affairs at Quang Ngai Province, testified that Barker would be on his own while operating in the area, ". . . without advising us of what they were doing. This was normal because they didn't want us to know what they were doing because there were too many leaks in the Vietnamese structure."

Although Koster was assured that the forthcoming task force assault would be even more successful than the two previous operations—Barker reported that he expected to find four hundred Viet Cong at Pinkville—the division commander acknowledged that he really knew very little about the planning. He was consulted about the mission, Koster said, simply because only he could authorize the use of the twelve helicopters Barker considered necessary. As Barker initially explained it to the general, the main target was the hamlet of My Lai 1, the center of the Pinkville area where intelligence said the 48th Battalion had its headquarters. Although Koster approved the mission, he really didn't attempt to analyze it, as he later testified: "I'm reasonably sure that he probably outlined the fact that there would be two blocking companies—one would get there overland, and the other two were air assaulted . . . But I don't recall that I even focused as to exactly where it was on the map, one of these little villages as opposed to another one. The one that had been the primary target was the one on the coast, and the only time I really heard [the word] Pinkville used was for that one on the coast [My Lai 1] as opposed to any of the others . . . Of course, that place was nothing but a bunch of rubble anyway. I know they had gone in there on many occasions and tried to blow the dugouts and tunnels, and I knew that this was a continuing thing. Every time we went through there we tried to blow a few more of them."

At no point were there any formal written plans outlining the tactical aspects of the operation. Barker's plan for the mission was not seen in any form by any top-level Americal Division officers, such as Lieutenant Colonel Tommy P. Trexler, the intelligence chief. In addition, Major Charles Calhoun, the task force operations officer, couldn't recall any specific concern about the citizens of Son My before the March 16 operation and even told the Panel he thought there were only about a hundred residents in My Lai 4, Charlie Company's main target (the population was at least

500). The major did note that "on a continuous basis leaflets were dropped in the area advising the civilians to move into the refugee center . . . they [task force personnel] had advised the civilians that it was an area they should move out of and some of them, I understand, left."

It's not clear whether anyone in Task Force Barker headquarters really understood that the civilians had no place to go, even if they wanted to, because the refugee camps were already overflowing, although many officers at Division level were aware of the situation. Major General Koster, asked about relocation plans, simply said there were none: "I didn't really look upon that area as our primary concern." "This was the primary concern of the 2nd ARVN Division . . . I wouldn't have said the [Americal] Division would have ever taken it upon itself to relocate these people. I don't know if I would have even encouraged ARVN to undertake the relocation of people in those hamlets, because it's just an impossible task. You wouldn't have had any place to put them."

Captain Kotouc, the intelligence officer who took over his job three weeks before the My Lai 4 operation, gave the Peers Panel one possible explanation for the task force's lack of any real concern about the civilians: "The civilian population was known to be rather active sympathizers with the VC. The VC was a local unit. The VC came from the families. There were mothers, fathers, and sons of the VC. The father was a VC, and the uncle was a VC." *

* Kotouc's assessment was made, of course, on the basis of limited experience. The captain told the Peers Panel that his shortcomings were compensated, nonetheless, by his service during a tour in 1962 as an adviser to an ARVN unit in Quang Ngai Province. "The adviser group was kind of loose and we traveled all over the area . . ." Kotouc testified. "I had driven up there [near My Lai 4] because, if I am not mistaken, I went swimming there one day."

It was a hopeless situation for the civilians in Son My, regardless of their political affiliations, if any. Captain Charles K. Wyndham, who served until March 16 as the task force civil affairs officer, testified that he had never participated in any planning for the handling and safety of civilians before any operation with Task Force Barker. He had learned while in Vietnam, he added, "it's kind of useless to go out there [into the field with an infantry company] and try to do civil affairs."

At one point in the task force planning for the operation, some unchallenged intelligence information about the civilians in My Lai 4 was received: The residents would leave their hamlet about 7 A.M. on the day of the operation, a Saturday, to go to market.

Since none of the planning details of the task force operation had been presented to higher headquarters, it was impossible for staff officers there to evaluate the intelligence assumptions with more sophistication.

However, amid all the conflicting testimony before the Peers Panel, one consensus did emerge: that there was no basis for assuming that all of the residents of My Lai 4 would leave the village to go marketing at about seven in the morning. In fact, Lieutenant Clarence E. Dukes, a well-informed intelligence officer at American Division headquarters, said that precisely the opposite might have been expected: "I would say that normally by sunrise if there were VC soldiers in a populated area they'd be moved out before dawn . . . Your women and children would be around town. Most of your male population would have moved out to their daily work." Lieutenant Colonel Trexler had a similar opinion: "An occupied village with any reasonable number of people, I would expect some of them to be there at any time of the day or night unless there was some other reason that they had been alerted to get out."

Under any circumstances, he was asked, "would there always be left behind children, toddlers, old women, old men, pregnant women, and persons in these categories . . . ?" Trexler replied yes.

With concern for possible civilian casualties out of the way, the task force attack plan was drawn up. Major Calhoun summarized his understanding of the plan this way: ". . . the main force of the 48th Battalion was again back in this area [Son My village]. And having had so much trouble before getting across . . . these open rice paddies around this area of My Lai 4, Colonel Barker decided he wanted to land as close to the village, or get as close to the village as fast as he possibly could, to take advantage of surprise and so forth. So he decided on a heliborne operation. Generally he was thinking of landing near My Lai 4 with a rifle company [Medina's Charlie Company], tying up this outpost or security line that they had, and then taking another company and landing in behind for a real fast advance into the Pinkville area proper [My Lai 1] to see if we could catch the headquarters before it moved, as had happened in other operations."

Yet Kotouc, the intelligence officer, gave the Peers Panel a much different interpretation of the importance of My Lai 4: "The reason we went to My Lai 4 was because that is where we thought the headquarters and the two battalions [of the 48th] were."

There was no misunderstanding, however, over one other basic military tactic that was put to use by Colonel Barker. He ordered the task force's four support cannons to fire a three- to five-minute salvo of shells into the hamlet proper of My Lai 4 beginning at 7:20 A.M., about ten minutes before the landing of the first helicopter-borne squad of men, led by Lieutenant Calley. The process is known in the military as "prepping the area."

Lieutenant Colonel Robert B. Luper was serving then as commanding officer of all the artillery units attached to the 11th Brigade. He testified that Barker "wanted preparation fire, but not on his landing zone. This is a little different than we would normally expect, because he felt that the area that he was going to make his combat assault into was open enough that he could see if there was going to be any problem. He wanted the preparation fired north of his landing zone, which would have put it on My Lai, the village of My Lai." Asked if the entire five-minute attack was to be placed on the village, Luper replied, "It was . . . Now, this evidently at one time was a very populated place, but at the time this operation took place, most of those houses and buildings had been blown up, and it was a fairly small area compared to what the map showed." Luper acknowledged, under questioning, that the placing of artillery fire on even a thinly populated hamlet was against brigade policy, but added that there was nothing about Barker's plan that was not known to Colonel Henderson.

The use of artillery on a populated village also was considered routine by the officers at the task force. One justification for such tactics—a clear violation of international law—was offered by Major Calhoun: "So on the morning of the fifteenth [the day before the mission], he [Barker] had to decide whether he was going to land that close to the village without putting a prep on the western part of that village. If he landed in there, he felt, and I'm now having to speak for him and this is, I'm sure, what he thought, if he landed there knowing we had already been down there, that they had some [heavy] weapons . . . and machine guns and automatic weapons, if he landed in there with nine or twelve helicopters within the distance . . . he might lose helicopters and Americans . . . of course, the most vulnerable time is coming down with the first landing; you have nothing there, no troops on the ground and the choppers are slow and they are sitting down like ducks on the water. Or he could put the fire into the area and, I'm sure, realizing that some civilians might be hurt. There is a difference between the sacrifice of American troops and the sacrifice of some civilians in this area."

Another justification for the shelling of the village was the fact that such action had been "cleared" by the South Vietnamese authorities responsible for the area of operations. The Vietnamese considered the whole area to be Viet Cong dominated, and long had declared it a free-fire zone. Clearance was needed only to make sure that no American or South Vietnamese troops were operating in the immediate area. Captain Wayne E. Johnson, who was a liaison officer for the Americal Division attached to the 2nd ARVN headquarters in Quang Ngai, was responsible for relaying requests from American commanders for artillery clearance to the proper Vietnamese authority. Approval was invariably granted. Johnson said he believed that both the Americans and South Vietnamese serving in Quang Ngai Province "felt that whatever people were out there in Son My village were enemy. If there was a target worth shooting at, it shouldn't be canceled because of the presence of civilians. The district people didn't hold too many civilians to be in the area. It didn't hold a large population."

This generally held view was tragically wrong, as a subsequent resettlement program demonstrated. Saigon authorities began an uprooting in Son My village in February, 1969, expecting to relocate 5,000 civilians; at its end there were 12,000 people shifted from the area.*

* The inability to learn from past mistakes, which has undermined so much of the American effort in South Vietnam, was tragically demonstrated in late March, 1971, when Vietnamese troops began yet another

Lieutenant Colonel Luper explained to General Peers that once the clearance was obtained through the South Vietnamese, his men would fire on any requested target. He was asked, "And if you are firing in populated areas and killing noncombatants, you as an artilleryman could care less. Is that what you are telling me?" Luper replied, "No, sir. I am not saying that I could care less. But I am saying that if a ground commander requests fire . . . I think that I have a responsibility to question it if I know it is on a populated area, yes, sir, but if the commander on the ground still insists that he needs it, it is my responsibility to fire."

On March 15, the day before the mission, Colonel Barker, Major Calhoun, and Captain Kotouc scheduled a complete operational briefing on the mission in a small tent just outside task force headquarters. Invited to the session were the men who were going to play the key roles in the March 16 attack: Captain Medina of Charlie Company; Captain Michles of Bravo Company; Captain Stephen J. Gamble, commanding officer of the four-gun artillery battery located at Landing Zone Uptight, five miles north of My Lai 4; and Major Frederic W. Watke, commanding officer of the Aero-Scout Company of the 123rd Aviation Battalion located at the American Division headquarters area at Chu Lai. Watke's pilots would fly support for the mission. Alpha Company, the third unit in Task Force Barker, was assigned no significant role in the operation.

Sometime before the briefing, perhaps a few hours, Father Carl Creswell, a division Episcopal priest, paid his first visit to the task force headquarters. "It was basically a social call," the priest recounted in an interview with me.

---

relocation program in Son My. As many as 16,000 civilians were uprooted, a total that, according to *The New York Times,* "surprised" officials, who had expected to find far fewer refugees.

"Barker and Major Calhoun were working on maps, laying on the operation. I stood and watched them." Creswell remembered the mood inside the headquarters as "very, very hostile. They were going to 'level Pinkville.' You could cut the hostility with a knife. Nothing was said about resettlement [for the civilians]. I told them that I didn't think we made war like that." Creswell wasn't sure which officer responded, but the answer was uncompromising: "It's a tough war." He was surprised at the vehemence of their comments. Although he was accustomed to rhetorical excess at the platoon level, he said, "You can usually afford to be more clinical at the battalion level."

The briefing itself was professionally crisp. The headquarters staff at Task Force Barker listened inside the crowded briefing tent as Colonel Henderson gave what amounted to a pep talk; Henderson had, only hours before, formally taken over command of the 11th. It was a short talk, and Captain Stephen Gamble was able to recall much of it for the Panel: ". . . He generally reviewed what was going to occur the next day and he mentioned that it was a very important operation, and the Viet Cong unit that was located in that area—they wanted to get rid of them once and for all and get them out of that area. He stressed this point, and he wanted to make sure that everybody and all the companies were up to snuff and everything went like clockwork during the operation."

Captain Ernest Medina remembered Henderson's demand that the companies get more aggressive: "Colonel Henderson . . . stated that in the past two operations the failure of the operations was that the soldier was not aggressive enough in closing with the enemy. Therefore, we were leaving too many weapons and that the other enemy soldiers in the area, as they retreated, the women and children

in the area would pick up the weapons and run and therefore by the time the soldiers arrived to where they had killed
a VC that the weapon would be gone."

Captain Kotouc spoke of Henderson's promise that
"when we get through with that 48th Battalion, they won't
be giving us any more trouble. We're going to do them in
once and for all." The captain was pleased with Henderson's tough talk: "I thought, personally, that was a real fine
thing to say."

After the Henderson speech, Kotouc gave a quick summary of the intelligence situation, including the report that
all civilians would leave My Lai 4 by seven in the morning.
Major Calhoun followed with a map review. Then Barker
stood up. Kotouc recalled his words vividly: "Colonel
Barker said he wanted the area cleaned out, he wanted it
neutralized, and he wanted the buildings knocked down. He
wanted the hootches burned, and he wanted the tunnels
filled in, and then he wanted the livestock and chickens run
off, killed, or destroyed. Colonel Barker did not say anything about killing any civilians, sir," Kotouc told General
Peers, "nor did I. He wanted to neutralize the area."

Captain Medina further testified that Barker "instructed
me to burn and destroy the village; to destroy any livestock,
water buffalo, pigs, chickens; and to close any wells that we
might find in the village." Major Watke, the helicopter commander, told the Panel that the "most significant thing I recall from the whole thing was the real anticipation that they
were really going to have a body of enemy out there. They
were just convinced that there was a battalion in that area
and they were going to get in there before the battalion ex-
tricated itself . . . The last contact had produced a substantial number and he was going to go in there and clean out
that battalion and finish them up. He felt sure where they
were, and with the time and element of surprise he was

going to bag them. He convinced me." Watke remembered there was great stress put on the element of surprise that was in their favor. "It was a very typical briefing that I have been exposed to previously," he added. "The briefing was professional in my exposure to briefings in Vietnam. Everybody was sincere. The operation was discussed in a professional manner."

Specialist Four Frank Beardslee had also listened to the briefings; his job as Barker's driver had enabled him to squeeze unchallenged into a corner of the briefing tent. "Barker told them that he wanted the village taken care of. My impression was that he wanted the village cleaned out," Beardslee related in an interview. "He didn't say 'I want every living thing wiped off the map'—he didn't say kill women and children. He just said 'Take care of it.' We were going to 'get it on' until the 48th was no more." Beardslee volunteered to join Charlie Company for the operation—he wanted to earn his Combat Infantry's Badge (CIB).

After the formal briefing was over, Barker flew with Captains Medina and Michles over the next day's target areas, pointing out their landing zones and showing them where their artillery would impact. Medina and Michles were dropped off later at their company bivouac areas, where they, in turn, were to give their briefings to their infantrymen. The captains, both impressed by what they had heard from their superiors, faithfully relayed the life-and-death significance of the operation. That night Sergeant Nguyen Dinh Phu, a South Vietnamese Army interpreter, wandered among the Charlie Company soldiers. The briefing had ended two hours earlier, but Phu hadn't been there. He testified: "Many of the soldiers were drunk, a large number. One of the soldiers told me that tomorrow they would go on an operation and they would kill women, children, cattle, and everything . . . 'I'm not joking, that's the truth.' That

person was drunk and I discredited it to some extent because he was. After that I drank with them." Later, Phu
said, he returned to the tent he shared with Captain Medina
and went to bed. The captain was already asleep.

7

The Intelligence

Who told Task Force Barker that all of the civilians in the hamlet of My Lai 4 would magically disappear—on their way to market—shortly after 7 A.M. on March 16?

Where did the task force receive information stating that four hundred members of the 48th Viet Cong Battalion would be in the Son My village on March 16?

These two questions remained unanswered throughout the lengthy hearings into the My Lai 4 massacre. Witnesses were consistently asked if they could cite any documents or individuals who provided such information; the answers were invariably vague. "No, sir, I cannot cite any document," Captain Kotouc said confusedly in response to one such question, "but it was through interrogation of people I had talked to. This was always—this was the part we were trying to figure out, how they moved in the area. They all came and went about the same time . . . If I recall, part of it [the intelligence] came from Colonel Barker. Information, I think, he received from his contacts or somewhere like that. It is very difficult for me to pin it down."

Other witnesses testified that the task force worked very closely with Major David C. Gavin, the senior American adviser to the Vietnamese at Son Tinh, one of the six administrative districts of Quang Ngai Province. Gavin's district headquarters was a few miles west of Son My village. The major was an aggressive adviser who longed for combat duty; he had accompanied Task Force Barker on its previous Son My operations missions. Gavin and Barker conferred a number of times before the March 16 operation, but Gavin, as he testified, was not the originator of much fresh intelligence. His district headquarters was then in the process of setting up a District Intelligence and Operations Coordinating Center (DIOCC) under the control of the Phoenix program. This was a joint American–South Vietnamese venture aimed at identifying and then "neutralizing"—either through imprisonment, assassination, or forced defection—local members of the Viet Cong "infrastructure," known as VCI. As defined by the military, the VCI "is the leadership structure of the Communist insurgency. It constitutes the political, administrative, supply, and recruitment apparatus. The VCI supports military operations of VC and North Vietnamese Army units by providing guides, caches of food, clothing, weapons [etc.] . . . to achieve Communist objectives." A secondary goal of Operation Phoenix was to collate all of the various information gathered by the multiplicity of intelligence networks run by South Vietnamese government agencies.

The original impetus behind the program came from the Central Intelligence Agency, which began similar operations on a smaller scale in the early 1960s. By 1968 Phoenix Committees were set up in each of South Vietnam's forty-four provinces and directed by an agent from the Central Intelligence Agency, who sometimes operated under cover as an employee of the Agency for International Development (AID). Most of the information about the VCI was gathered through paid informants or from interrogations of Viet Cong and civilians captured or detained during military operations. Elaborate, and sometimes computerized, file indexes were kept on suspected VCI in villages and hamlets; many covert military operations were launched to "neutralize" such persons. These operations, largely made up of South Vietnamese but often led by American military men, were supplied with "blacklists" of known VCI by a Phoenix Committee member. The teams eventually became known as Province Reconnaissance Units (PRUs) and often included Nationalist Chinese and Thai mercenaries. By 1968, most of the provinces and districts had monthly or weekly quotas of VCI neutralizations that had to be met. Behind the program was a vast amount of American money, paid to informants and to the assassination teams. Two separate branches of police, financed by American funds, had been developed. The more elite Special Police teams were given the responsibility of collecting, collating, and evaluating the VCI intelligence at the district and province levels. National Police Field Forces (NPFF) teams became the paramilitary arm of the National Police, and also conducted operations against the VCI.

The Phoenix system works this way: once Vietnamese civilians are identified by the district or province operations center as VCI suspects, most are quickly arrested and taken to the Province Interrogation Center (PIC) for questioning. Others are killed on the spot. After interrogation the suspects, still in custody, are brought before the Province Secu-

rity Committee, an all-Vietnamese panel of seven that includes four representatives of the police and military. In
effect, the civilians are tried by a group of men sitting in
judgment of arrests made by their own police agencies. The
sentences for those thought to be Viet Cong sympathizers or
VCI usually are two-year maximum terms which, however,
can be renewed indefinitely. After sentencing, the prisoners
may be sent to repressive political prisons such as the one at
Con Son Island. Any other citizen for whom the evidence
was less persuasive could be jailed for up to one year with
no judicial review.

The basic governing document for the Phoenix program
is known as SOP-3, and is provided by the Vietnamese government to its operatives. A translation of that document
also is made available to the Americans in the program.
SOP-3 clearly sets forth the type of data it desires from local
agents: "Information on a person, residents of the area who
make suspicious utterances such as . . . expressions which
distort Government of Vietnam policies and the action of
Government of Vietnam cadres." Informants are given the
following guidelines by SOP-3 to determine whether a
neighbor should be reported: "Those who act suspiciously:
(a) the hesitation or fearful attitude of a dishonest person;
(b) contact with those whom we suspect; (c) regular secret
colloquies of a certain group in the area."

American and South Vietnamese officials have been in-
genious in their attempts to establish clandestine sources of
information on the elusive VCI. At one stage, officials in
Saigon announced the formation of a new ombudsman program, known as census grievance, which called for Vietnamese government employees to visit local villages and
hamlets and give residents a chance to air grievances and
complaints against the central government without fear of

local reprisal. The program's real function was to create a new method of determining which villagers were members of the VCI; many American dollars have been spent to finance such teams in contested areas of Vietnam. In Quang Ngai and other provinces, separate offices for census grievance were set up, with CIA agents in charge.

American officials have gone to great lengths publicly to deny the much-published assertions that the Phoenix operation was primarily an "assassination program." In private, however, the military publications tend to confirm that prior to 1970, a policy of assassination was closely identified with the program. A May, 1970, directive published by the Military Assistance Command in Vietnam (MACV) warned American soldiers connected with the Phoenix program that they were "specifically unauthorized to engage in assassinations or other violations of the rules of land warfare . . ." Official statistics compiled by MACV listed 15,776 persons as "neutralized," that is, those who were jailed or renounced the National Liberation Front, by the Phoenix program in 1968. This included 2,259 VCI who were killed. In 1969, the military high command in Saigon set a quota of 21,000 "neutralizations" for the Phoenix program. End of the year statistics showed that 19,534 persons were "neutralized," with 6,187 deaths. A government document noted in 1970 that the 1969 quota was not reached, in part, because of "an end of year slump." These statistics, like all others in Vietnam, are highly suspect.*

---

* On July 19, 1971, William E. Colby, a former CIA official who became head of the American pacification program in 1968, acknowledged during a discussion of the Phoenix program that South Vietnam in 1967 and 1968 was in a "wild and unstable period and a lot of things were done that should not have been done. We have been trying to get it stopped with some measure of success." During testimony before a subcommittee of the House Foreign Operations and Government Information Committee, Colby also reported that 8,191 Vietnamese were killed by the Phoe-

Patrick J. McGarvey was assigned as an undercover agent for the Central Intelligence Agency in South Vietnam during the 1960s in a program that was a forerunner of the present Phoenix operation. Then a Washington, D.C., salesman, McGarvey told me about his work, during an interview early in 1971: "It was very glibly dubbed the 'Four Eyes and Four Ears' program then . . . We worked with the National Police in each province. What we wanted was to have two informants in each hamlet and village who didn't know each other, who didn't know they were working for the same people. Their main purpose in life, for which they got about thirty bucks [a month], was to keep detailed books on everybody who moved in each hamlet. Every week the National Police would go down and get reports for us [the CIA operated at the province level]. We had files set up for each hamlet and each village, and what we'd do is once a month pull out all of the material and review it. Then the crunch came because you'd find some guy's pattern of activity was unusual, so right away you'd brand him a VCI suspect. Then you ask one of the informants to follow the guy, and then he graduates to the confirmed VCI list.

"We had a tiger by the tail. Many times the case officers were writing phony reports, saying they had thirty-five informants in a lot of villages, while they were just sitting back doing nothing except collecting money. The big thing was to show how pervasive our network was becoming. We had to get statistics, performance figures, stuff to pump back up the pipeline to Washington.

"The whole thing just kind of slid in one direction. I

nix program in 1970, and defended the operation as "an essential part of the war effort . . . to protect the Vietnamese people . . . from the Communist clandestine organization in Vietnam."

mean, you can't prove that anybody ever said, 'Okay, we're going to go out and start killing people,' because it just started happening. The information was there and the enthusiasm was there—at least among the National Police and the CIA staff—and it was inevitable. It started right after we got in big with the [American] ground forces in the fall of 1965. MACV sent a captain or major in counterintelligence [CI] into our province, and by being exposed to the Army penchant for body count—kill, kill, kill—the attitude sort of rubbed off by osmosis on the Vietnamese National Police. It was almost by accident, sort of like, 'Okay, we got the information. What the fuck are we going to do with it— play with it or act on it.' "

The judgment of the men running the programs left much to be desired, in McGarvey's eyes: "Once some psychological-warfare guy in the CIA back in Washington thought of a way to scare the hell out of the villagers [in a hamlet that was known to be friendly to the Viet Cong]. When we killed a VCI in there, they wanted us to spread-eagle the guy, put out his eye, cut a hole in his back, and put his eye in there. The idea was that fear would be a good weapon. The funny thing was, people got squeamish about cutting out his eye, so they got hold of some CBS eyes [the network's logo] and began dropping them all around the body."

On February 4, 1968, the Central Intelligence Agency sent a new man into Quang Ngai Province—third largest in South Vietnam—and assigned him the job of running the Phoenix operation. Robert B. Ramsdell was new in every respect; although he was about forty-five years old, this was his first assignment with the agency. It was also the first time he had been in South Vietnam.

Ramsdell had enlisted in 1941 in the Army as a private; he was discharged in 1958 as a captain, because of deafness in his right ear. He had been a police investigator for the Army, and was serving in its Criminal Investigation Division at the time of his discharge. He moved to Poughkeepsie, New York, where he applied for and received a private investigator's license. He also gave the local police force some training in investigative techniques. In 1960, he moved his family down to Orlando, Florida, where he eventually opened a private investigator's office. "I wasn't doing so well," Ramsdell told me during an interview in his office, "and I wrote a letter to the agency looking for a job. This was in 1967. I took my training in the States and they hired me." After his service in Vietnam, his employment contract was not renewed by the agency and in August, 1969, he returned to the United States and went back into the private investigation business.

Ramsdell described his functions in Vietnam during his incognito appearance before the Peers Panel (newsmen were told he was an AID employee): "I was the adviser to the Special Police Branch of the South Vietnamese police. I think this branch would best be described as a combination of the FBI and the CIA rolled into one . . . As the Phoenix coordinator, I also handled intelligence nets, chains, and so forth . . . I think it can best be described as a pool where we brought in all intelligence from members of all organizations, including Vietnamese, American, civilian, and military and everything, and pooled it, and then fed it back to organizations where it could be used either in the Vietnam area or the American . . . I, in my capacity, had very little actually to do with the military, the American or the Vietnamese—other than the fact that I fed them information. Their principal duty was to assist us, cooperate with us, on the elimination of the VCI . . . Perhaps it would best describe my position in terms of a wheel and I was in the hub position . . ."

Ramsdell's enthusiasms and ambitions astounded the military members of the intelligence team who were working as advisers to the 2nd ARVN Division or with the province advisory staff. He immediately began wearing the outfit which seemed to appeal to many CIA agents in Vietnam: beret, camouflage Army jacket with corduroy collar, Levis, and white fuzzy sox. A large, heavy-set man, Ramsdell often carried an exotic Swedish-made high-velocity submachine gun or a Browning automatic pistol, two more trademarks of many agents.

Ramsdell quickly became controversial. Most of the young military intelligence officers working in Quang Ngai City had never met his predecessor, who ran both the Phoenix program and the Province Interrogation Center anonymously. The CIA men assigned to Quang Ngai generally kept to themselves, spending their off-duty hours at their quarters—cryptically known in the city as the "Embassy House." Gerald Stout of Syracuse, New York, now a law school student but then an Army intelligence officer, vividly recalled his first meeting with Ramsdell: "This big fat guy burst into my office one day and he wanted 'this and that thing.' The first thing I heard out of his mouth was, 'Well, we all know who I am—I'm the Fuller Brush man.' " Stout and other officers were invited to a meeting of the Phoenix Committee, many for the first time, and learned that Ramsdell had "lists and lists of Vietnamese. He said he was going to get them [the blacklists] out to the district so they can eliminate the VCI."

One of the CIA agent's first steps was to begin rounding up the residents of Quang Ngai City whose names were on the Phoenix blacklists. As Ramsdell explained it in the interview, the citizens were actually undercover members of the shadow Viet Cong government which was ready to begin operating in the open after the Tet offensive. The

heavy Viet Cong losses in the attack on Quang Ngai City
during Tet had set back the timetable. "After Tet," Ramsdell said, "we knew who many of these people were and we
let them continue to function because we were controlling
them. They led us to the VC security officer for the district.
We wiped them out [the Viet Cong] in Tet and then went
ahead and picked up the small fish." During his testimony
before the Panel, Ramsdell also alluded to the operation:
"We, in the first part of March, had wrapped up forty-four
VCI within the city of Quang Ngai . . . This was the play-
over from the Tet affair." The forty-four civilians who were
alleged members of a shadow government were arrested
and "eliminated," that is, put to death, by the Phoenix Special Police. It was a remarkably quick response from a CIA
operative who had only arrived in Quang Ngai after the Tet
offensive had begun. "Ramsdell simply eliminated everyone
who was on those lists," said Stout. "It was recrimination."

Army Captain Randolph L. Lane, who was in charge of
the intelligence section of the advisory team, recalled learning later that the Ramsdell victims "were not Viet Cong." In
fact, he said he and others had never heard of a "shadow
government" composed of civilians inside the city waiting
to take over after Tet. Ramsdell's operation may have been
conducted with good intentions—after all, eliminating Viet
Cong was his job—but it added to his souring reputation
among the younger intelligence officers.

"I remember the praise heaped on us after Tet," Lane,
now an insurance salesman in Atlanta, Georgia, said caustically during an interview. "I recall some official praise coming from Da Nang [regional headquarters for the CIA] for
rounding up the 'coalition.' "

Ramsdell, apparently trying to increase his stature among
the Army men, unsuccessfully offered to build them a new
office, with new equipment. His purpose was clear: he

wanted to develop a working relationship with the American military units nearby.

"Ramsdell wanted to start a program whereby small American units would go out and take the lists and go out and round up villagers," Stout said. "The idea was to drop down early in the morning, surround the village, and round them up."

Lane remembered Ramsdell as "an empire builder. He tried to get the intelligence people behind him. His idea was that American Army units would be more effective in combating the infrastructure" than the Vietnamese Army. One of Ramsdell's first moves was to get the intelligence personnel working at the local district headquarters to begin reporting directly to him, instead of through the province advisory outlets. Some of the districts immediately fell under his influence, Lane said, among them the Son Tinh headquarters run by Major Gavin. "Ramsdell came on too strong," Lane said. "I didn't like him. He didn't have enough experience in the country, despite his attempts to disguise it."

One of Ramsdell's chief problems with the intelligence personnel arose over the Phoenix chief's insistence that he be allowed to interrogate captured high-ranking enemy officers before the military men at Quang Ngai. The officers knew that Ramsdell's jurisdiction was limited to the civilian infrastructure and did not encroach on military matters such as Viet Cong unit location and strength. In addition, there were doubts about his interrogation techniques. "Ramsdell would come along and draft them away from us and take them to the interrogation center," Stout said. "They would never come back. He'd say they'd gone over to the Americal Division. We knew what was happening—but it was out of my hands."

Lieutenant Norman Freemyre, who was serving as an intelligence adviser to the 2nd ARVN Division at Quang Ngai, also had some doubts about the interrogation techniques at the PIC. "I was there one time," Freemyre, now a law student at the University of Colorado, recalled. "My counterpart [the Vietnamese officer he was advising] and I went down to talk with a prisoner. Allegedly they had a man who was number three in the VCI infrastructure in the province. When we got there, his tongue was severely bitten." Freemyre wondered what had happened to the man and was told, he said, that the prisoner "had done it to himself." Such self-destruction seemed unlikely. Other officers recalled the night that Ramsdell came rushing up to the bar in the officers' club, looking for the Army doctor assigned to the advisory team. The men later said they learned from the doctor that a Viet Cong suspect had been severely burned with a branding iron on his stomach.

Ramsdell, in his interview with me, emphatically denied any mistreatment of prisoners. "I wanted prisoners," he said, "and I wanted them in good shape." Yet Dr. Margaret Nelson of New Haven, Connecticut, declared during a July, 1970, Congressional hearing into Con Son Island and other alleged South Vietnamese prisoner abuses, that she had treated dozens of PIC prisoners in Quang Ngai who had been tortured. Dr. Nelson testified that she worked for the American Friends Service Committee as a physician in the province from October, 1967, to October, 1969, and began regularly treating the civilians inside the province prison in the summer of 1968.

Dr. Nelson gave the following account: ". . . I also regularly examined and treated prisoners who had been tortured. This seems not to have occurred in the prison itself but in the Province Interrogation Center. I saw dozens of patients with bruises of varying severity. I also examined patients who had coughed up, vomited, or urinated blood after being beaten about the chest, back, and stomach. On at least two occasions I was able to document by x-rays fractures of bones following beatings. Prisoners also told me of being tortured by electricity with wires attached to ears, nipples, and genitalia; by being forced to drink concoctions containing powdered lime and other noxious substances, and by being tied up and suspended by ropes often upside down from the rafters for hours. On at least three occasions, patients seriously ill or injured and under my care were removed to the Province Interrogation Center without my knowledge for further interrogation."

Captain Jon Fasnacht headed a special Marine interrogation team that had been assigned by III MAF headquarters to Quang Ngai, with orders to report directly to the higher MAF headquarters. Fasnacht was constantly battling with Ramsdell over the interrogation of military prisoners. "The first time I met Ramsdell I'd gone to the interrogation center with Quy [Le Quang Quy, a Vietnamese interpreter working with Fasnacht] and we attempted to elicit some information from a Vietnamese prisoner. There was Ramsdell with his beret and spook outfit. He went up to Quy and said, 'I hate to tell you this, little buddy, but you know who I'm with—the biggest.' "

Similar stories about Ramsdell's arrogance and lack of judgment were rife throughout the military staff at Quang Ngai; feelings ran so high, said Stout, that when the CIA personnel would come to the officers' club for a drink, "they were asked to produce their ID cards and stuff like that. Eventually they stopped coming around."

One of the most perceptive critics of Ramsdell was Lieutenant Jesse Frank Frosch, a former journalist who worked in intelligence under Captain Lane. After leaving the Army, Frosch joined United Press International in Atlanta, Georgia, and began writing a book on Quang Ngai Province; he had kept assiduous journals and smuggled home, so his colleagues believed, copies of many important documents. Frosch never finished his book—he was killed in late 1970 while covering the Cambodian war for UPI—but in his one published article he caustically described the techniques of an intelligence agent, although the agent was not mentioned by name. "A CIA operative," Frosch wrote, "who went under a code name . . . was a former Army man who had only recently joined the agency; this was his first assignment. He arrived long on enthusiasm and energy but woefully low on judgment. His intelligence estimates were so ludicrous that he was ignored by serious intelligence officers in the province. But if anybody could pull a snow job, it was this operative. Shortly after his arrival, even the experienced military-intelligence team at Quang Ngai City was sucked in by his bubbling confidence. Based on CIA information, a Special Forces team was sent to reconnoiter a supposed Viet Cong industrial-hospital complex. The only thing it found was an ambush.

"The CIA operative liked to think big, and it showed in his intelligence estimates. He estimated the 48th Battalion at a strength of 450 men . . . He could produce report after report to reinforce his statements, but there was a reason for that. Just as he thought big, so, too, did he pay big for information. Indeed, he was known to pay as much for a single, unconfirmed piece of information as the military intelligence team paid its entire agent net in a month. The Vietnamese agents—who were not as financially ignorant as the operative thought them to be—quickly recognized that he paid well for overblown reports. They responded with the big reports he wanted. The agents ended up wealthy and the operative, happy."

All of the former intelligence officers I talked with were privately convinced that Frosch was referring to Ramsdell

in his article; they recalled that Frosch was more knowl-
edgeable about the workings and politics of the province
than most junior officers.

Ramsdell acknowledged to me that he was indeed the
prototype for Frosch's anonymous agent, but discounted
the criticisms as sour grapes: "Frosch was operating at a
lower level; I had nothing to do with those people. My job
was at province level. I wasn't in a position to be liked and I
wasn't trying to be liked." In fact, Ramsdell had far more in
common with senior commanders such as Major Gavin and
Lieutenant Colonel Barker than the young intelligence
officers—who were even then anxiously counting the numbers of days they had left in the Army—realized. For one
thing, there was his attitude toward the Son My area, as expressed to the Peers Panel: "Very frankly, anyone that was
in that area was considered a VCS [Viet Cong suspect] because they couldn't survive in that area unless they were
sympathizers. I mean this is something that you can't print
for the American public, but it's a known fact among anyone who's in Vietnam. The VC wouldn't have left them
alive. They had to cooperate to stay in that area."

Ramsdell refused to speak specifically about the information he provided Task Force Barker before the My Lai 4
operation, but acknowledged that his intelligence undoubtedly was a factor in the planning for the mission. "The 48th
VC Battalion was in and out of there [Son My]," Ramsdell
said. "They used it as a staging area . . . We had a Viet
Cong area and we had a highly infiltrated area. We cleaned
it up." He definitely recalled, he said, getting reports about
the Viet Cong unit from that area at the time of the March
16 operation.

Ramsdell said he had directly provided intelligence to
Captain Kotouc, the intelligence officer for Task Force
Barker, but had never met its commander, Lieutenant Colo-

nel Barker. He added, however, that Kotouc "got the same kind of information" from Phoenix as was provided to all units upon their request. Part of that information included a blacklist—Ramsdell suggested a better phrase would be "identification list"—of suspected VCI in the area of operation. "We knew there was a VC setup" in Son My, Ramsdell explained. "What we did was—if they would notify us they were planning a sweep of an area—we would give them an identification list."

I asked Ramsdell about the intelligence indicating that all of the civilians would leave My Lai 4 by seven o'clock in the morning. He replied, "Most of the time people did in fact come out to sell their goods—this was a common practice. If it was the time of the year for harvest, they would go into the cities to make their market trips. And because of the heat, they would go in the morning." * Cecil Hall, the task force communications sergeant, told me that Major Gavin and Captain Kotouc had picked up the information in

* Captain Kotouc, who received Ramsdell's evaluation, similarly told the Peers Panel, "In the civilian population area, there were several markets, large markets, where all the people would gather each day because they had no refrigeration or anything like, and normally in the morning, from the VC reports that I have heard, numerous reports from people that I have personally interrogated and talked to, the people would leave to go to the market in the morning, and they would leave about seven o'clock in the morning or so and then they would return, depending how far it was. They would return after they bought the food that they had when they returned." Some of the other statements made in the defense of that intelligence also bordered on the ludicrous. Captain Dennis R. Vazquez, who served as liaison officer between the task force and its main artillery support group, told the panel that ". . . in most of these populated areas they always plan them [operations] for certain days of the week like Sundays or Saturday, or whenever . . . I considered it sort of peculiar that they said something like this." One of the two previous operations into Son My had been on a weekend, and Vazquez' suggestion that certain operations were planned for weekends was not mentioned again, either during the Peers Panel investigation or during my interviews.

Quang Ngai City a day or two before the mission. "They considered the source of the intelligence *impeccable,*" Hall said.

The link between Ramsdell and the poor intelligence for the March 16 operation was never explored by the Peers Panel. For one thing, none of the high-ranking officers on it had any reason to suspect that Ramsdell was poorly informed about Vietnam; Ramsdell's statistical record while in Vietnam, like Barker's high enemy body counts, was excellent. Shortly after the My Lai 4 operation, the number of VCI on the Phoenix blacklists was sharply reduced. Ramsdell eventually received praise from his superiors for the large numbers of VCI he eliminated. In his progress report for March, James A. May, the senior American adviser for all of Quang Ngai Province, described the Phoenix operation as finally getting "into full motion . . . The general intelligence flow in the province has greatly increased, both in efficiency and speed . . ." (May added this bit of special praise: "Task Force Barker . . . of the Americal Division [has] been extremely active and responsive and continues to merit high praise.")

General Peers, who served as a high-ranking CIA official after World War II, was exceptionally courteous during Ramsdell's hearing. "One of the reasons I have been rather desirous to talk to you," he told the private investigator, ". . . is the fact that you did have this rapport and understanding and fine working arrangement with the Vietnamese. Perhaps, if anybody within the province advisory staff should have had the information [about the My Lai 4 massacre], it should have been you." Ramsdell testified that he had never learned about the massacre, and then added, "If anything of this nature had occurred in that time, I would have known it. I've gotten word when a GI truck has gone through the village too fast, or run over a cow, so that there would be no misunderstanding or hard feelings."

The thought that he had not heard of the massacre because his intelligence network was incompetent did not occur to Ramsdell, who suggested without any challenge that since he had not learned of the massacre, it could not have happened: ". . . I'm saying that if something did happen, it might have been an incident, but I think it's an incident that's been magnified to a point to try to almost destroy the image of the United States Army . . . I think it's been magnified by the VC, and very cleverly done . . . I base that opinion solely on the fact that if such a thing had occurred in there of such a size . . . I think some of our own paid sources would have [told me]."

Undoubtedly the men of the task force had some basis of their own for believing the 48th Battalion was in the Son My area; evidence of the unit—old documents and civilians who knew, perhaps, of some of the unit's recent movements—could be found at any time throughout the Batangan Peninsula, which was, after all, the base of operations for the 48th. After Ramsdell and Gavin agreed the information looked solid, while adding information of their own, such as the market patterns of civilians, no further attempt was made by Barker to confirm the enemy unit's location, because none was needed. If Barker or any of his aides had checked, they would have found that every intelligence desk at the provincial headquarters in Quang Ngai placed the 48th Battalion at least fifteen kilometers to the west of the city. They would also have learned that the unit was considered to be in poor fighting condition because it had suffered heavy losses while attacking Quang Ngai City during the Tet offensive the month before. "Whatever was left of them was out in the mountains," Gerald Stout recalled. His information, in part, was based on highly classified reconnaissance flights over the mountain area.*

There was no conspiracy to destroy the village of My Lai 4; what took place there had happened before and would happen again in Quang Ngai Province—although with less drastic results. The desire of Lieutenant Colonel Barker to mount another successful, high enemy body-count operation in the area; the desire of Ramsdell to demonstrate the effectiveness of his operations; the belief shared by all the

---

* Intelligence officials of the 11th Brigade also had no more than a vague idea where the local force of the 48th Viet Cong Battalion was located during February, when Task Force Barker was in such apparently heavy contact. Lieutenant Colonel Blackledge, the brigade intelligence chief, told me during a mid-1971 interview: "Any intelligence officer in Vietnam will tell you that you *can't tell* at any time where a main-force Viet Cong or local-force battalion is located. You just can't turn to an office map and say, 'Hey, that's where the enemy is.' It's like playing blind man's bluff—you stick pins up on a map [to mark the location of enemy sightings] and then point to the middle." Yet during February and March at least three other intelligence offices—not including province—managed to agree on a location for the 48th. The Americal Division, its higher headquarters, the III Marine Amphibious Force, and the overall headquarters for Vietnam, the Military Assistance Command—Vietnam (MACV), each published separate classified intelligence summaries listing the 48th Viet Cong Battalion as undergoing an extended rebuilding and resupply drive west of Quang Ngai Province in the mountains near Laos. The 300-man unit had suffered at least seventy and perhaps a hundred casualties during the Tet offensive, when it joined other Viet Cong units in storming the provincial headquarters at Quang Ngai City. Bitter hand-to-hand fighting took place at a province hospital, two schools, and a Catholic church inside the confines of the city. The American analysts at Quang Ngai considered Tet a significant and bloody defeat for the Viet Cong, an evaluation that was being repeated in province headquarters throughout Vietnam and one that overlooked the demoralizing aspect of the deep penetration into the similarly fortified province capitals. Though it was reasonable to believe the 48th's two subsequent defeats in Son My during February had left the unit with less than a hundred fighting men by mid-March, the task force—in a statistical evaluation that was not challenged anywhere—evaluated the strength of the 48th at up to 400 men as it began the planning for the March 16 attack.

principals that everyone living in Son My was staying there by choice because of Communist sympathies; the assurance that no officials of the South Vietnamese government would protest any act of war in Son My; and the basic incompetence of many intelligence personnel in the Army—all these factors combined to enable a group of ambitious men to mount an unnecessary mission against a nonexistent enemy force, and somehow also to find the evidence to justify it all.

8

The Operation

*I*t began, like almost all combat assaults in Vietnam, with artillery and helicopters.

Lieutenant Colonel Frank Barker arrived over My Lai 4 in his command-and-control helicopter just in time to watch the beginning barrage of artillery shells fall into the hamlet. At least sixty—and perhaps more than a hundred—shells were fired without warning. Colonel Oran K. Henderson's helicopter—filled with high-ranking officers—flew over the hamlet a few minutes later; a faulty radio had delayed the colonel's takeoff from his headquarters at Duc Pho. Major General Samuel Koster flew in and out of the area throughout the early morning—watching the men of Charlie Company conduct their assault.

The task force staff journal for March 16, which was submitted in evidence to the Peers Panel, shows that Calley's first platoon landed precisely at 7:30 A.M. at the landing zone outside of My Lai

4. The nine troop-carrying helicopters were accompanied by two gunships from the 174th Aviation Company. The ships, guns blazing, had crisscrossed the landing zone moments before the combat troops landed, firing thousands of bullets and rockets in a fusillade designed to keep enemy gunmen at bay. Of course, there were no enemy gunmen, but it didn't matter that day: within minutes the statistics began filling the daily log for the task force. At 7:35 Charlie Company officially claimed its first Viet Cong; the victim was an old man who had jumped from a hole waving his arms in fear. Seven minutes later the gunships—known as "Sharks"—claimed three Viet Cong killed; the dead men reportedly were seen with weapons and field gear. By eight o'clock seventeen more Viet Cong were said to be killed. At 8:03 Charlie Company said it had found a radio and three boxes of medical supplies. At 8:40 Charlie Company notified headquarters it had counted a total of eighty-four dead Viet Cong. By this time My Lai 4 was in ruins. Lieutenant Calley and the other men of his platoon had already slain two large groups of civilians and filled a drainage ditch with bodies. The second and third platoons, too, had committed wholesale murders, and some men had systematically begun to set aflame anything in the hamlet that could burn. Wells were fouled, livestock slaughtered, and foodstocks scattered.

The Sharks from the 174th also committed murder that morning. Hundreds of civilians streamed from the hamlet in fear after the killings began, most of them traveling southwest toward Quang Ngai City. The two gunships flew overhead and began firing into the crowd. The time was about 7:45; it was noted by Captain Brian W. Livingston, a pilot from the 123rd Aviation Battalion who was flying in support of the mission. Livingston later flew over and took a close look at the victims; they were women, children, and old men—thirty to fifty of them. Scott A. Baker, a flight commander with the 123rd, also watched the civilians leaving the village. He told the Army that the Sharks made a pass over the group with their guns firing, and moments later, saw twenty-five bodies on the road to Quang Ngai City. The troops from Charlie Company had yet to move that far south, Baker said. "Do you think the Sharks got them?" he was asked by the Peers Panel. Baker replied, "Yes, sir."

The killing continued at random for at least ninety more minutes, but no more enemy kills appeared on the task force log. Charlie Company's statistical day officially ended at 8:40 on March 16; it had killed eighty-four Viet Cong and captured documents, a radio, ammunition, and some medical supplies. The Sharks had reported a total of six enemy kills; later that day Bravo Company concluded its operation with an official body count of thirty-eight. The total number of dead Viet Cong—128—would make the front pages of American newspapers the next morning. It was the most significant operation of the war for the 11th Brigade.

The smoke over My Lai 4 could be seen for miles. Lieutenant James T. Cooney was flying Colonel Henderson's helicopter over My Lai 4; he told the Panel: "I did notice several hootches burning, several buildings burning, possibly rice stores. I do remember there being burning going on on the ground at that time." Warrant Officer Robert W. Witham was flying General Koster's helicopter; he similarly recalled "smoke and things like this, artillery . . . There was a lot of smoke." Even Captain Johnson, the Americal Division liaison officer at Quang Ngai City, six miles to the southwest, saw it: "I remember seeing smoke in the area and knowing that Task Force Barker was in the area. I accepted this. I assumed that I knew what was happening."

The pilots saw it, but the commanders claimed they did not. General Koster, asked if he recalled seeing the village "pretty much up in smoke at that time when you flew over," responded simply, "No, sir, I don't." Colonel Henderson, asked a similar question, declared, "I did not see My Lai 4 in flames or having been burnt or burning." *

Warrant Officer Jerry R. Culverhouse was piloting a helicopter that morning in support of Charlie Company. Culverhouse was attached to the 123rd Aviation Battalion; as such, he was part of a new concept in the Vietnam air war. The 123rd was an aero-scout battalion; its mission was to cut off enemy troops attempting to flee Task Force Barker's trap in My Lai 4. Culverhouse usually teamed up with a second gunship, and both would fly above a small observation helicopter manned the morning of March 16 by Warrant Officer Hugh C. Thompson, Jr. Above the gunships, in turn, were two or three helicopters carrying infantrymen. The concept called for the observation craft to flush out the enemy so the gunships could force them to stop. If the enemy avoided the gunships, the infantrymen would be landed (the 123rd pilots described this process as "inserting the animals") to engage the Viet Cong.

Culverhouse arrived at his duty station sometime after nine o'clock and joined up with Livingston and other pilots. The hamlet was still aflame. He began flying back and forth

---

* However, Lieutenant Colonel Blackledge, who flew over My Lai 4 with Colonel Henderson on a later trip that day, told of seeing widespread devastation: ". . . They [the homes] were not actually burning, they were smoldering. They had been burning; they were pretty burned down when we went over. . . . This was a little unusual in that the huts were all burning." Major Robert McKnight, the brigade operations officer, also testified that "there were some hootches burning in the My Lai 4 area."

across My Lai 4 and the nearby rice paddies, on the prowl for the Viet Cong: ". . . It appeared to us there it was fairly secure. We heard no shooting and didn't receive any fire ourselves . . . And we immediately noticed the bodies surrounding the village . . . There were numerous bodies scattered both in the inner perimeters of the village and in the outer perimeters leaving the village . . . I was especially . . . amazed at one group of bodies encountered . . . Over on the east side of the village there was an irrigation ditch, which appeared to me to be about six or seven feet wide . . . [and] probably five or six feet deep . . . There were numerous bodies that appeared to be piled up. In some places I don't know, maybe four or five or I suppose as high as six deep . . . For an area about thirty to thirty-five yards, the ditch was almost completely filled with bodies." Warrant Officer Daniel R. Millians also saw the carnage while piloting the ship with Culverhouse that morning. He recalled that he and his fellow pilot both wished "we had a camera so we could take pictures of it."

Thompson was enraged; he had spent the morning watching Charlie Company murder. At one point, Millians testified, Thompson complained over the radio "that if he saw the ground troops kill one more woman or child he would start shooting [the ground troops] himself."

Finally, observing no more than ten women and children huddling in fear as Lieutenant Calley and his men approached them, Thompson landed his craft, ordered his two machine gunners to train their weapons on Calley, and announced he was going to fly the civilians to safety. "The only way you'll get them out is with a hand grenade," Calley replied. Thompson radioed to the pilots and asked them to land their helicopter and begin evacuating the civilians. They did so, although their costly gunship was still heavy with unexpended ammunition and fuel. The decision to land was heresy for combat helicopter pilots: the aircraft are exceptionally vulnerable to enemy fire during the slow moments of descent and ascent. As they landed, Thompson and his door gunner began coaxing the terrified civilians into the craft. "We took four of them in the gunship," Culverhouse recalled, and "set them on the ammunition trays in the back. He and Millians made two trips to rescue the civilians.

Perhaps two dozen combat pilots and crewmen saw and heard some of what happened at My Lai 4 on March 16. William Bezanson was flying over My Lai 4 that morning with the infantrymen assigned to the 123rd Aviation Battalion. "There was a lot of shooting and a lot of people laying there," he recalled in an interview. "We were happy at first because we thought they were enemy. But by the end of the mission, the sergeant manning the radio told us what was going on. He repeated what Thompson had said—that he'd like to open up on them [Charlie Company] because they were killing civilians."

Captain Livingston testified that he heard Thompson make three separate radio transmissions about unwarranted killings, beginning sometime after nine o'clock. Thompson complained twice about a captain—apparently Ernest Medina of Charlie Company—who shot and killed a Vietnamese civilian, and a third time about a Negro sergeant who did the same thing. "The reason this stuck in his mind was he [Thompson] was a boy from Atlanta," Livingston told the Panel. "I guess you could say he was kind of prejudiced . . . He was real unhappy about this."

Major General Koster kept up with the swirl of action by monitoring three or four different radio frequencies; he was constantly on the alert for the first signs of trouble or enemy contact anywhere in his area of responsibility. Such signs can always be heard over the air waves: calls for reinforcements, medical helicopters, more ammunition and more firepower. His helicopter had an elaborate radio console, and if he chose, the general could tune into communications between helicopters and ground forces, the task force and the companies, or the brigade and the task force.

But Koster, in his testimony before the Peers Panel, could not specifically recall any details of the My Lai 4 operation. Asked if he had seen the hundreds of Vietnamese civilians fleeing the hamlet that morning, the general made a noncommittal reply: "I can't tie it to this particular operation. I've flown over several of them, and this one doesn't distinguish itself from any other as far as this type of thing is concerned." Colonel Henderson, however, testified that he saw six to eight bodies during his early-morning flight over My Lai 4. He said he immediately checked with Barker about the bodies and was told they were the result of artillery fire. Those were the only bodies he reported seeing, although he overflew My Lai 4 on three occasions that day.

At least one other passenger aboard Henderson's aircraft, however, testified he had seen much more. Michael Adcock, Henderson's radio operator, told the Panel that he observed thirty-five to forty bodies in all during his trips over My Lai 4. The command and control helicopter, he said, usually flew at an altitude of 1,500 feet—out of the range of small-arms fire—but traveled much lower during the morning trips over the hamlet, occasionally going "low enough to make the rice wave." The other passengers on the flight were Major Robert McKnight, the brigade operations officer, who testified he saw perhaps five dead bodies; Lieutenant Colonel Robert Luper, the artillery officer, who said he saw fifteen to twenty bodies; and Air Force Lieutenant Colonel William I. MacLachlan, assigned to coordinate air strikes, if necessary, who saw only a few bodies. None of the passengers, including Adcock, specifically recalled hearing anything about Americans murdering Vietnamese. One hint of discord came from MacLachlan, who said "the general impression I remember was that this was a day that it wasn't really successful . . ." There were many statistics to prove otherwise.

The only known complaints before nine o'clock were made by Thompson and other members of his unit. The helicopter unit, normally stationed at the Americal Division headquarters at Chu Lai, had set up a special operations van and refueling station at Landing Zone Dotti to increase the support it could provide Task Force Barker. Specialist 5 Lawrence J. Kubert, who served as operations sergeant for the battalion, told the Peers Panel that he and others in the van heard pilots' complaints early that morning about the excessive shooting of civilians by the Sharks from the 174th Aviation Company. The complaints were relayed to the task force operations center, only three hundred yards away at Dotti, with a warning that most of the persons fleeing the village were women and children. Kubert recalled that Colonel Henderson, identifying himself by his radio code name, Rawhide 6, subsequently warned the combat units by radio: "I don't want any unnecessary killing going on." A similar statement also was heard at a radio relay station at Landing Zone Uptight, site of the artillery batteries. Kubert said he assumed the warning was directed at the gunships.*

---

* At least two pilots also heard warnings. Captain Thelmar A. Moe, a section leader for the 123rd Aviation Battalion, testified that he heard Henderson say, "I don't want any unnecessary killing down there." Moe was in the operation van at the time. Captain Randolph E. Sabre, a flight platoon leader for the 123rd, told the Peers Panel that he heard some transmissions while flying near My Lai 4. Asked if he heard something like "Stop the killing," he said, "I don't know if that was the verbatim transmission made or a transmission something like 'Let's not have any

By that time Colonel Henderson was back at the task force operations center. The brigade commander had spent more than an hour over My Lai 4, only leaving for a few minutes around eight o'clock to watch Bravo Company begin its assault on My Lai 1—a target it never reached. At about 8:30 Henderson ordered his helicopter landed near My Lai 4 and picked up two suspected Viet Cong soldiers who were flushed from the hamlet. The prisoners—who later were found to be members of the Saigon government's regional forces—were turned over to military police at Dotti after Henderson and his staff returned to the task force headquarters area.

Within the next thirty minutes the colonel was joined by most of the senior officers of the task force and 11th Brigade. Major Calhoun and Sergeant William J. Johnson were monitoring the radios in the operations center. Captain Charles R. Lewellen, the assistant operations officer who ran the night shift at the operations center, stayed up to transcribe the operation with his tape recorder. A copy of that tape was later made available to the Peers investigators, and provided a minute-by-minute timetable for the first hours of action. The tape also helped prove, in the eyes of the Panel, that a cover-up—involving the manipulation of battlefield statistics—did take place between 8:30 and 9:30 at Landing Zone Dotti.

Barker was still flying over the combat area; he had been out there for more than an hour. At 8:28, according to the Lewellen tape, Barker messaged Captain Medina, saying, "I'm heading back to refuel. Have you had any contact down there yet?" Lewellen's tape did not record Medina's response, but Barker, apparently informed the company

---

needless killing' . . . or, 'Stop the burning,' or something to slow down something or caution the troops . . ."

was checking for body count, told them to "dig deep. Take
your time and get 'em [Viet Cong] out of those holes." Medina gave him the body count, and Barker queried, "Is that
eight . . . ah, eight-four KIAs?" Told yes, Barker then radioed Sergeant Johnson: "Returning to your location to refuel."

A few minutes later Barker landed at Dotti and rushed to
the operations center, just as the official task force log was
noting that "Co. C has counted 69 VC KIA." The map coordinates for My Lai 4—716788—were listed alongside the
entry, which was filed at 8:40. The log statistics were not cu-
mulative, and the new report of sixty-nine kills, added to
the earlier claim of fifteen victims, gave Charlie Company
its total body count of eighty-four at that point.

By this time the operations center should have been in a
state of jubilation, but most of the personnel there were
acutely aware of the fact that there were none of the normal
sounds of combat coming from the radios, just a steadily
climbing total of enemy kills. The only casualties reported
by nine o'clock were a lieutenant and some enlisted men
from Bravo Company who had triggered land mines. The
Peers Panel suggested, during one of its interrogations of
Colonel Henderson, what really was going on: "They
[Charlie Company] went through this place in less than an
hour. By the time you were ready to come back [to Dotti]
they had been practically through the village . . . There
were dead civilians all over the place. There wasn't any resistance. There wasn't a shot fired after that . . . Hootches
were burned by this time." About nine o'clock Lawrence
Kubert, the operations sergeant for the 123rd Aviation Battalion, relayed the reports from his pilots over My Lai 4 to
the task force. A number of witnesses testified that at about

this time Barker and Henderson—the two commanders—
had a private talk with each other on one side of the room.
Major Calhoun said that he may have discussed the operation with his direct superior, Major McKnight. Calhoun's
memory, like everyone else's at this point, became extremely vague: "It might have been . . . I made a mention
that I thought that we might have killed some civilians in
that body count, sir. This sixty-nine, some of them might
have been civilians. I don't know whether it was Major
McKnight, or later on, but I remember mentioning that at
some time to somebody."

Just before nine o'clock Lieutenant Colonel Barker again
left Dotti and flew to the Bravo Company area near My Lai
1 to evacuate the men wounded by mines and approve the
change in mission for Captain Michles' men. He returned
about forty minutes later, well after the first of Warrant
Officer Thompson's agonized complaints. Captain Eugene
Kotouc, who spent the morning dashing in and out of the
operations center, said that he heard one of Thompson's
protests over one of the task force radios: "There was a report from . . . the helicopter pilot . . . The report was
something about someone getting shot with a machine gun.
'Looks like they are shooting them with a machine gun.
Someone is going across the road and is getting shot with a
machine gun.' The helicopter pilot, whoever he was, said
something like: 'He doesn't have a weapon' or words to that
effect." The operations center was hectic. By the time
Thompson made his complaints, Bravo Company had been
given permission to forget its main target, My Lai 1, the
headquarters base of the 48th VC Battalion, and instead
proceed to My Khe 4. Yet Major Calhoun did not know
until it came out during the testimony before the Peers

Panel that Bravo Company had never entered My Lai 1 on March 16.

Under Army regulations, all of the task force's significant actions had to be promptly relayed to the 11th Brigade for inclusion in that unit's daily report to the Americal Division. The brigade staff journal, however, listed the following entry at 9:30 from Task Force Barker: "Counted 69 VC KIA as a result of Arty [artillery] fire." Suddenly and inexplicably, Charlie Company's 8:40 report of sixty-nine kills was attributed to artillery. The map coordinates for the engagement also were changed to an area about six hundred meters north of My Lai 4. The altered information—which was filed to the Brigade fifty minutes after the task force received it, an unheard-of delay for such "good" news—became a focal point of the Peers investigation, which was never able to learn who filed it. The 8:40 entry was the last Charlie Company report logged by the task force for the day, although one witness told the Peers Panel that he was with Captain Medina when he radioed a body count of 310, later that morning. (Medina and all others involved denied any knowledge of such statistics.)

Peers and his staff questioned closely the artillery officers connected with the My Lai 4 operation, in an attempt to determine how they accepted without question or investigation credit for the killing of a remarkably high total of sixty-nine Viet Cong as a result of a short three- to five-minute artillery barrage. Captain Dennis R. Vazquez, the task force artillery liaison officer who spent that morning aboard Colonel Barker's helicopter, claimed that the report of sixty-nine Viet Cong being killed by artillery was provided to him by an artillery forward observer assigned to Charlie Company. He said he accepted the statistic without question. The Panel tried to pin him down:

Q. Did you ask Colonel Barker what this was all about, this sixty-nine being killed by artillery which you can't see?

A. I think I asked him what the situation was to verify with him. And all he did was he nodded to me that everything was okay. That's what I took it to mean.

Q. Did you think it was okay? . . . You looked right down there where the artillery went in, you didn't see anything?

A. The only thing I thought at the time, I was pretty pleased with the artillery, the effects that it had achieved.

Captain Medina and Lieutenant Roger L. Alaux, Jr., the artillery forward observer at Charlie Company, both testified that they knew nothing about deaths due to artillery and had no idea how the total of sixty-nine originated. According to Alaux, he had learned of the statistic after the operation. "I accepted that number," he said, adding, however, that it did "not impress me as being a particularly valid number . . . There was no way for me to make a body count."

The statistic similarly went without challenge from any of the senior artillery officers in the battalion and division. Lieutenant Colonel Luper, the 11th Brigade artillery commander, who flew over the area after learning of the sensational score of his men, testified that he, too, made no attempt to investigate the statistic. Asked what he did do during the second ride with Henderson over My Lai 4, Luper responded, "I assume I rode in a helicopter, sir. I must have looked out some, but I'm telling you that I don't recall anything, sir." *

---

* The Peers Panel made clear it thought that Lieutenant Colonel Luper and his superiors had a higher duty to investigate the sensational enemy kill. Luper was drawn into a revealing discussion of what he thought was his obligation to report artillery incidents. He acknowledged to General Peers that he had seen fifteen to twenty bodies, most of them women and children, inside My Lai 4, before learning that his artillery unit had been

At 9:35 General Koster himself landed at Dotti and was met by Colonel Henderson. They discussed briefly the status of the two prisoners who had been brought in, and then, according to Henderson, Koster "asked me how the operation was going and I gave him the results as I knew it at that time . . . I did tell him, or he asked me, about any civilian casualties, and I do recall telling, 'Yes, I had observed six to eight,' but I had no other report from Colonel Barker as to civilians killed, but I had observed these."

In an earlier version of that statement, Henderson testified he had told Koster that some of the civilians appeared

credited with such a high enemy kill. But even if they had been killed by artillery shells, Luper said it would not have to be reported as an artillery incident if the shells were fired on target. As for My Lai 4, the artillery officer said, "This is in connection with an operation, and the fires were fired where they were requested, and this would not be considered an artillery incident." Luper's reasoning suggested that anything goes if ordered in combat—at least in Vietnam. His superior, Colonel Mason J. Young, the Americal Division artillery commander, similarly defended Luper on the grounds that "at no point in connection with this incident was there any allegation that it [the death of civilians] was a result of misdirected artillery fire or that artillery fire had in fact killed anybody. I don't remember any such allegation." There was this subsequent exchange between General Peers and the colonel:

Q. Well, do you have to have an allegation? If you see dead bodies out there, that isn't an allegation, that's a fact. Isn't that enough to kick off an investigation?

A. Well, if the infantry commander had said that there was some of them killed by artillery fire, but they didn't.

Q. Oh, well . . . You're not going to investigate anything even though you suspect they were killed by artillery or gunships if you can possibly blame it on somebody, and as long as somebody doesn't raise it up, then just forget it. That's basically what you're telling me.

A. No, sir. That's not. If there had been any allegation that anybody had been killed by artillery. Now there was none that came to my attention or apparently to Colonel Luper's attention . . .

Q. My point is that your battalion commander [Luper] was there and was seeing it. Isn't this authority for him right there to initiate an artillery incident report . . . ?

A. Well, he was under Colonel Henderson's command.

to be victims of an errant artillery shell, and
Koster's memory was foggy, and would be
throughout his interrogations by the Panel. He
denied any recollection of specific conversations.
example, that Colonel Henderson had suggested ⟶ ...e
general initiated the questions about civilian casualties, and
asked why, Koster said, "Nothing other than this was a
populated area and I would have had concern, because, assuming I had been flying over the area of operations and
had just seen a lot of civilians moving along the road." He
could not recall if he was over the area that morning, but
"assumed" he had been. Both men did agree, however, that
Koster ordered Henderson to find out how many civilians
were killed during the operation.

Henderson then took off for another tour of the My Lai 4
area, again accompanied by his large staff. He said that he
radioed Barker and passed along Koster's demand that civilian casualties be tabulated. Henderson further testified
that on this trip he noticed some burning homes and again
radioed Barker "to ask him why those buildings were burning. To the best of my recollection," Henderson said, "he
told me that the ARVN or—not the ARVN, the National
Police or the company interpreters . . . that was with the
companies were setting them afire. And I told him to stop
it." But at that point, there were no National Police on the
mission.* Medina testified, moreover, that he never received
any orders regarding the burning, which continued well
after the shooting ended.

But Medina acknowledged that Major Calhoun, as a re-

---

* As Henderson described it to the Peers Panel, he was the model of a
stern commander: "I informed Colonel Barker that regardless of who
was burning them . . . whoever he had with him, they were still under his
control and we had no authority to burn houses and [I told him] to see
that they were gotten under control immediately."

sult of Thompson's complaints, radioed the following message to both him and Captain Michles: "Make sure we are not shooting anyone that is not necessary. Let's not be killing any civilians out there." * At this point, Medina testified he had seen "anywhere between twenty to twenty-eight" dead civilians in My Lai 4, but claimed, nonetheless, that Thompson's complaints were based solely on his—Medina's—killing of a woman in a rice paddy outside the hamlet. (Lieutenant Alaux, who was at Medina's side throughout the operation, testified that he had observed sixty to seventy bodies in My Lai 4.) Medina said he had shot the woman,

---

* Calhoun's message to Medina was the first of at least four transmissions about the mass murders that were made over Charlie Company's frequency on the radio, a maneuver that would have precluded the messages from being overheard by officers or staff personnel at higher headquarters. Sergeant Lawrence C. LaCroix, a squad leader in the second platoon, testified that at some point during the morning someone in a helicopter complained over the radio that "From up here it looks like a blood-bath. What the hell are you doing down there?" The message was probably made by the pilot of a medical evacuation helicopter who flew into My Lai 4 at 10:25 to pick up the sole casualty of Charlie Company's assault—a GI who had shot himself in the foot. Sergeant Thomas J. Kinch, a member of the company's mortar platoon, told the Peers Panel that he overheard Lieutenant Colonel Barker ask Captain Medina about the pilot's report. "He [Barker] had gotten a call from the dustoff chopper, and he wanted to know why there were so many bodies laying down there," Kinch said. "Medina replied, 'I don't know. I'll call forward and find out.' He called up in front of him," Kinch added, "I imagine it was the First [Calley's] Platoon, and told them to stop the shooting, and words similar to that—'The party's over.' " A similar account was given to the Army investigators by Sergeant William E. Watson, who was operating the mortar platoon's radio. He testified that he overheard Barker radio Medina and ask, "Do you know anything about any civilians being killed down there?" Watson said Barker told Medina he had received a report of civilian casualties from higher headquarters. Watson then recalled: "Captain Medina said that he was positive it wasn't his people. After Colonel Barker got off the net [radio], Captain Medina . . . called all the platoon leaders to check and make sure that it wasn't any of his people."

with Thompson's helicopter hovering overhead, after she made a threatening gesture.

By eleven o'clock the men of Charlie Company were preparing to have lunch, and Jay Roberts, an Army combat correspondent who had landed with Charlie Company and witnessed the murder of women and children, thought it was time for him to hop a helicopter and check in with Bravo Company near My Lai 1. "I guess I was looking for a story of American heroics in combat," the correspondent told the Panel. "Maybe I could go somewhere else and see what was going on. There might be a story some other place." Ronald Haeberle, the combat photographer from Ohio who had joined Roberts on the mission, also jumped aboard the helicopter.

Warrant Officer Thompson returned to the improvised helicopter base at Dotti before noon. The pilot and his two crewmen were enraged and frustrated. Their last mission had been to fly a wounded Vietnamese boy to the civilian hospital at Quang Ngai City; they had spotted the youth— still alive—amidst the blood and gore of the huge ditch at My Lai 4. Thompson landed his helicopter near the ditch— the third time he had been on the ground during the morning—and his crewmen rescued the child. His clothes bloody, the young Georgian walked into the operations van to describe the scene to Major Frederic Watke, his company commander. A few other pilots went with him. Lawrence Kubert, the operations sergeant, listened and watched closely: "They were white, their faces were drawn and . . . They were very tense, very angry . . . The whole feeling—it wasn't just one man, it was three or four saying the same thing, the look, the force that they put out was one of seeing something terrible. And these are men that are used to seeing death." Kubert heard the word "murder" and re-

called thinking that at least a hundred civilians—possibly
more—had been killed. Many of the pilots told their commanding officer that they would never fly again in support
of Task Force Barker unless the unnecessary killings were
halted.

Watke did not share his pilots' rage. He was left with the
impression that perhaps twenty to thirty civilians were
killed, "people that obviously could have been construed, I
guess, as not having been hostile." He told the Panel that he
did not recall hearing details from Thompson about the
ditch full of bodies. The fact is that Watke was immediately
more concerned about Thompson's landings at My Lai 4—
the interference with the prerogatives of a ground commander—than with Thompson's story of massacre. "In my
mind, sir," Watke testified, "after I had talked with them, I
was left with the impression that it was just in their minds.
Maybe there was a little shooting in the areas that wasn't
called for. That was the only impression that I went to
Colonel Barker on." Watke spent fifteen minutes debating
what would happen to him if he reported it. He finally decided to go to Barker: "I was compelled to. My people
brought it to me and I could not resolve the problem for
them to their satisfaction . . . so I went to Colonel Barker
to bring it to his level. It was his troops, plus I was concerned more that my people had entered into a heated argument, so to speak, with the ground troops, and this is an un-
tenable situation. You just can't have this going on."

Watke walked the three hundred yards to the task force
operations center at Dotti and reported the incident to
Barker, stressing the confrontation between his helicopter
pilots and the ground troops, and not the murders. By then
Barker had at least received reports of indiscriminate
shooting from the radios, and had personally flown over My
Lai 4. Watke recalled his relief at Barker's first reaction:

"Colonel Barker didn't get indignant when I brought it to his attention. His first action was to call out—as best as I can recall, Major Calhoun was airborne—and he told Major Calhoun, in effect, to look into this." Major Calhoun testified that after receiving Barker's request, he checked with Captain Medina and told him "to make sure that there was no unnecessary killing of civilians and no unnecessary burning." The major also said he flew over Bravo Company's operational area at roughly the same time to check with them. This, perhaps, prompted Lieutenant Thomas Willingham of the first platoon to order his men to cover the bodies of the slaughtered civilians at My Khe 4 with straw.

Medina didn't mention this second warning in his testimony, but it really didn't matter by then; My Lai 4 was no more.

Charlie Company finished its lunch break shortly after noon; the men ate amidst the sprawled bodies of their victims. On orders from Medina, the men trudged to the east, toward the nearby hamlet of My Lai 5. Sergeant Phu, Charlie Company's interpreter, told what happened there: "We met some civilians. Captain Medina instructed me to tell the people they had to get out of this area because this area was a Communist area, and when they returned the next time on an operation in this area, anybody left in this area would be all killed just like in the area they had just left.

"As soon as I finished talking to them," Phu continued, "they started picking up their gear, equipment, household belongings, and their children and left . . ."

9

The Cover-Up Begins

*B*y noon it was clear to most of the men on duty
at the 11th Brigade operations center in Duc Pho
—as it had been for some time at task force headquarters—that something was seriously wrong at
My Lai 4. "Nobody was proud of the body count,"
John Waldeck, the intelligence clerk, told me in an
interview. "The officers seemed to kind of restrain
themselves." Waldeck clearly remembered hearing
the radio reports from Thompson: "They came in
only for a few moments. I remember him saying
that civilians were running all over and they [the
men of Charlie Company] were zapping them."
Roy D. Kirkpatrick, operations sergeant for the
brigade, similarly recalled, as he told the Peers
Panel, hearing Thompson's claim that Charlie
Company was shooting civilians. The sergeant, a
career Army man, added that he wasn't too upset
by the report: "We called back to Colonel Barker
. . . and asked him what was going on. The indica-

tion that I took from my position in the TOC [operations center] would have been to not give credit to this because the people that we were combating there were dressed as civilians." \

The brigade staff spent much of the day on the telephone to the task force operations center, urging them to pursue the enemy and capture more weapons.*⸣ Everyone was aware, Waldeck said, that "we weren't taking any weapons and had no casualties. And there were no calls for help, medevacs [evacuation helicopters], or gunships—none of that." At one point, the youth said, Lieutenant Colonel Blackledge, the brigade intelligence officer, came into the operations center and expressed concern. Yet Blackledge, when he appeared before the Panel, said, "The only thing I was really aware of was how many casualties we had taken that day. It was quite light and I just attributed this to the fact that we had caught them with their pants down . . . It appeared to be the case because we never had this kind of figure in such a short time." The mood was equally grim at Task Force Barker's operation center at Landing Zone Dotti. Describing that afternoon more than three years later, Sergeant Cecil Hall explained simply, "None of us wanted to admit that it actually happened." Hall recalled that Barker returned to the operations center angry at the mounting complaints about the My Lai 4 operation. "What the hell's the matter with these people?" he quoted Barker as saying. "I don't know what they expect. There's bound to be some civilians killed out there."

The brigade's complaints to the task force about the

---

* Task Force Barker's two earlier operations in Son My also had generated high body counts with few captured weapons, but the statistics in those cases were not reported until hours after the operations had ended, and thus, brigade officials had no chance to make any demands.

delay in its reports of captured weapons and equipment were intensified by pressure from Division. Captain James A. Logan was in charge of the operations center for the Americal Division in Chu Lai that day; he testified that "we queried the 11th Brigade TOC throughout the day about when they were going to start getting weapons and things like that. And the answer came back, as soon as they could get into the bunkered area."

Colonel Henderson said that he discussed the operations at least two times with Lieutenant Colonel Barker during the early afternoon. He added, "I received a report from him that the total of some 128 enemy and twenty-four civilians had been killed in the operation. He was still attempting to secure additional information regarding the manner in which the civilians had been killed."

Jay Roberts, the 11th Brigade combat correspondent, also saw Barker that afternoon. He returned to Landing Zone Dotti disturbed about what he had seen and unsure about what to write. The truth, he knew, wouldn't do—not only would it get him in trouble, but it would never leave the Brigade public information office. Roberts told the Panel that he interviewed Barker about the mission inside the task force operations center: "I asked him for a statement, 'Give me a quote on your opinion of the operation'; things like that, and he said something to the effect that it had been highly successful, that we had two entire companies on the ground in less than an hour and they had moved swiftly with complete surprise to the VC in the area . . . And I asked him, of course . . . about the high body count and the low number of weapons, and he just indicated to me that—you know—that I would do a good job writing the story, and said, 'Don't worry about it.' . . . He did . . . indicate to me that he didn't feel that it was necessary for him to comment on it. It wasn't part of my story, particularly, anyhow, and I would do a fine job with the information that I had." Roberts' subsequent story, as rewritten by the Army public information offices up the chain of command, was the basis for that day's news of the "victory" in the United States.

A few hours later Barker told Major Watke that he had found nothing to substantiate Thompson's story. Watke didn't believe Barker, and told the Peers Panel why: "I didn't believe that he couldn't find the man [Calley] in the field, for one thing . . . Somebody, even if you have to line up the company, someone is finally going to admit that somebody else saw somebody speak to somebody else. In my mind he went out and had stopped the killing of the people, and that was it."

Sometime after three o'clock Colonel Henderson decided that he wanted Charlie Company—then moving a few thousand meters to the east of My Lai 4—to retrace its steps. He ordered Medina back into the hamlet to determine precisely how many civilians were killed. By that time Michael Adcock, his radio operator, had seen thirty-five bodies scattered throughout the area, and the official body count for the mission was 128 Viet Cong killed and three weapons captured. Henderson, perhaps, had also heard the complaints from Thompson over his helicopter radio, or had at least been informed of them during this lunch stay at his headquarters. Medina said he protested Henderson's order. "I told him [Major Calhoun, who transmitted the order] that due to the time and the distance that I did not recommend moving back from my location to the village . . . because we were trying to prepare our night defense position." *

---

* During Colonel Henderson's subsequent court-martial in late 1971, Medina acknowledged that there were other reasons for not going back. "I was afraid of what I would find," he testified.

Charlie Company's work for the day was nearly over; it had burned two more villages to the east of My Lai 4 and rendezvoused with Bravo Company in a joint defensive position at a cemetery near the South China Sea. Barker learned of the order almost as soon as Medina did and took an immediate and unusual step to stop it; he went over his brigade commander's head and discussed the demand by radio with Major General Koster, who was flying nearby. Koster rationalized the call when he described it to the Panel: "He [Barker] indicated to me that the troops were to be sent back . . . He did not recommend it in view of the late hour . . . To me, sending the infantry troops in to examine bodies . . . I have seen a lot of bodies and I can't tell what has killed them most of the time—I didn't think it warranted the risk of putting people into minefields." Koster, using his call sign, Sabre 6, broke in during the discussion between Calhoun and Medina and said, according to Medina, "Negative, don't send them back to go look at that mess." Medina testified that the general next asked, "How many does the captain say . . . he's actually seen." Medina said he told him between twenty and twenty-eight; Koster responded, according to the captain: "Well, that sounds about right."

Koster denied using the word "mess," but neither he nor Calhoun quarreled with Medina's description of the encounter. Henderson was told of the countermanding—in effect, a slap in the face to a new commander on his first day of operation—by Major Calhoun a few moments later. Like every ambitious colonel, Henderson was trying to please his superiors; and Koster's action in countermanding the order could have been interpreted as a sign to "cool it" in terms of pursuing an investigation into the just-completed operation. Henderson's order to Medina was the most direct attempt anyone made at the time to determine what actually happened at My Lai 4.

By now Barker had taken four steps which, in effect, obscured the events at My Lai 4: he had indicated to his artillery liaison officer that he should accept without question the report that artillery had killed sixty-nine Viet Cong; he had assured Watke that there was no basis to Thompson's report; he had urged a distorted news story about the operation to be written; and he had prevented Medina from returning to the village.

The killing of Vietnamese had yet to end. Dozens of GIs from Bravo and Charlie Companies witnessed the interrogation of a group of Vietnamese prisoners that culminated in executions later that afternoon. The Peers Panel assembled voluminous testimony indicating that between three and eight Vietnamese civilians were shot to death by National Police in front of at least six American officers, some of whom took part in the mistreatment. Captain Kotouc of the task force had assembled a team of South Vietnamese soldiers and National Police to help him interrogate the men and women who had been detained during the operations in My Lai 4 and near My Lai 1. There were about fifteen Vietnamese prisoners—most of them had been detained by Bravo Company—at the task force bivouac area, east of My Lai 4. Kotouc and Lieutenant Dennis H. Johnson, an intelligence officer assigned to Charlie Company, began interrogating eight of the Viet Cong suspects. Captains Medina and Michles watched the procedure, along with two forward artillery observers attached to the task force—Lieutenants Alaux of Charlie Company and Boatman of Bravo Company.

Boatman told what happened next: "At the time when
we [Bravo Company] linked up . . . [Charlie Company] had
with them four or five National Policemen with eight VC
suspects. When I arrived there they [the National Police]
were beating them and I saw them shoot all eight of them,
one by one. They were interrogating them of sorts. I saw
one, for example, they hit him in the head and hit him in the
middle of the back, and then he [one of the policemen] shot
him. I was with Lieutenant Alaux, and we both saw that,
and, well, I didn't have too many comments and neither did
he; but I can't remember exactly what was said." Boatman
said the Vietnamese civilians were shot by carbines and left
in a ditch near the two companies' command post area. He
did not report the shootings to anyone, he said, because "I
just thought it was the way the National Police operated. I
guess it was under their jurisdiction."

Other witnesses said the National Police shot two or three
Viet Cong suspects at the most. Captain Kotouc testified
that he saw "them take [one] man behind the hootch, and I
heard a rifle go off. I saw a National Policeman come back
without the man. And Captain Medina said, 'Let's knock
that off, that is not the way we handle our people around
here.'" In his account, Medina also acknowledged two
shootings, but indicated he was not near the scene: "As
Earl [Michles] and I were implacing the companies in defensive positions, I heard two shots. The National Police
had executed two of the VC. Captain Michles and I went
over and told them to stop this, that this was not supposed
to be going on. The only thing that we wanted them to do
was to identify the VC for us, and then they would go with
us on the remainder of the operation to get the VC that they
had identified to show us where weapon and rice caches
were located and where any mines and booby traps might
be located."

Sergeant Du Thanh Hien, the interpreter for Kotouc, provided details left out by Kotouc and Medina: "We found three men [among those assembled] who had their name in the black book of VCI . . . The police, when they came in, had with them the list. Also, one of the policemen was from that village, and he knew the VCI in the village. So, immediately, he selected the ones . . . Shortly after that, Captain Kotouc, myself, and Sergeant Phu took this man to one of the family bunkers in the area to interrogate him. So then we asked the policeman again, 'Are you sure that this man is who you say he is, VCI?' He said, 'Yes, he is a member of the Communist Party, I am sure.' We tried to interrogate the man, but he refused to say anything . . . Captain Kotouc took a knife from his scabbard, placed the man's hand up on a rock and threatened to cut his finger off. I turned away to meet Sergeant [Duong] Minh [another Vietnamese interpreter], and a moment later I came back. At that time I saw that he had lost a little bit of his finger, not very much. Just a very, very small part of his finger. But his hand had been beaten a good bit; it had been beaten red."

Sergeant Hien said that Captains Medina and Michles were talking with Lieutenant Johnson about twenty meters away at the time. After the man had part of his finger cut off, Hien said, "He continued to refuse to say anything, but he did say, 'I haven't done anything. Why are you beating me and treating me this way?' He asked me to help him out . . . For about fifteen or twenty minutes after that, I tried very hard to get some information from this man . . . I told him for his own good to give me some information, but he continued to refuse. So I checked with the police again to make sure they were certain that this was who they thought he was . . . One of the policemen . . . continued to ask me many times to let him kill the man because he was certain who he was. So, finally, the one policeman plus the other two policemen asked me to ask the Americans to let them kill one of them. I told them, 'No, we want to take the man back to LZ Bronco [at Duc Pho] and interrogate him.' But they were very insistent. They finally persuaded me to check with Captain Kotouc what he thought about it and he approved it. He said 'Okay' and raised his hand and signaled to the man that his spirit was going to heaven . . . We laughed together . . . He turned to me and smiled." The prisoner was then taken to a nearby ditch and shot, Hien said. The sergeant, queried sharply by the Peers Panel about the fate of the other prisoners, testified further: "Honestly, I can't remember clearly. I can't because I have gone on a lot of other operations and in some cases have had other similar incidents . . . It is very common to have their [prisoners'] hands beaten or a bit of the ear cut off by the Americans, the police and PF [popular forces] in order to make them talk." Asked specifically if he had witnessed such actions by American units, Hien said, "Yes, sir, a few times."

Sometime later that afternoon the pilots from the 123rd Aviation Battalion completed their assignment at Landing Zone Dotti and flew en masse back to their home base at Chu Lai. Captain Gerald S. Walker, a section leader of the aero-scout company, met the angry men at the flight line. Some of the pilots jumped off their aircraft and threw their helmets to the ground. "They all seemed quite upset," Walker told the Panel. "In fact, some of them seemed disgusted." Thompson was still complaining about what he had seen as he walked to the operations room to prepare his after-action reports. Major Watke, who already had been told by Barker that Thompson's story could not be substantiated, was also in the operations room. Walker recalled that Watke "tried to quiet some of the people down to try to keep it within our own group . . . [He] was interested in trying to console the people. Trying to get them back in the right frame of mind again . . . and as we were moving toward the operations, I know that someone mentioned, 'Well, let's keep it here, and we'll report it to the commander.' "

(At this point in the proceedings, Colonel J. Ross Franklin, a Peers Panel member, angrily criticized the captain: "Walker, I don't mean to vent any anger on you, but frankly, what you're saying and the tone of what you're saying [is] what we have heard from so many people. We have yet to have a man [testify] who said, 'I was vitally concerned about this and I wanted to know what happened. I was concerned about my subordinates and my duties and my obligations to really go into this.' This is all water under the bridge and you don't stand alone, by any means, but listening to people talking the same way you do day after day, where was the man, where was the officer who would take enough interest and concern for what Warrant Officer Thompson has to say to track this thing down? . . . It's just hard for me to understand when you've got these people coming off a flight line, how this doesn't have an emotional effect on you. You've got a pilot who asks why he is in Vietnam when things like this are happening. 'Just take it easy; forget about it.' ")

At 3:55 on the afternoon of the sixteenth, this self-serving entry was filed in the official Task Force Barker log: "Company B reports that none of VC body count reported by his unit were women and children. Company C reports that approximately ten to eleven women and children were killed due to artillery or gunships. These were not included in the body count." The task force log noted that the information had been forwarded to the 11th Brigade, but it did not appear in the brigade or the division logs for the day. Neither Major Calhoun nor Colonel Henderson could explain the entry. Following a series of sharp probes about the questionable log entry, Major Calhoun, on the advice of his counsel, decided to exercise his legal right to stop testifying on the grounds of self-incrimination.

That night, the briefing officers at the Americal Division at Chu Lai reported a total Viet Cong body count of 138 for the division, all but ten resulting from the Task Force Barker operation. Lieutenant Colonel Francis R. Lewis, the division chaplain, was one of about fifty officers who attended the briefing that night. "We were told a hundred and twenty-eight VC were killed in the incident," Reverend Lewis, a Methodist, told the Panel, "and I heard the G5—I think it was Colonel Anistranski—say, 'Ha ha, they were all women and children.'" Lewis added, "We were talking about it, were buzzing about it, on the way out of the room . . . also three weapons. This was another item that was buzzed about." There was no official mention of civilian casualties in connection with the task force operation.

Generals Koster and Young left the briefing together and discussed the disparity between enemy killed and weapons captured. Captain Daniel A. Roberts, Koster's aide, was walking a few feet behind the men. "General Koster made some—there must have been some comment made—about the disparity," Roberts testified, "and General Young was very annoyed. General Young said he was going to find out, he was going to continue to research the problem and determine what caused this disparity. It was my impression at the time that the 11th Brigade had lied about their body count, that the weapons were correct but the body count was inflated." Roberts added that the incident took place "during a period in which there was a great deal of concern of inflated body counts. We'd had many people come down investigating this thing . . ."

Thompson's clash with Charlie Company and the reports

of excessive shooting dominated the talk at the nightly
cocktail hour in Colonel Henderson's air-conditioned mess
hall at the 11th Brigade headquarters. According to Captain
James H. Henderson, who ran the brigade operations center
during the day, Task Force Barker's operation was one of
the main topics of conversation among the twenty-five or
thirty officers there. Yet Henderson testified that the only
story he heard at any time about My Lai 4 concerned "the
. . . helicopter pilot stopping and having his door gunner
ward off an American soldier while the helicopter pilot got
out and did something to a Vietnamese . . . We couldn't
actually visualize one of the helicopter pilots sitting down
up there and having one of his door gunners holding off or
stopping a U.S. trooper while one of the pilots got out to
check a Vietnamese or something. We were just discussing
how impossible it seemed at the time."

There were at least three attempts made that evening to
bring some of the truth about My Lai 4 to the attention of
higher authorities. Captain Barry C. Lloyd, a section leader
with the 123rd Aviation Battalion, underlined some of the
words in Hugh Thompson's bitter after-action report and
wrote the word "NOTICE" in capital letters next to a statement about civilians being killed at My Lai 4. Such reports
were filed after every mission with the battalion intelligence
office. He hoped his small action would make some of the
senior officers begin asking questions. Lawrence Kubert
also filed an after-action report. "I wrote that there were approximately one hundred to one hundred and fifty women
and children killed," Kubert testified. "And that was about
it as far as our action was concerned." Copies of his report
were sent to both the division air office and its intelligence
office. Investigators for the Peers Panel were unable to find
either of the after-action reports or any officer at division
headquarters who had any knowledge of them.

Major Watke spent much of the evening in his office at Chu Lai brooding over the discrepancies between what he had learned from his men and what he had been told by Lieutenant Colonel Barker. Around ten o'clock Watke decided to take his story to his immediate superior in the chain of command, Lieutenant Colonel John L. Holladay, the aviation commander for the Americal Division. Much of his worry was over his own future, Watke acknowledged in his testimony: "I still didn't at the time put all that much significance in the allegation . . . but I told him [Holladay] because I didn't want someone to come back and surprise him [by saying] that I was out charging people and creating incidents which weren't true and he wouldn't be able to at least halfway come to the defense." Watke's greatest concern was over the possible ramifications of Thompson's unprecedented interference with the commander on the ground in My Lai 4. He told Holladay about Thompson's reasons for making the unusual landings on the ground, but apparently wasn't himself convinced that the pilot's actions had been justified.

Holladay warned him, Watke recalled, that "my charge was quite something and if it proved to be false . . . that I would just basically be ruined. I sat there and accused people of needlessly killing people and I certainly wouldn't be asked to perform another mission for anybody again, because I was definitely hurting a number of people . . ." But Holladay was more concerned about the reports of indiscriminate killings than with the possible violations of procedure by Thompson. He had sat through the evening briefing at Division, and perhaps he, too, had been wondering about the high body count and small number of captured weapons reported by Task Force Barker. "At the conclusion of my little story . . ." Watke said, "Holladay asked me if I realized what I was doing, and he told me I had better make sure if I was going to stand on it. I thought about it for a while and I said, 'Yes, I stand on what I said.' " There was no question in Holladay's mind after Watke's visit that a great many civilians had been murdered, perhaps as many as 120. Holladay told the Panel that he had considered waking up his immediate superior, General Young, that night to relay Watke's account, but decided to wait until the next morning. He ordered Watke to meet him shortly after seven o'clock.

Sometime late in the night of the sixteenth, Colonel Henderson telephoned General Koster at his headquarters to report formally that at least twenty civilians were inadvertently killed during the operation at My Lai 4—something Koster already knew from Captain Medina. Henderson's information, however, came from Barker, who had prepared a three-by-five index card for him, detailing how each victim was killed. Barker's list claimed that the deaths were caused either by artillery or helicopter gunship fire. Henderson's report should not have been surprising to Koster, yet the colonel recalled that the commanding general "evidenced considerable surprise and shock at the number. General Koster was unhappy, as was I, over this abnormally high number of civilians [who] have been killed. But there was no further instructions from the general."

Over at the barracks for the 123rd Aviation Battalion, Captain Brian Livingston was writing to his wife. A portion of the letter was submitted to the Panel: "Well, it's been a long day; saw some nasty sights. I saw the insertion of infantrymen and were they animals . . . I've never seen so many people dead in one spot. Ninety-five percent were women and kids. We told the grunts on the ground of some injured kids. They helped them all right. A captain walked up to this little girl, he turned away, took five steps, and fired a volley of shots into her. This Negro sergeant started shooting people in the head . . . I'll tell you something: it sure makes one wonder why we are here . . . I can also see why they [the Vietnamese] hate helicopter pilots. If I ever hear a Shark [pilot from the 174th Aviation Company] open his big mouth I'm going to shove my fist into his mouth. We're trying to get the captain and sergeant aforementioned reprimanded. I don't know if we will be successful, but we're trying. Enough for that."

10

The Day After

Shortly before eight o'clock on the morning of Sunday, March 17, Lieutenant Colonel Holladay and Major Watke walked into the Americal Division headquarters to report the My Lai 4 massacre to General Young. Young was at his desk. Both officers were nervous: reporting a massacre to a general was no way to get ahead in the military. Holladay began the conversation, as he told the Panel: "I went into General Young's office and told him . . . that something had occurred that I felt he should know about right away. And he invited us in, Major Watke and me. I turned to Major Watke, as near as I can recollect. I said, 'Go ahead, you tell General Young the same story you told me last night' . . . He told the same story to General Young that he told to me on the night of the sixteenth. And here, again, the points of that conversation that stick most clearly in my memory are the fact that there was some excessive killing down there that day, the sergeant standing on the ditch, firing an M-16 or an M-60 machine gun into the ditch, into a number, a great number, many civilians, and Mr. Thompson threatening to fire upon the advancing Americans . . . Fred told the story with little or no variation . . . and General Young sat there and listened to it very attentively . . . When the portion of the story unfolded that Mr. Thompson threatened to fire on the Americans, he was visually taken aback by this and showed great concern . . . He may have said 'My God' or some exclamation or revelation to that portion of the story."

Holladay recalled that the number of apparent killings was given as 120 during Watke's conversation. General Young made no interruptions nor did he make any demands for more information. "There were several 'How's that' . . . 'What do you mean by that?'—and then going back," the lieutenant colonel testified. "The only specific words that I remember General Young stating that morning were 'We don't want Americans shooting Americans.' Those were his precise words." The general seemed more upset over Thompson's action in landing his helicopter and threatening ground forces than in the numbers of civilians slain, Holladay said. "I'm not saying unconcerned," he specifically noted, "I'm saying less concerned . . . I recall very clearly that it sort of surprised me because I had it just the other way around in my mind."

Young testified, however, that he came away from the forty-five-minute meeting with no knowledge of any murders. "I gained the impression," Young said, "that civilians were in a crossfire between the friendly forces and the enemy forces. That in an effort to save the civilians and to insure that they were not injured, the pilot landed his airplane . . . I would say, to the best of my knowledge, there was no mention made of any noncombatant casualties. I cannot recall being informed of any noncombatant casualties . . ." The only confrontation Young was told about, he said, concerned Thompson and the ground troops. His version of that incident had little relationship to the facts: "He [Thompson] landed simply to tell them that this fire was being received out there by people . . . that were without weapons and were predominantly women and children." In Young's view, the dispute between Thompson and Lieutenant Calley on the ground centered over Calley's concern that the pilot wanted Charlie Company to take unnecessary risks to save civilians, because of the heavy enemy fire. Young's recollection at this point seems suspect; the only excuse for Thompson's admittedly extreme actions in landing his helicopter was the indiscriminate slaughter he was witnessing. Holladay and Watke had no possible reason for omitting the allegations of murder.

Perhaps because of his fears over the impact of his testimony on his career, Watke gave a number of varying accounts to the Peers Panel of what he had, in fact, told General Young. Much of his report was obviously aimed at justifying Thompson's action at My Lai 4. But at no time, the major testified, did he convey to General Young the impression of a hotly contested action with civilians caught in a crossfire. ". . . I certainly would not have gone to anybody and tried to portray there was one [a crossfire]," Watke said. "Because, in my mind, there just never was one. This is why I questioned the total [body] count in the first place . . ."

When General Koster returned to his headquarters for lunch, Young took him aside to relay the Holladay–Watke report. Koster said he learned only the following information: "As best that I recall, it was a question of indiscriminate firing on the part of the ground troops, and it was a case of there being some difficulty between the pilot and the ground commander . . . I'm not sure that I got all this at one time . . ." Koster testified that Young explained the helicopter incident in the following manner: "The pilot had wanted to bring in some ships for evacuation of personnel, and I guess the ground commander at the time hadn't thought this was the time or the use of gunships for that mission." He said he was not told about the murders at My Lai 4, nor was he told that Thompson had trained his machine guns on fellow Americans in order to evacuate some Vietnamese civilians. The indiscriminate firing that he did learn about was perhaps understandable: ". . . The troops were firing at targets as opposed to identified enemy which they were supposedly there to fire at. They were covering a wide range, and just by this type of coverage they were bound to hit some of the civilians that were in the area." (Yet, in an earlier statement to the Army's Criminal Investigating Division, Koster acknowledged that he had been told by Young during the meeting that there had been some "indiscriminate shooting of Vietnamese civilians.") After hearing Young's report, Koster said, he ordered him to "find out what went on down there; interrogate the people involved and the leaders concerned and let's have the facts." Shortly after his meeting with Young, the major general either telephoned or personally visited Lieutenant Colonel Barker and asked him about the conduct of his troops. Barker replied that he or Major Calhoun had been overflying the area at various times throughout the operation, Koster said, and "they had not witnessed nor heard things of this type being discussed or taking place. I . . . received no indication from him that there had been unusual firing or incidents . . ."

The Peers Panel posed the inevitable, and unanswered, question to both Young and Koster: If the only reports presented to them concerned some civilians killed in a crossfire and a pilot who had a dispute while attempting—perhaps recklessly—to rescue some civilian noncombatants, what was there to investigate? None of those incidents were specific violations of any Army regulations or international law. Neither officer could provide a clear or satisfactory answer.

By midday on March 17, of course, Koster had already heard from both Captain Medina and Colonel Henderson about the killing of civilians; he had also expressed disgust, along with General Young, over the patently absurd disparity between the body count and the captured weapons reported for the Task Force Barker operation into Son My. He had personally countermanded an order from Henderson to Medina calling for a careful check of civilian casualties. He had flown over My Lai 4, and should have seen for himself the extensive fire damage or heavy smoke resulting from the operation. He had asked General Young and Lieutenant Colonel Barker to investigate the civilian casualties, Thompson's action on the ground, and the reports of excessive firing, but had not reconsidered his order countermanding Henderson's demand that Charlie Company return to My Lai 4.

(That morning Charlie Company passed within a few hundred yards of the hamlet. The company had broken camp early and begun moving south. The first platoon moved to the west to search a hill and perhaps set up an operation base. Private Paul Meadlo got careless and tripped a booby trap; fragments blew off his foot and slightly cut Lieutenant Calley about the face. My Lai 4 was still smoking. The survivors, who had begun digging large open graves, hid in panic as the Americans walked by.)

At least one officer in the 123rd Aviation Battalion, however, did order an overlight of the area that day. Warrant

Officer Charles H. Mansell testified that he and his crewmen "were instructed to just go back and check the general
area out." He noticed perhaps two hundred dead bodies all
over the hamlet of My Lai 4, and added, "I don't remember
seeing any living Vietnamese in this area at all." Many refugees were still streaming south, apparently toward Quang
Ngai City, as Task Force Barker continued its operations in
Son My.

Early Sunday, Hugh Thompson, still angry, visited his
chaplain, Father Carl Creswell, and told his story again. He
came in and "sat down very upset." Father Creswell particularly recalled Thompson's angry denunciation of a
"sawed-off runt of a lieutenant" who had challenged him on
the ground at My Lai 4. "He . . . wanted to know what to
do from that point on. It was my suggestion that he lodge
an official protest in command channels, and I'd do the
same thing through chaplain channels . . ." Creswell immediately went to see the Reverend Francis Lewis, the Americal Division chaplain and his superior in the chain of
command. "I told him about these allegations that had been
made," Creswell related, "and that I had an awful lot of
confidence in Mr. Thompson and that I would—well, I'll be
perfectly honest. I said that if there was not going to be an
examination into these charges, I was going to resign my
commission . . ." Lieutenant Colonel Lewis planned to
forward the complaint immediately through Jesmond Balmer, then the operations officer for the division. When he
learned Balmer was on leave, Lewis decided to wait.

By Sunday, everyone in Thompson's aero-scout company
of the 123rd Aviation Battalion knew what had happened,
in very specific detail—unlike the information the high
command of the division claimed it was receiving. Captain
Brian Livingston told the Panel that My Lai 4 was "common knowledge" among the company. That afternoon

Barry Lloyd walked over to the intelligence section at battalion headquarters, trying to find out what had happened
to Thompson's strongly opinionated after-action report that
he had underlined for emphasis. It was a Sunday and there
was only a clerk at the desk. Lloyd said he "asked the specialist at the desk if anything had come from our operation
with Task Force Barker, and he didn't know anything
about it."

At division headquarters, Holladay decided to tell the
chief of staff, Colonel Nels Parson, about his report to General Young. Parson had criticized Holladay earlier for not
keeping him informed of all his actions with the generals;
under Army procedure, messages to the commanding general or his deputies should come through the chief of staff.
Holladay testified that he went to Parson's office and "told
him the story as Fred [Watke] had told it to me . . . I can
recall Colonel Parson using the term 'that's murder,' and I
can recall him saying, 'We're trying to win these people over
and we do things like this' . . . He was visibly and forcibly
shaken up about this story." But Parson also berated the
lieutenant colonel for not bringing the story directly to him.

That afternoon General Young immediately began his investigation, as ordered by Koster, by flying to Landing
Zone Dotti. By the time Young arrived at the task force
headquarters, much of the area to the east was shrouded in
heavy smoke. Both Charlie and Bravo Companies had continued their search-and-destroy mission in Son My during
the day, burning at least six hamlets along the South China
Sea coast near My Lai 1 and inland. The Peers Panel investigated the weather conditions for March 17 and learned
that skies were fair with some scattered clouds at 4,000 feet;
visibility was put at seven miles. Young acknowledged to
the Panel that he probably did fly over the operational area
that afternoon but hedged when asked if he had seen the

fires: "I don't know whether I did or not. I probably did,
sir. I don't recall specifically. I can't answer your question
yes or no."

Young's aide at the time, Lieutenant Donald T. White,
had a much clearer recollection: "I remember one time
there was a big operation out here especially, because I remember there was a lot of smoke flying over the area. A lot
of villages were burned." Henry E. Riddle was a door gunner aboard General Young's helicopter that day. He testified that at some point as they were flying along the South
China Sea coast near Son My, one of the pilots shouted,
"My God, look at the fires . . . I sat on the same side as the
general," he added. "There was a lot of smoke, so I just
took it . . . that it was hootches and so on burning." Riddle
didn't recall any specific comments from General Young
that day: "I remember General Young when we was flying
over the smoke. He seemed a little bit touchy. Several times
he'd be trying to light a cigarette or something, but the way
the wind was he couldn't light it. He got mad and jerked the
cigarette out and threw it out of the ship. He wouldn't light
it . . . I remember this because several times [previously]
. . . he would ask me for my cigarette lighter. I remember
because he didn't this time."

At Landing Zone Dotti, Young was given an extensive
briefing on the mission. Major Calhoun testified that he told
the general that "sixty-nine were killed by artillery and that
I thought that possibly some of those were civilians that had
been killed by the artillery fire." Young asked him no direct
question, Calhoun said, although the general "said something about that they were aware of some incident." The
talk of artillery killings must have surprised the general;
there had been no mention of artillery at the division
briefing the night before.

Sometime after his briefing at the task force, General

Young ordered Colonel Henderson, Major Watke, and Lieutenant Colonels Barker and Holladay to attend a meeting with him the next morning at task force headquarters. Whatever he had heard or seen that afternoon apparently troubled him. Lieutenant Colonel Trexler, the division intelligence chief, recalled that sometime that day—or perhaps early on the next day, the eighteenth—he was flying with General Young when they began a private discussion on the intercom. Young was unhappy about the task force: "The main thing that stands out was [Young's] concern . . . that the people had gone beyond what he conceived was proper conduct . . . Units had indiscriminately burned hootches, burned villages. He was most concerned . . . They had been more destructive than the situation called for . . . I think maybe that he did discuss the value of retaining Task Force Barker." Trexler claimed he did not remember much of the conversation: "The significant thing was that we switched to private conversation [altered frequency so others on the helicopter could not overhear] and discussed this incident in very, very general terms. That stuck with me and that's the basic thing that stuck with me."

That same afternoon Task Force Barker headquarters ordered its two companies in the field to stop burning; from that moment on, the operation suddenly became a mercy mission—to the amazement of the GIs. Medical teams were flown to the area to inspect and treat the civilians who had been collected by Charlie and Bravo Companies during their two-day reign of terror.

Task Force Barker's log for the Sunday was modest—only four Viet Cong were reported killed. There was one significant entry: Charlie Company had captured three Viet Cong suspects, along with an elderly man. Captain Medina gave a vivid description of how he tried to make the suspects talk: ". . . The one Vietnamese woman, the nurse, and the three men were brought to my position. The woman did not have a blouse on. All she had was pajama bottoms. I did not know if she ever had one on or if it was ripped off of her. A GI was carrying her. She was acting like she was out of her mind and she was kind of bubbling at the mouth. It was like a child bubbles. I looked at her and knew she was faking. My medic said that she was faking. So we laid her on the ground and I asked him if he had any ammonia capsules. We put an ammonia capsule in her nose and she immediately snapped to. I took the blouse off of one of the VC and I placed it on her to cover her up."

Gregory Olsen, one of the GIs in Charlie Company, had a different understanding of the reasons for the woman's poor state. She had been pulled from a hut during the company's sweep of My Khe 2, stripped, and paraded around the area by a GI who flung her over his shoulder. "He said he was going to 'put it' to her, but she was too dirty," Olsen told me during an interview. Sergeant Thomas Kinch, who served with Charlie Company's mortar platoon, went even further during his testimony. He cited the incident when asked if he thought Medina was aware of the company's practice of abusing and raping women detainees during operations. "The guy that found her said that he was going to rape her until he looked at her and changed his mind," Kinch said. "So anyway, just as the chopper came in to pick up these suspects, Captain Medina—I guess Captain Medina had heard about this guy was planning to rape her or something. So the girl, she wore no blouse or nothing, she just had a skirt on . . . and Captain Medina grabbed her by the breast and pulled her to the chopper." Other GIs told me that the woman eventually remained in the bivouac area and—after it was determined that she was a "North Vietnamese nurse"—a number of men from the second platoon repeatedly raped her.

Medina never mentioned the assaults; his account of the woman's interrogation ended with the provision of a blouse. He turned next to the men. "There were two individuals that were definitely VC," the captain said. ". . . We started going through their pockets. One had a small embroidered cloth that had, I think the translator said, 'Honor to the VC,' or 'Death before dishonor to the VC,' or something like this. The other one would not talk. The other individual was very mature, an executive-looking individual. He was not the type of individual that you would find out in the hamlets or villages in that area. He was definitely not a rice farmer . . . They were tied up. The executive-looking individual, for a better term to describe him, shouted out a command. It was definitely a command. It was not like the normal Vietnamese sound, talk, and I turned around and I told him, in American, that he was to shut up and be quiet. I hit him with the back of my hand. I cracked his skin open on the forehead. It was starting to bleed very profusely and I didn't hit very hard. It was running down his nose . . ."

The captain claimed that his interpreter then suggested the suspect would talk if he could be frightened: "So I had a .38 [caliber] pistol with me. I had removed all the ammunition from the chamber. The individual did not see me do this. I showed him one round, pretended to put it in the weapon and put it up to his head. Now, apparently, he knew that the weapon was empty because I could not scare him." At this point, Medina testified, Sergeant Phu again suggested that "if you shoot at him very closely he might talk." Medina followed the advice: "I put him up against a tree, a coconut tree, and I moved back approximately ten to fifteen meters and I took my M-16 weapon . . . and I told Sergeant Phu to tell him that I was going to ask him one more time and he'd better talk or I would shoot him."

The captain then described how he fired two shots—each

closer to the suspect's head—but the man remained silent:
"So I propped him up against the tree sideways, and I
showed him where the two rounds were with my fingers. I
put my finger in the last [bullet] hole and then I put him up
against it and somehow or other, it came almost between
his eyes, indicating that the next round, the third round,
was going to go right between his eyes. So I propped him up
against the tree, facing me, I walked back ten or fifteen meters. I raised my M-16 rifle and the individual started talking. The weapon was on safety the third time. I would not
have killed the individual, have shot him in cold blood. If
he hadn't broken and talked he would still be alive today."
Medina added quickly, "By that I don't know whether he is
dead or alive." Other GIs have testified that at this point
Medina had a photograph taken of himself drinking from a
coconut in one hand and holding a sharp knife at the throat
of the "Viet Cong."

By Sunday, the seventeenth, intelligence officials at Division had received a classified summary of Task Force Barker's operations in Son My the day before, as prepared by
Lieutenant Colonel Blackledge. The document was in many
ways as erroneous as the simultaneous newspapers reports
in the United States describing the task force's "victory."
Task Force Barker's log had listed the accidental shooting
of a GI in the foot—Charlie Company's only casualty on
the sixteenth—straightforwardly as "Co. C . . . reports 1
EM [enlisted man] . . . shot in foot." Yet Blackledge's summary reported "one U.S. wounded by sniper fire." An early
Charlie Company report that fourteen Viet Cong soldiers
were killed was rewritten by the brigade to say that the Viet
Cong were "evading" when shot. A further Charlie Company report that thirty to forty Viet Cong had left the village at seven o'clock was never forwarded to Division, al-

though that would have been a prime piece of intelligence in evaluating the operation, particularly in light of the later high enemy body count.

The Peers Panel suggested that such alterations hinted of a massive and conspiratorial cover-up. Undoubtedly, the intelligence report for the 11th Brigade was deliberately altered that day, as were other documents and reports throughout the task force and brigade. But such embellishments were not necessarily created by one officer or a group of men; the evidence indicates that on a day-by-day basis the cover-up or fabrication of intelligence to dramatize combat engagements or to minimize operational fiascos was a routine matter. Still, by Sunday, the day after the mission, Blackledge should have been in the field seeking copies of enemy documents and other data to forward to Division. He made no trips and, apparently, division intelligence never asked for documents.*

---

* Some questions were being asked by lower-ranking officers in the division G2 office, but none of the senior commanders took the obvious step of demanding a reevaluation of the mission's results. Clarence Dukes, a division intelligence officer, recalled questioning the statistics during a briefing for Lieutenant Colonel Trexler, the intelligence chief. He not only questioned the results, Dukes told the Peers Panel, but also found no evidence that Charlie Company in fact had been in contact with the main force of the 48th Viet Cong Battalion. "It was never truly identified," Dukes said. "You have to have two or more bits of evidence to prove that you are in contact with a certain element." Trexler, questioned about his reaction upon learning of the operation's results, gave the standard response: "Well, it's a little bit abnormal [to kill 128 Viet Cong while capturing three weapons], yet not so much that it would be extremely unusual because in the particular area that this operation was taking place. Very frequently many of the enemy was just simply armed with a hand grenade." Asked if Division had demanded an explanation for the statistical imbalance, the lieutenant colonel replied, "I was made aware of this within a day or so, or maybe the very next day, which makes me quite positive it was done." There is no evidence, in fact, that an explanation was sought.

Blackledge did not even attempt to determine the home units of the dead Viet Cong, normally a basic intelligence requirement. Asked about the lapse, Blackledge replied, "Most times you couldn't tell what unit the enemy casualties were from. It was very unusual, even though you had people lying there dead, to ever find anything on them." Colonel Franklin, of the Peers Panel, interrupted harshly: "Are you that stupid to make that statement? Now if you kill civilians it would be highly unusual to find anything, but I believe the experience in Vietnam is that when you get in with a local force or NVA [North Vietnamese Army], or a main force unit, and you kill anywhere near the quantity of sixty-nine, you got so darn much documentation you are submerged in it; with diaries, and letters, and the rest of this business." The panelist apparently thought Blackledge was lying. Another possibility is that Blackledge, whose combat experience was nil, really did not know very much about the type or number of documents found after a big enemy kill. During his tenure with the 11th Brigade, there simply may not have been any large kills of Viet Cong at all—Task Force Barker's successes to the contrary. The Peers Panel also gathered much testimony indicating that the quality of the training in intelligence procedures—or perhaps the quality of the men taking such training—was extremely poor.

By late evening of the seventeenth, all the signs of a serious atrocity were present; one which could force an official investigation and perhaps widely publicize courts-martial that could ruin the careers of many high officers. Over the next few weeks, however, the growing evidence that a massacre had taken place at My Lai 4 was either disregarded or covered up.

11

A Day of Denial

*A*t nine o'clock on Monday morning Colonel Henderson, Lieutenant Colonels Barker and Holladay, and Major Watke arrived for the unique meeting called by General Young. The five men moved, at Young's suggestion, into Frank Barker's personal living quarters, a small house trailer that was located a few dozen yards from the task force operations center. Young sat on Barker's bed; the junior officers stood. Holladay told the Peers Panel what happened next: "General Young opened up the meeting . . . by saying . . . 'We are the only five that know about this.'" His message was clear: no unnecessary talking about either the meeting or the complaints. Young turned to Holladay, the aviation officer testified, and said, "John, go ahead." Holladay, in turn, asked Watke to retell his story for the third time. The only person in the room who hadn't heard Watke's account firsthand by that time was Henderson.

Holladay and Watke both agreed in their testimony that the major gave the same account as he had previously of the My Lai 4 confrontation between Thompson and the ground troops and the unwarranted shooting of civilians. Holladay recalled that Henderson did not seem surprised or shocked by Watke's tale. When Watke had finished, Holladay said, Young again exclaimed, "We don't want Americans shooting Americans," and told Colonel Henderson, "I want you to investigate this and have it to me." Holladay thought that the brigade commander had been given seventy-two hours to complete his inquiry. Holladay left the meeting convinced that Henderson had been ordered to pursue both the reports of the Thompson confrontation and the indiscriminate killings, although no specific directives had been given. Watke recalled that Henderson, after hearing the account, suggested that Barker be assigned to investigate it, but was told by the general, "No, I want you to look into this and render a report." *

But Colonel Henderson testified that he left the meeting convinced that the Thompson confrontation was to be the crux of his investigation, although his subsequent inquiry belied this testimony. "The primary point that we were talking about," Henderson said, "or the initial point, at least, was the confrontation between United States troops, between Warrant Officer Thompson and the troops on the ground . . ." Henderson denied hearing any information at the meeting about American GIs doing indiscriminate shooting at My Lai 4, "except for the one incident of Cap-

---

* That night Major Watke wrote his wife about the meeting: "My people observed an unfortunate act the other day and I reported it. Colonel Henderson has been directed to investigate and report it to the commanding general. I didn't make any friends, but my conscience is clear." Watke supplied the letter to the Peers Panel.

tain Medina." He also insisted that he had not been ordered to compile a formal investigation, but was only told to "look into it" by Young and report his findings.

General Young similarly had conflicting recollections of the meeting. He testified that he spent just a few moments in the van, during which time he relayed a request from General Koster that the incident be investigated quickly. Young emphatically denied the contention—raised by Colonel Henderson and no one else—that he criticized at length the actions of Hugh Thompson in landing at My Lai 4: "I admired the warrant officer for the action he took, and the fact that he did what he did." The general added that during the meeting he had asked Barker what he knew about Thompson's accusations regarding indiscriminate firing. The task force commander "acted quite surprised and gave every assurance that there had not been any casualties resulting from his troops," Young said. "He had indicated that he had received this report, but he . . . did not actually believe what had been reported." Young also denied making a statement indicating that the participants should keep the meeting quiet. The general's main thesis, despite the Calhoun briefing at Landing Zone Dotti the day before, was that he was not told at any time that "there had been civilian casualties resulting from either ground troops' engagement or helicopter . . . I was not aware that friendly casualties, I mean noncombatant casualties, had occurred," he said. Moreover, Young said he thought the investigation Henderson had been ordered to begin would basically deal with the charges that civilians had been inadvertently caught in the crossfire at My Lai 4.

The conflicts over who said what and when were inevitable, given the fact that men's careers and reputations were

at stake. But if Young had not learned from Watke that
there had been a needless killing of civilians at either of his
meetings with him, the question still remains: what did he
ask Colonel Henderson to investigate? Shooting civilians
accidentally in the heat of battle is not a war crime.* At any
time, too, Young still could have ordered one of the units in
the Americal Division to make an on-site inspection of the
area, and thus find out firsthand—instead of relying on
comments from those who had the most to lose—what had
happened. (Ronald Ridenhour and his 11th Brigade helicopter crew did inadvertently fly over the hamlet while on a
patrol a few days after the massacre. The young GI, as he
later told me, was appalled by the complete desolation at
My Lai 4—"not even a bird was singing . . . There were no
people around. No signs of life anywhere.")

After the meeting in Barker's van, Colonel Henderson—
beginning his inquiry—asked Watke to send some of the
complaining pilots to him for interviews. Watke walked to
the 123rd's operations van and ordered Thompson, Jerry
Culverhouse, and Lawrence M. Colburn, one of Thompson's door gunners, to report. The aviators had been pulled
off flight duty the day before and ordered to stay near their
quarters in case they were needed for official questioning.
Thompson testified that he spent twenty to thirty minutes
telling Henderson his account of the massacre at My Lai 4:
"I told him that I had seen the captain [Medina] shoot the
Vietnamese girl. I told him about the ditches and the bodies

* One clue to Young's state of mind was provided by Lieutenant John P.
Newell, the general's personal pilot. He testified that while the crew was
waiting at Landing Zone Dotti for the meeting to break up, Young's aide,
Lieutenant Donald White, "told me that the general was meeting Colonel
Holladay and Major Watke down there, and that heads were going to
roll, that he was going to relieve somebody of their command because of
something that happened."

in the ditch . . . I told him about the sergeant saying the
only way he could help them was to shoot them . . . I told
him what I said to Lieutenant Calley . . . I told him about
how I had gotten the people out of the bunker." Thompson
said he estimated the number of bodies in the ditch at between seventy-five and one hundred.

Henderson denied being told anything about his troops
wantonly killing large groups of civilians. He also baldly denied being told of a machine-gun confrontation between
Thompson and Calley. He did quote Thompson as telling
him, "Sir, your soldiers on the operation of the sixteenth
were like a bunch of wild men and were wildly shooting
throughout My Lai—or throughout the area, including the
gunship." What he did remember, Henderson said, was a
report from Thompson of a Negro sergeant who murdered
a civilian after the helicopter pilot had marked the position
with a smoke signal indicating that there were wounded civilians in the area. Thompson also repeated the accusation
about Medina's shooting of the women. "He . . . told me
that he saw a lot of dead civilians in the area," Henderson
testified. "I recall asking him if he knew what were the results of the infantry units he had supported in this operation. And I informed him that what the results were that
twenty civilians had been killed and one hundred twenty-
eight VC. And he said, 'Well, yes' . . . but these civilians
that he saw on the ground were . . . not VC, that they were
old men, old women, and children."

At this point Henderson's testimony became almost incredible. Thompson, he claimed, did not mention his dispute with Calley, and, therefore, Henderson said, he did not
connect the confrontation and subsequent evacuation of civilians from the area with the reports of indiscriminate
shooting: "Although it [the Calley confrontation] happened

perhaps the same day or part of the same operation, I did not tie this in with the report I had from Warrant Officer Thompson. I know I didn't have the full story of what went on up there. I know I didn't have a full story from Warrant Officer Thompson . . . I know that when he was talking to me he was in tears." By this time Henderson had made up his mind about Thompson: ". . . It appeared to me that a young warrant officer who was apparently new—I didn't know this, but he appeared to be new and inexperienced; and apparently what was a fierce fire fight going on down below appeared to the warrant officer that it was an act of savagery." Henderson had already received the assurances of Lieutenant Colonel Barker about the "fierce fire fight"; and he had been told that the only persons killed by Charlie Company that day were Viet Cong and a few civilians.

On the other hand, the colonel was immediately provided details of the extent of the massacre from two other eyewitnesses who saw him one by one, following the Thompson interview. Jerry Culverhouse of the 123rd Aviation Battalion, who had seen more than one hundred bodies at My Lai 4, testified that Henderson seemed most interested in determining whether a Negro sergeant was firing into a ditch. "He asked me how I could say that it was a colored soldier and that he was an NCO [noncommissioned officer]," Culverhouse said. "I told him that we were making very low passes over the village and not really flying that fast . . . I told him that there was no doubt in my mind that the individual was colored [and] . . . that I could definitely see chevrons above his rolled-up sleeves." Culverhouse said he described the blood-filled ditches full of dead Vietnamese in some details for the colonel: "It seemed that some of the things that I told him did seem to put him . . . more or less on the defensive . . . It made him uneasy . . . He seemed to be quite uneasy when I'd make a rather bold or brass statement as to the hard facts, like so many bodies—that there was blood actually running off from the bodies into the ditch." According to Culverhouse, the colonel scribbled some comments in a notebook during the session.

Lawrence Colburn similarly recalled telling the colonel about the ditch, estimating the number of bodies at sixty to seventy. He also described Thompson's landing and his evacuation of the civilians over Calley's protests. But much of the youth's emphasis was placed on Medina's shooting of the woman: "I was so close. And I think that was what really shocked. I had no idea that he was going to do that."

Again Henderson repeatedly denied any recollection of either of the two men or of his talks with them, although other testimony established conclusively that the interviews took place in Barker's van shortly after the morning meeting on March 18. Henderson did acknowledge, however, that at some point during the day, probably at noon, he told his staff and Colonel Barker that he wanted the allegations and his investigation of them to be kept "close to our belt, because I didn't want to demoralize the troops if they had gone out and done a damn fine job. There is nothing worse in my mind—and I know I relayed this to these people—than coming in and finding out they have been accused of shooting up the countryside." The message to the Task Force Barker staff was one it did not need to be told: Keep it quiet.

After lunch the colonel then flew out to see Medina, bringing along two of his key aides, Major McKnight and Lieutenant Colonel Blackledge. Henderson said he was angry and embarrassed, because within a few days his commanding general had overruled one of his orders and also ordered the investigation of Task Force Barker's operation. "I think some of my thinking was that I had just assumed command of this brigade," Henderson explained, "and that it was my brigade, and dammit, I wanted to run it. I wanted to find out what in the hell was happening. I didn't yet have control, I recognized that. I know when I went out there to see Medina that I expected to relieve him . . . I was seeing red after receiving this report [of the shooting of a woman] from Warrant Officer Thompson." Amazingly, Henderson claimed at this point that he only had "one item that I could dig my teeth into, and that was the positive identification of a dark-complexioned captain and he [Medina] was the one in that particular area."

Charlie Company had completed its mission by noon of the third day, and was waiting for helicopters to airlift them back to their quarters at Landing Zone Dotti. Henderson landed near a potato field, and moved a few dozen yards away with Medina and some staff members in tow. The men talked while flattened on the ground as a precaution against enemy snipers. "I told him I had a very serious report from a pilot who was flying over the operation on the sixteenth," Henderson related. "There had been possible indiscriminate killing of civilians, and specifically, a captain had been identified shooting a woman. And I remember saying, 'Dammit, Ernie, I want the truth from this, was that you?' " According to Henderson, Medina's initial response dealt with the killing of the woman and "it was almost step for step what the warrant officer had relayed to me, the only difference being the hand movement that Medina had seen out of the corner of his eye as he was moving away from the wounded woman who he had earlier assumed [was] dead. I then asked him about any killing of civilians that his troops could be involved in that he couldn't have seen. He said he had had no such report from his platoon leaders, and he was certain he would if it had happened . . . I asked Captain Medina how he determined the number [of civilians] killed and he said they were reported by his platoon leaders as they came upon these bodies while moving through the area. And I asked him if all of them had been killed by artillery and by gunships, and he said yes."

Any other answer to that question, of course, would have contradicted the contrived reports that had already been forwarded to higher headquarters. Henderson testified that he concluded his interview by questioning Medina about the high body count for the operation. "I didn't believe the body count," the colonel said, "but I asked him where were the bodies, that I hadn't seen them, where were they? He said that there were a great number of them that were spread out in bushes and among trees. The gunships had taken them under fire. Others were in the defensive bunkers around the village. And it is possible you can't see a body. I didn't see any," Henderson noted, "and it is pretty hard to see from the altitude I was flying." Medina confirmed much of the conversation during his appearance before the Panel, but added that Henderson "asked me if I thought my people could do such a thing, and I told him I did not think American soldiers would do such a thing. He said 'Okay.' " *

---

* Nearly two years after his testimony before the Peers Panel, Medina—then a civilian—publicly acknowledged that he had lied to Colonel Henderson about the extent of civilian casualties at My Lai 4. Testifying as a defense witness during the court-martial of Henderson in November, 1971, Medina said he reported the twenty to twenty-eight civilian casualties as victims of gunship or artillery fire when, in fact, "I had a suspicion they had been shot by members of my command . . . not wanting to believe my people would do this, I tried to give the impression they wouldn't." At the time, Medina testified, he already had been informed by his three platoon leaders that at least 106 villagers had been slain in My Lai 4, but he did not give Henderson that information. Medina further admitted lying to the Peers Panel and also to the Army Inspector General's office during its investigation of the atrocity in mid-1969. Medina resigned his commission one month before his appearance at Henderson's court-martial.

Lieutenant Colonel Blackledge, who heard most of the conversation, recalled some talk about getting in medics to treat the civilians: "I believe that Colonel Henderson and Captain Medina . . . had an understanding that medics were on the way, that whatever could be done for civilians was being done." The reference may have been to the medical teams that were treating hundreds of civilians along the coast of the South China Sea. Colonel Franklin was curious about the fact that Blackledge, who rarely flew with the brigade commanders, was taken along on this sensitive mission. "You've heard the expression CYA [Cover Your Ass], haven't you?" the Peers investigator asked Blackledge. "Was that a little CYA operation? Why did he take you along?" The suggestion was clear: Henderson wanted a witness to demonstrate that he had conducted an investigation. Blackledge claimed his only thought as he climbed aboard the colonel's helicopter for the rare trip was, "Well, here it looks like with a new commander I'm going to get a chance to go out."

After his field visit to Medina, Henderson returned to Landing Zone Dotti to wait for the return of Charlie Company. When the first group of GIs climbed off the helicopter, the colonel continued his investigation: "I walked up to them and grabbed the first NCO, whom I do not know, but told him, 'Just hold these people here, I'd like to talk to them for a moment' . . . I started talking to this group of individuals—thirty to forty individuals . . . So I told them . . . they had done a damn fine job and that I was their new brigade commander and appreciated the fine job they had done for the brigade. I also told them that I had heard a report that we had injured and killed some noncombatants; that this was an unsubstantiated report; that, if true, it would certainly discolor the fine record that they had. I spoke along this vein for a few moments . . . and then I asked them in a group, 'Does anybody here, does any individual, any of you observe any acts against noncombatants, any wild shooting? Did any of you, or do you have knowledge of anybody killing any civilians during this operation?' And I got silence. I then pointed to three or four individuals and I don't think they had name tags on, but I identified the man and I believe said, 'How about you?' . . . I got back from the first individual a loud response 'No, sir.' And I pointed to three or four individuals and in each case I got back a loud and clear 'No, sir.' The men had their heads high. There was nobody trying to ignore my eyes. I looked at every individual there. They seemed to be in good spirits. They didn't appear to me to be a bunch of soldiers who had just gone out and shot up the countryside and killed a bunch of women and children."

Henderson added, "Although I wasn't thinking along these lines of a bunch of women and children being killed at the time." He continued his account: "The impression I got of them at the time was that they were a bunch of normal fighting infantrymen whom I have served with in three wars. Again I said I was delighted to see this, 'I think you have done a damn fine job, and again I deeply appreciate it.' I think I went ahead to say, 'I know what a rough, dirty damn job you've got and appreciate it.' " Henderson then ordered one of the sergeants to dismiss the men: "He called them to attention and gave me a salute and dismissed them, and they moved back down the hill and I stood there and watched them pass by me. No individual soldier made any effort to speak to me. I made myself available."

Of course no GI would admit to mass murder under those conditions; in later interviews with me, many of the Charlie Company men described Henderson's efforts with contempt and derision. And, contrary to Henderson's recollection, many soldiers described the meeting as a moment of feet-shuffling and head-averting. "Some colonel came up and asked me if there was anything unusual going on in the village," said Isaiah Cowen, a senior sergeant in Calley's platoon. I said 'No comment' and he passed on."

Jay A. Buchanon, the second platoon sergeant, had a strikingly different recollection of Henderson's remarks, as he told the Peers Panel: "Well, he [Henderson] said, 'You're back off this operation. Do you think the VC will be happy with this operation. Do you think it will leave the impression that when they see the American soldier they will say, "Here comes my buddy, he is here to help me." And he looked at me and said, 'What do you think, Sergeant?' I said, 'I have no comment, sir.' . . . I didn't say anything else. He said, 'We're here to protect the people from the evils of Communism,' and he said, 'I want that known,' or something like that. He didn't ask any further questions from me. He did not ask me why I didn't have no comment, or anything. I didn't know what to say, to tell you the truth."

One of the panelists dryly asked Colonel Henderson after his description of the interrogation if he had considered that "psychologically, this was a very poor time and very poor circumstances to be asking individuals if they committed atrocities?" Henderson agreed in retrospect: "I really didn't stop and think of it. I have thought of it since and I agree, psychologically it would have been a bad time. And I wouldn't expect a man to stand up and say, 'Yes, I killed a bunch of people.'" The concept of asking men to own up to mass murder shortly after they participated in it could be considered an example of deliberate blundering or inadvertent naïveté—yet Generals Koster and Young both accepted Henderson's subsequent findings with little question.

Before he left the task force headquarters area, Henderson had an argument with Barker. Frank Beardslee, Barker's driver, who had spent three days in the field with Charlie Company, returned to the headquarters area in time to overhear part of a violent confrontation between Colonel Henderson and the task force commander. "They yelled for a half-hour" inside Barker's van, Beardslee told me. "I wasn't close enough to hear all of what they were saying, but they were really going at it."

The Barker–Henderson dispute also was alluded to in a statement by David F. Meyer, a former 11th Brigade clerk who was interrogated by the C.I.D. but did not testify before the Peers Panel. Barker told Meyer that he was "very upset and angry about the fact that Medina's unit had gone through a village and had shot up the village . . . In fact, Barker told me that he had reprimanded Medina for this action . . . When I was discussing this particular operation with Barker, I recall asking him if he intended to formally charge Medina for what had happened. Barker told me that the brigade commander, Colonel Henderson, was quite concerned about it all, but that he, Barker, intended to just let it lie and cool off." Nevertheless, Barker began asking questions himself, although General Young had specifically made clear earlier in the day that he wanted Henderson to handle the investigation. What Henderson might find out could be crucial to Barker's ambition to command a battalion in the Americal Division.

Medina testified that he was greeted by Barker as soon as he climbed off a helicopter at Dotti: "Colonel Barker . . . stated there was a colored NCO, a colored soldier that [witnesses] had seen shoot into, or point his weapon into the bodies of dead civilians or shooting into civilians. Colonel Barker asked me to conduct an informal investigation to see if I could find out if any of this took place." Medina, in turn, asked his platoon leaders about it. "I talked to one colored NCO, a Sergeant [David] Mitchell [of Calley's pla-

toon]. He denied ever shooting any civilians . . . He said
that it could have been any colored sergeant, so why was I
picking on him. I said, 'Just forget about it. Right now I'm
not accusing you of anything, or anything like that.' " Medina claimed he reported his findings to Barker and suggested that some other officer conduct the investigation. At
that point, the captain said, Barker told him, "Ernie, you
have been doing a real fine job. Go on back to the company
and just continue doing the good work that you have done."
That was the last official word, Medina claimed, he heard
about My Lai 4 while in Vietnam.

Later that day Medina called his company together and
told them that "there was an investigation being conducted
into the alleged accusations, there were atrocities committed at My Lai 4 and that I myself, as the company commander, was being investigated. I told them that it would be
best if they did not discuss it amongst themselves or with
anybody else and that the investigation would be conducted." Thomas Kinch of the mortar platoon had a different recollection of the meeting, as he told the Panel: "He
got us all together and said they were going to run an investigation into what happened the last couple of days, and
said, 'As far as anyone knows, we went in there, we caught
fire, and we returned fire.' " Sergeant Michael A. Bernhardt
of the second platoon similarly testified that Medina promised to "back up anybody who was going to get into any
trouble for this . . . 'I'll back you up in any way.' " Bernhardt later considered sending a protest letter to his Congressman about My Lai 4 but dropped the idea after he was
accosted by Medina in a mess hall and urged not to do so.

Colonel Henderson testified that sometime that evening
he asked Major Glenn D. Gibson, commander of the 174th
Aviation Company, to "look into this matter, both of his
own gunships firing and also whether they had observed

any of my soldiers shooting at civilians." Henderson said he told Gibson of the charges made by Thompson and Watke, and asked him to "get me a report . . . from each of his pilots." Within twenty-four hours, the colonel added, Gibson told him that "none of them had heard or seen any indiscriminate shooting, nor had they participated in any. He got a complete negative response from his people." On his part, Major Gibson steadfastly denied having any conversations at all with Henderson about My Lai 4.

By late afternoon the investigation had run the gamut from a two-star general to a battlefield captain, with one common denominator that would exist for the next two months: every denial was accepted at face value.

12

The First Reports

Sometime on Tuesday, March 19, Colonel Henderson gave General Young an oral report of his investigation into My Lai 4. Young had flown into the 11th Brigade headquarters at Duc Pho for one of his routine briefings, and by now Henderson had received an indirect account from Major Watke; eyewitness reports from Hugh Thompson, Jerry Culverhouse and Lawrence Colburn; denials from Medina and Barker; and what he interpreted as a negative response from the men of Charlie Company.

The colonel reassured Young that Thompson's report of indiscriminate killing was incorrect: "I believe I told General Young that the only way that I could rationalize or understand what he [Thompson] had reported to have seen as opposed to what my troops and what other people had told me had occurred may have been as a result of his recent assignment. And I was under the impression that he had not been with the 123rd very long."

Henderson said that the troops on the ground had been confused over the use of smoke signals by the helicopters; and they had misunderstood a marking indicating a wounded civilian as an alert for Viet Cong. This, unfortunately, may have caused some deaths, but the men of Charlie Company, Henderson recalled telling Young, did not have any "dog-tail" look about them: "I know I passed on to General Young this reaction that I had gotten out of these men. I don't mean they were whooping and hollering, but they were tired . . . There wasn't a man who was trying to hide or failing to meet my eyes.

" 'Fine,' Henderson quoted Young as saying, 'make the report to General Koster.' "

On the next day, Henderson reported, he traveled to Chu Lai to pass along the results of his investigation to Major General Koster. He began his presentation by showing Koster a three-by-five-inch filing card that Barker had prepared, purporting to list the reason for each of the twenty alleged civilian casualties, as well as the victim's sex and approximate age. Barker had given Henderson the card on the night of the sixteenth. Koster was annoyed. "I can't recall his exact words," the colonel told the Panel, adding that the general said something like "Damn it! This is just thoroughly unacceptable, and we've got to provide in our plans so this doesn't happen any more." Henderson continued: "I assured him that it would receive my continuing attention . . . I went into what Thompson reported to me . . . I did report to him that the machine gun confrontation problem had apparently been whipped or put to bed, that the rapport between Major Watke and Colonel Barker was going well . . . I told him that I had talked to Captain Medina. Captain Medina had been able to satisfy one aspect of this to my satisfaction . . . I told him that I had observed personally only the six to eight bodies that I had reported to him previously in the area . . . Warrant Officer Thompson was the only individual that I placed as observing [an atrocity] in that area."

Henderson said Koster then told him that he had heard about the Thompson confrontation from General Young "and that he would discuss this with General Young further. He gave me no further instructions and I departed." Henderson added that before leaving he finally screwed up the courage to ask Koster why he had countermanded his order on the afternoon of the sixteenth: "And he indicated to me, in sort of a disinterested way . . . that he didn't believe it was that important to find out how these twenty may have been killed. I did not open the issue that there might have been more than twenty." That was the last word he heard about My Lai 4, he said, for two weeks.

Later Generals Koster and Young each claimed that the other had the major responsibility for dealing with the results of Henderson's investigation. Young acknowledged that he had many discussions with Henderson throughout late March and early April, but only to determine the status of the report he thought Henderson was preparing under orders of General Koster. His role, he indicated, was that of a liaison man between Henderson and Koster: "I never got the impression that I was to supervise the conduct of the investigation . . . And I did not get the interpretation that I was involved as deeply as Colonel Henderson or General Koster was." He said that he did not specifically recall receiving Henderson's oral report on March 19 nor did he recall suggesting that Henderson bring his findings to the attention of Koster. Young also said he was somewhat surprised that Henderson had decided to conduct the investigation of his own unit himself. The thrust of Young's testimony was that he was merely a bystander while Henderson completed an investigation which was requested by the division commander.

Koster's recollection was precisely contrary. In his eyes, Young was responsible for overseeing the investigation and he, as commanding general, was totally reliant on his deputy's reports. Koster claimed—and his testimony continued to be marked by vagueness—the first report on the My Lai 4 incident came not in person from Colonel Henderson on March 20, but from Young, who said that Colonel Henderson had found some discrepancies in Thompson's story. At no time, Koster said, was there any hint that many more civilians than twenty had been killed. ". . . It seemed to me we both expressed some relief that the helicopter pilot . . . perhaps exaggerated and imagined to a certain extent, because at the time that was really the item that was causing us to investigate further." Koster testified he then told General Young to follow through with the investigation: "I believe I did in the words along the line of 'Will you ride herd on this thing?' "

In any case, neither senior officer made any attempt to investigate personally any aspect of the charges, but instead permitted Colonel Henderson to conduct an inquiry within his own unit. They did not offer Henderson any staff help for the study, although the new brigade commander was known to be woefully short of headquarters personnel. On March 19, the same day that Henderson made his oral report to Young, General Westmoreland's office inadvertently made the job of investigating the atrocity much more difficult. A telegram of congratulations routinely forwarded under Westmoreland's name by the military command in Saigon was sent to the officers of Task Force Barker, lauding them for the unit's "heavy blows" to the enemy. The message arrived at the American Division headquarters. The next step was not routine, however: the message was relayed to both the 11th Brigade and the 123rd Aviation Battalion, with an additional comment by Major General Koster: "I add my congratulations for the teamwork and aggressiveness exhibited by the above-mentioned companies and to all others participating in this operation." The message was sent by courier to the aviation battalion headquarters at Chu Lai, where it was received with suspicion by Lieutenant Colonel Holladay, the commander who didn't feel that his unit's participation that day deserved such special praise. He interpreted it "as a sort of reward, if you will, just to keep quiet."

After his endorsement of Westmoreland's telegram, Koster chose not to press the investigation. Instead, on March 24, eight days after the incident, he sent an unusual letter dealing with "The Safeguarding of Noncombatants" to each commander in the American Division. The general acknowledged, during one of his appearances before the Peers Panel, that the letter "was probably as a result of the My Lai 4 operation which resulted in what I thought to be something in the order of twenty civilian casualties." Chief of Staff Parson later issued a memorandum to commanders urging that the term "search and destroy" be dropped. "Unfortunately," Parson wrote, "this term has been taken out of context and the emphasis placed on the word 'destroy.' It is then used to describe an area in which heavy fighting has occurred. Further, 'search and destroy' has occasionally been used to foster the impression that military operations wantonly create, without regard to human suffering, large numbers of refugees." *

---

* Parson's order listed this glossary of recommended terms: "Phrases which are fully descriptive are sweep operations, search and clear, search

On March 28 the 11th Brigade received Frank Barker's self-serving subsequent after-action report for the My Lai 4 operation. That document covered only a ten-and-one-half-hour period of March 16, although the filing of an after-action report for a one-day operation, let alone ten hours of it, was highly irregular. Barker claimed his men were under enemy small-arms fire from the moment they landed at My Lai 4 and "pressed forward." Bravo Company was said to have run into more enemy troops as it approached the area of the "VC base camp"—apparently Barker meant My Lai 1, which was never entered that day by his men. As Barker further reported, "One platoon from Co. B flanked the enemy positions and engaged one enemy platoon resulting in thirty enemy KIA [killed in action]." By 4:30 that afternoon, Barker wrote, "the surviving enemy elements had broken all contact with friendly forces by infiltrating with civilians leaving the area, or by going down into the extensive tunnel systems throughout the area." Barker concluded: "This operation was well-planned, well-executed, and successful."

Barker's conclusion about the My Lai 4 operation was officially shared by that time at every level in the 11th Brigade and American Division. Nearly two weeks after the operation, Captain Medina received a special letter of commendation from Colonel Henderson in connection with the Westmoreland telegram. "I wish to add my personal congratulations to those already stated by General Westmore-

and hold, cordon and search, and search and reconnaissance in force. Other applicable but less commonly used descriptive phrases for consideration are meeting engagements and movement to contact." The colonel added, "These instructions do not preclude the use of words or phrases indicating offensive or defensive actions, providing they give the reader no basis for assuming a lack of compassion on the part of members of this command."

land and Major General Koster for the outstanding action, team work and aggressiveness exhibited by your unit," Henderson wrote. "The success of this operation and the praiseworthy role of units of the 11th Infantry Brigade directly reflect your expert guidance, leadership, and devotion to duty. The quick response and professionalism displayed during this action has enhanced the brigade's image in the eyes of higher commands." Medina was also told to "convey my sincere appreciation to those personnel responsible for a job well done." Medina, of course, kept the praise to himself.*

In early April, as Colonel Henderson recalled, he was asked by Koster to put his oral report—the one presented March 20—into writing. General Young, he said, approached him ten or fourteen days after the oral report and "advised me that General Koster wanted my report in writing . . . I recall very vividly asking General Young, 'Has there been some new development or is there something I do not know about?' He stated, 'No, there is nothing new developing. General Koster wants it for the record.' " Henderson then wrote his report and delivered it to General Koster's headquarters at Chu Lai.

Henderson, Young, and Koster disagreed again as to

---

* Less than a month after the letter of commendation was sent, however, American Division headquarters disapproved a recommendation for an award of the Bronze Star for Achievement to Medina, in connection with his work as Charlie Company commander from January 25 to April 9, 1968. But within six months, as Medina moved into responsible staff positions in the 11th Brigade headquarters and at the American Division tactical operations center, and as the talk about My Lai 4 ended, he received two awards: a Silver Star dated August 22, 1968, for his role in rescuing some of his infantrymen stranded in a minefield on February 25, 1968; and the Bronze Star, for his overall service from December 1, 1967, to November 30, 1968.

what actually happened. Neither Koster nor Young recalled either seeing the written report or telling Henderson to prepare it. Young, however, did remember "seeing Colonel Henderson in General Koster's office several days after I had been told he made his oral report and he had a paper with him . . ." Koster recalled receiving a report in writing, but not until May.

Part of the confusion probably arose because Henderson wrote more than one report of the investigation. The early-April report, which simply may have escaped General Koster's mind, probably did exist and dealt briefly and inaccurately with Thompson's charges. Captain James Henderson, the 11th Brigade operations officer, recalled seeing a piece of paper that had "something to do with the helicopter bit on it." Roy Kirkpatrick, the brigade operations sergeant, similarly testified that he saw a document which he described as an investigation of Thompson's challenge to the My Lai 4 operation: "They had investigated it and they found, to the best of my knowledge, the report to be not true."

The Peers Panel spent many hours trying to establish the timing and content of the early-April report, not because of its intrinsic value, but because the Panel was operating in the dark; by the end of 1969, all but two of the reports and documents dealing with My Lai 4 and its aftermath, including investigations and after-action summaries as well as their copies—each of which should have been on file at brigade and division headquarters—had vanished.

13

Those Who Knew

Charlie Company collapsed in the days and weeks following My Lai 4. "I think after a while everybody was pretty well ashamed of it, you know," Frank Beardslee testified, "because so many, what they term 'innocent people' were killed." Beardslee himself was bothered by the babies who were shot that day. "They just got in the way . . . they were either on their mothers' backs or something like [that] . . ." Later Beardslee explained in an interview with me, "It never dawned on us what really happened until it was all over." Roger Alaux, the artillery observer, told the Panel that "throughout the entire company, there was a general feeling of depression after this entire operation was completed, and it lasted—I talked to quite a few men during the time—for a week or two weeks afterward, and a lot of them had very many doubts in their minds as to what actually had gone on and why it had gone on . . ."

By mid-April, Task Force Barker was routinely disbanded, Lieutenant Calley had been relieved as leader of the first platoon,* and Captain Medina was getting ready to take over a brigade staff job. His company, which had been given the honor of leading the brigade's advance party to Vietnam, was a shambles.

One of the Peers panelists relayed a description of the post-My Lai 4 group to Lieutenant Colonel Edwin D. Beers, commander of the 1st Battalion of the 20th Infantry, Charlie Company's home unit: "Subsequent to the time that Medina left . . . we were told by one well-experienced, combat-noncommissioned officer, that he had never seen such a ragtag, undisciplined hoard, so to speak—no control by the officers . . . the men sometimes went two months without getting haircuts. They would move from daylight to dark with no opportunity to get themselves cleaned up. Their night discipline was practically nothing. Never digging in at night. Never providing any cover for the men. The officers absolutely failing to do the jobs that they were supposed to do as officers to insure protection for their men. A pretty sordid story that comes out . . ."

Beers agreed that "the Charlie Company that I got back [from Task Force Barker] was not the Charlie Company that landed in Vietnam in December with me . . . Somewhere along the line, obviously, there was a breakdown of leadership and communications between Captain Medina and his platoon leaders and the noncommissioned officers." † Beers had briefly visited with Medina at Land-

---

* In June, 1968, Calley was given a new job as civil affairs and pacification officer for another of the battalions in the 11th Brigade. "He did remarkably well," his commanding officer, Lieutenant Colonel William D. Kelley, told the Peers Panel, "considering that he had no experience. He was energetic. He did everything that I . . . told him to do."
† By June, Charlie Company had been returned to its parent battalion

ing Zone Dotti sometime in mid-March, he recalled, when the men were completing the My Lai 4 operation. The GIs' anxiety over what had happened at My Lai 4 was shared by Captain Medina.

Major Harry P. Kissinger, III, the assistant chaplain of the 11th Brigade, spent a few days near Charlie Company shortly after the Son My operation. Knowing how highly company commanders value a large body count, "I said congratulations [to Medina]" for the 128 Viet Cong his men had helped kill. "I proceeded to ask about it, but I didn't get too much response. I can't remember any details of what he told me except a little nod and 'Yes, it was so,' or something like that . . . I did not receive the impression that he was proud . . . I proceeded to ask someone [else] about it and didn't get too much of an answer. I just felt that he didn't want to talk about it and left it hang, didn't say any more."

for more than a month, but was still disorganized. Captain Jerry W. Swenson, then serving as the unit's third commander in two months, talked about the men in a mid-1971 interview: "They lacked pride in themselves; their appearance was poor, they weren't caring for their weapons . . . I knew that something had happened; that there was some type of incident." Swenson had served with the 11th Brigade in Hawaii in 1967, when Charlie Company led its battalion in all competition. "I'm not a psychiatrist," the young officer said, "but it wasn't the same company that I knew before." In some ways, it was the same, however. One Charlie Company member gave to the Peers Panel part of a daily diary he kept. It included the following extract, written in May, about two months after My Lai 4: "We went down to the valley. We took a path all the way down. When we got down to the bottom the first element saw some gooks running. They shot but missed. We took left flank and when we went about two hundred meters [another Charlie Company GI] saw three of them hiding in the brush—one woman, two men. They had food and medical supplies. Some of the guys messed with the girl; went down further into the valley. Some huts were there. We all ransacked the places and messed with the girls; tore off their clothes and screwed them. Sal beat up one. We left and came up a hill to break for chow and also to set up for night. I took some pictures."

As an afterthought, the chaplain noted he had stayed over-night in the field with the men, even going on a patrol. "Nothing was ever said to me by any of the men," Kissinger went on. "I talked to a number of them there, and you'd think that someone would say something to the chaplain if there was anyone's conscience bothering them."

Yet within ten days, one GI told an Army lawyer about My Lai 4, and the shocked officer asked the soldier's permission to report it. Because of some minor infraction, Medina had given the soldier an Article 15—nonjudicial company-level punishment that usually involves extra guard duty or more kitchen work. "This soldier began indicating a complete disgust with the Army in general and Co. C and CPT Medina in particular," the lawyer—Captain Maurice E. Vorhies, then serving in the Americal Division's legal office at Chu Lai—subsequently said in a private letter that was made available to me. "The substance of his complaint was that he simply could not understand how a man who had committed murder and ordered others to commit murder would now seek to impose punishment on him for some trivial misconduct."

Vorhies quickly learned that the story of My Lai 4 had preceded him throughout the division; he also learned that no one was going to do anything about it. He took it up first with his immediate superior, Major Robert F. Comeau, then assistant staff judge advocate for the division. Comeau had served with the 11th Brigade before joining the staff at Chu Lai and knew of Medina by reputation. "After discussing the incident and the personalities involved," Vorhies wrote, "partially from the standpoint that there was a possibility that my client was fabricating, or at least exaggerating, the facts in an effort to 'get back' at his CO [company commander] for giving him an Article 15, the discussion was dropped. Major Comeau indicated to me that he would 'take care of it.' " (Comeau, during his brief testimony before the Panel, was asked if he recalled any "inquiry, investigation, report, or anything of that nature concerning the My Lai incident . . ." His answer was "No, sir.")

Captain Vorhies then began asking questions down at the 11th Brigade headquarters in Duc Pho, when he found that Charlie Company's high body count and low weapons report was "almost a joke." Later he discussed the incident with an agent of the C.I.D., who was assigned to Duc Pho. "He told me that he had heard rumors of the incident on 16 March and other incidents involving C Co. . . . He informed me that he intended to investigate the matter. However, when I next spoke with him sometime later, he told me that he had been told by someone to 'forget about it.' To the best of my knowledge he did not actually conduct an investigation." After that, the letter said, the lawyer discussed the accusation with some officers around Chu Lai, and gradually drifted into other matters. "Quite frankly, it was not that extraordinary. This was neither the first nor the last story I was to hear of alleged atrocities. It was unusual only by its magnitude."

Some details of the massacre at My Lai 4 quickly became widely known throughout the 11th Brigade. Frank Beardslee, who went on the operation with Charlie Company, described his experiences to a number of enlisted men at the Duc Pho headquarters. Jay Roberts and Ronald Haeberle, the reporter and photographer who witnessed much of the killing, also told their friends about what they had seen. Clinton P. Stephens, the task force intelligence sergeant, said that he heard some GIs jokingly—he thought—remark "that Task Force Barker killed a lot of innocent civilians or Task Force Barker got a bunch of innocent civilians."

At the 123rd Aviation Battalion, Captain Brian Livingston noticed with disgust that all of the newspapers published by the division and brigade information offices were reveling in "Barker's Bandits" and their newest success against the crack enemy troops. One headline read: "TF Barker Crushes Enemy Stronghold." On March 19, in the midst of the publicity drive, Livingston wrote another letter to his wife: "You remember I told you about the massacre I witnessed, well, I read a follow-up story in the paper. The article said, I quote, 'The American troops were in heavy combat with an unknown number of VC. Two Americans were killed, seven wounded and 128 VC killed.' That's a bunch of bull."

Most of the aviation company shared Livingston's view. A few weeks after My Lai 4, Lawrence Kubert recalled, Major Watke assembled his company for a routine briefing by a young officer from division intelligence. "They reported one hundred and twenty CD, civil defendants, were killed at My Lai," Kubert testified. ". . . I don't remember who it was said, 'Oh, you mean those women and children?' . . . There were several comments made. The man who was briefing said, well, that they were known civil defendants who had worked for the VC. And then another comment was made. 'They didn't look like they could do much to us.' And Major Watke stepped forward and said, 'Let's not have any more of that. It's an old horse, we've already done what we can as far as these people are concerned . . . We're going to start over again, more or less.' "

William Bezanson, who had flown above the hamlet in one of the troop-ferrying helicopters attached to the 123rd Aviation Battalion, told during an interview how he was able to live with what he had seen: "The first night we got back and were sitting in the bunker smoking dope. One of my buddies started shaking—it really freaked him out. He kept saying something like 'What are we turning into?' It was truly the first time I ever thought about that—I can remember. But it didn't really matter that much; they were just gooks. The next day we were out flying again and killing again. You just put it in the back of your mind."

Those GIs who did not participate in or witness the massacre enjoyed gossiping about it. According to Lieutenant Colonel Charles Anistranski, the Americal Division's civil affairs officer, "there was a lot of talk about . . . near the end of March . . . GIs were talking in the mess halls . . . When we walked by the division headquarters, by the chapel . . . we could hear people talking about it. But it was all done very jokingly, 'Hey, did ya hear about this? Hey, did ya hear about that?' " On a few occasions, the officer said, he also heard the names Lieutenant Calley and Sergeant Mitchell mentioned around headquarters. "Surprisingly," Anistranski added with perhaps a touch of irony, "none of the commissioned personnel talked about it, none of the general staff members, at the mess or at any other place."

The concern over loose talk and the obvious fear among most senior officers of a career-ruining scandal was confirmed by the frustrating experiences of Reverend Francis Lewis, the Methodist chaplain, who attempted during the next few weeks to discuss the report of an atrocity with the top leaders in the division. Chaplain Lewis, who heard Hugh Thompson's story from an irate and persistent Father Carl Creswell, Thompson's priest, took up the matter first with Lieutenant Colonel Jesmond Balmer, the operations officer for the division. "I told Balmer that I had heard some pretty bad things," Lewis testified. "And he said he had, too, and that this was going to be thoroughly investigated." Later the two men—Lewis and Balmer—discussed the operation again in the presence of Lieutenant Colonel

Tommy Trexler, the intelligence chief. Lewis told the officers what he had learned from Creswell, and "both of them together said that they'd heard of these things. I remember that specifically. I didn't get the full impact of atrocity, but I did get the impact of women and children being killed . . . [Balmer] said that there was a sergeant that fired into women and children." At this or a later meeting, Lewis testified he said to Balmer, " 'Gee, who in the world goofed on this? Who in the world goofed?' He said, 'Well, we can't always know exactly what gives.' " Lewis said he next brought up the subject of the investigation in a separate meeting with Colonel Nels Parson: "I said, 'I wonder what's the situation on My Lai and I'd like to talk to General Koster about it,' or words to this effect. He said, 'Well, it's being investigated and we're not to talk about it.' In other words, he put me off in seeing the general on this." The cleric then had a third discussion with Anistranski, who had already completed his abortive effort to inquire about the massacre. The civil affairs officer cautioned him not to talk about it, as did other lower-ranking officials in the headquarters.

During the testimony before the Peers Panel, most of the division officers heatedly denied any conversations with Reverend Lewis about the My Lai 4 investigation. Only Anistranski confirmed that he had told the priest not to pursue his questions. Anistranski explained why he did so: "Chaplain Lewis was the type that walked around and looked for a lot of information. If I knew the commanding general was conducting an investigation of some type, then it was my advice to him that he shouldn't side-shoot the commanding general, if that's what you want to call it."

Chaplain Lewis even pursued the matter with Lieutenant Colonel Barker himself. He accidentally spotted Barker in division headquarters at Chu Lai one afternoon, and asked him about the report of wild shootings. Barker said, according to the chaplain, "Well, Lewis, as far as I'm concerned, it was combat. These occurred. It was tragic that we killed these women and children, but it was in a combat operation." Lewis said Barker mentioned that he had discussed the operations with his officers and the men on the ground, and concluded that "the report [of an atrocity] we had heard at Division of something happening . . . was not true."

Lewis was not the only officer to approach Barker privately. Another inquiry came from Captain Keshel, the 11th Brigade pacification officer who had heard many rumors about the incident in March and April. His discussion with Barker came after the task force had ended operations and the lieutenant colonel was working as executive officer of the brigade. "In the day-to-day activities," Keshel testified, "I'd almost completely forgotten about this thing and I was sitting up in the hootch one night and I was reading the book *The Rise and Fall of the Third Reich*. And I was getting into the part about the German atrocities, and this pronged my mind a little bit about this thing, and I—as I said, it sort of bothered me, and I said, 'Hell, you know this is ridiculous; I'm just going to go and ask the colonel whether this thing has any truth. But I debated this for a couple of days—now because he is a colonel and he was also my boss, my rater . . . I figured I'd ask him, because I knew him, and I was real close to him, he liked me, and I held him in great respect . . . and so this conversation took place in the mess hall prior to dinner . . . Prior to dinner the officers—the staff officers, would make small talk, have a beer or a drink, and on this particular day, I asked him if I could talk to him, and he said, 'You certainly can,' and he came over to my side, and I just asked him. I said, 'Sir,' I said, 'I have heard a couple of rumors . . . I heard a couple of things about Task Force Barker, when you had that task force, killing civilians,' and I said, 'I just want to know did this actually happen?' And he just a—well, he looked like I had slapped him, you know. 'The United States Army doesn't operate this way, we don't make war on innocent people, and that I, as commander, certainly had no knowledge of anything like this happening, and if it did happen, I wouldn't condone any activity of this type' . . . or words to this effect. And that was the end of the—our conversation . . . I walked away and I thanked him." *

The seeming lack of official information within the Americal Division could have been remedied by questioning that group which was most affected by the massacre—the survivors of My Lai 4.

---

* Some staff officers of Task Force Barker became increasingly defensive in the waning days of the task force's existence. There was one open clash involving Captain Winston Gouzoules, who handled pacification matters for another battalion of the 11th Infantry Brigade that operated near the task force in early 1968. Gouzoules chanced to make a sarcastic comment in late March about the killing of civilians by Task Force Barker in front of some young officers who had been on the mission. A few days later Gouzoules was told that he was no longer welcome in Barker's area of operations. Weeks later, as the task force was disbanding, the captain visited Landing Zone Dotti and asked Major Calhoun about the incident. "He told me he didn't want to hear any more comments on Task Force Barker, and I tried to tell him at the time that I hadn't made any . . ." the captain said. "After that, it was forgotten."

14

The Vietnamese

*I*t took less than three days for details about the atrocities at My Lai 4 and My Khe 4 to become available to South Vietnamese government officials in Son Tinh District and Quang Ngai Province. The first word came from the survivors themselves —who were never interrogated by the officers of the 11th Brigade and American Division.

Do Dinh Luyen, the government's village chief for Son My, told the Peers Panel that he had first heard of the shootings from the survivors of My Lai 4 who straggled into Quang Ngai during the afternoon.* A few days later he heard that hun-

---

* The Saigon government and the National Liberation Front each supported village and hamlet bureaucracies in Son My, but Luyen, as the government's representative, suffered the indignity of living in exile—and in the safety of Quang Ngai City. Asked by the Peers Panel why he did not travel the half-dozen miles to the hamlet to see for himself what had happened, the village chief replied, "It was just not, in my opinion, a sensible thing to do—to go out and get this information from these people

dreds of people had been killed in My Lai 4 [known to the Vietnamese as Thuan Yen] and My Khe 4 [known also as My Hoi].* "I heard they were killed by artillery, gunships, and small-arms fire during the battle to enter the village," Luyen said through a translator. He relayed his information orally to his immediate supervisor, Lieutenant Tran Ngoc Tan, chief of Son Tinh District.

Reporting information on American atrocities was a bold step for a Vietnamese Army officer in 1968, but Tan, then in the midst of a long-standing feud with his counterpart, Major David Gavin, the chief American adviser to Son Tinh, was offended because he had not been informed of the task force operation in advance. On March 22, six days after the atrocity, the lieutenant relayed the village chief's report in writing to his Vietnamese superiors at Quang Ngai Province headquarters. The message claimed that 480 civilians had been killed at My Lai 4 and ninety more at My Khe 4. "Besides persons killed," the report said, "animals, property, and houses were ninety percent destroyed." It further listed Viet Cong casualties at forty-eight killed and fifty-two wounded; as such, it was the first time in any re-

who were from outside the ARVN-secured area and from a VC-controlled hamlet . . . I was somewhat fearful of being assassinated."
* On Vietnamese maps, My Lai 4—or Thuan Yen—actually was one of five subhamlets in Tu Cung hamlet. The other subhamlets were Binh Tay, Binh Donh (listed on American military maps as My Lai 5), Trung Hoa, and Trung An. There were three other hamlets which, along with Tu Cung, made up the village of Son My: Co Luy, which included My Khe 4 (or My Hoi); My Lai, which included My Lai 1, 2, and 6; and My Khe, which included My Khe 1, 2, and 3. The subhamlet of My Lai 4 also was known as Xom Lang to some Vietnamese. In addition, the Viet Cong usually had its own names for most of the villages, hamlets, and subhamlets in the area. Quang Ngai was one of the few provinces in South Vietnam which had subhamlets under the jurisdiction of hamlets.

port on My Lai 4—American or Vietnamese—that anyone suggested Viet Cong had been wounded.

By the twenty-second, however, the Vietnamese province officials already had heard of the massacres through a different source, the Census Grievance Committee, a program which was covertly being financed by the Central Intelligence Agency.

Ostensibly, the grievance committee was set up to provide a central source in each Vietnamese village for bureaucratic complaints against the Saigon government; its ulterior and overriding purpose was to furnish intelligence on Viet Cong or suspected Viet Cong in each area.*

By March 18, two days after the massacre, a census grievance field worker had reported from Son My village that "after a fierce battle the allies killed 320 people" at My Lai 4. "At Co Luy hamlet," the report added, "eighty people young and old were killed. The total civilians and guerrillas

---

* Donald R. Keating, chief of the CIA mission in the province, depicted the operation in glowing terms to the Peers Panel: "The best way I can describe it or what I used as a comparison is the ombudsman . . . The idea was to take an individual who was known in his particular hamlet or village and had a certain amount of respect due him as a person and set him up with a place that he could talk to all of the people in the hamlet and take a census. It provides a place . . . where every individual in the hamlet was required to go and give certain vital statistics about where he was born and how many children he had and who he married and this sort of thing. The intent was to provide an individual with a requirement that he must go to this particular office so if there were any, and there were, Viet Cong sympathizers or cadre in the hamlet, no individual could be singled out as pointing the finger or giving information about the Viet Cong [and thus face enemy retribution]." Both Keating and Maurice M. Prew, another agent of the Central Intelligence Agency assigned to operate the grievance committee in Quang Ngai Province, testified that they had not seen the report. Prew also revealed during his secret appearance before the Panel that less than ten percent of the reports processed by his office in Quang Ngai had to do with legitimate grievances against the Saigon government; the bulk of the information was intelligence on suspected enemy movements and the like.

killed during the last three days—427, including young and old. At this time allied operation is continuing . . ." The Peers Panel found that most senior Vietnamese officials working at province headquarters in Quang Ngai City quickly learned of the census griev nce report, but only one American—Lieutenant Colonel William Guinn, the deputy province adviser—seemed to have received it. Guinn described the document as "just a penciled copy that the translator had taken from the original. And I remember it specifically because it was so poorly translated, and the handwriting was so poor I could hardly read it." Guinn said he didn't believe the allegation, but added that even if it were true, "I didn't consider it a war crime . . . The report indicated to me that these people had been killed by an act of war . . . because that was a free-fire zone out there, and they were operating in that area." Guinn, however, did personally pass on the allegedly insignificant information to Colonel Henderson at his headquarters in Duc Pho: "I thought he should know about it . . . I passed this on . . . simply because the allegation had been made. And I told him that these reports were usually very unreliable because of the source, and I didn't put any confidence in it at all." According to Guinn, Henderson expressed disbelief in the report but said that he would "check it out."

Colonel Henderson denied any knowledge of the meeting; in fact, he testified, he didn't even know what a census grievance team was. It's not clear why no other Americans on the province advisory team was told—as testimony before the Peers Panel indicated—of the census grievance report. The possibility exists that Guinn simply did not share this information, but unilaterally took it to Henderson. At the time Guinn was being considered for an appointment as battalion commander in the 11th Brigade, a job that would

have helped ensure his promotion to full colonel. There was
no evidence developed by the Panel that he reported the allegation—as he technically should have done—to the Military Assistance Command—Saigon (MACV), the next
higher step in the province chain of command.

On March 28, Lieutenant Tan received more information
from Do Dinh Luyen. Again Tan forwarded a report to
province headquarters, with copies to the intelligence and
operations advisory staff of the 2nd ARVN Division, which
was stationed in the city. The document was entitled:
"Confirmation of Allied Troops Shooting at the Residents
of Tu Cung hamlet." The report incorrectly claimed that
Viet Cong units had initiated the gunfire at My Lai 4. Before forwarding it, Lieutenant Tan discussed the allegation
with Major Gavin, the district adviser, and Captain Angel
M. Rodriguez, Gavin's assistant. Rodriguez got the impression, as he later testified, that "since it was VC and that was
a VC chief, the one who reported it, well, it was taken as
propaganda rather than any other thing." At that point a
Panel member reminded him that Luyen, who initiated the
report, was a government sympathizer.

The Vietnamese investigation might have ended with
Tan's second inconclusive report, except that Do Dinh
Luyen decided to forward to Tan a list of the known dead
at the two hamlets. More than 440 names were on the list. A
few days later the National Liberation Front committee in
Quang Ngai began circulating three-page leaflets about the
murders, filled with specific details—rare for such propaganda notices. The documents, except for some gross er-
rors—the wrong Army division was accused of the assault
on Son My—was amazingly accurate and obviously was
based on many interviews with survivors.

The leaflets said, in part: "The morning of 16 March 1968
was a quiet morning, just like every other morning, with the

people of Tinh Khe village [the Viet Cong name for Son My] about to start another laborious day of production and struggle. Suddenly, artillery rounds began pouring in . . . After the shelling, nine helicopters landed troops who besieged the two small subhamlets. The U.S. soldiers were like wild animals, charging violently into the hamlets, killing and destroying. They formed themselves into three groups: one group was in charge of killing civilians; one group burned huts, and the third group destroyed vegetation and trees and killed animals . . . Wherever they went, civilians were killed, houses and vegetation were destroyed and cows, buffalo, chickens and ducks were also killed. They even killed old people and children; pregnant women were raped and killed. This was by far the most barbaric killing in human history." The leaflet said the dead included 67 old people, 170 children, and 127 women. "After the massacre," the document concluded, "the people of Tinh Khe village wiped away their tears, hate deep in their hearts, and bravely rebuilt their homes, clearing away all traces of tragedy . . ."

A similar, although less detailed, National Liberation Front radio broadcast was monitored and translated by an Army intelligence listening outpost at Quang Ngai and disseminated throughout the intelligence offices of the advisory system: "Crazy American enemy used light machine guns and all kinds of weapons to kill our innocent civilian people in Tinh Khe village. Most of them were women, kids; there were some just-born babies and pregnant women. They shot everything they saw; they killed all domestic animals; they burned all people's houses. There were twenty-six families killed completely—no survivors."

By early April many Vietnamese officers in Quang Ngai Province knew of the census grievance reports and the two reports from the Son Tinh district chief; they also knew of the Viet Cong propaganda broadcast and leaflet, whose details were confirmation of what they had learned from their own sources. But only a few Americans shared that knowledge, largely because the Vietnamese simply kept what they knew to themselves. It is difficult to understand why such a specific allegation—involving an American unit and the slaughter of nearly five hundred civilians—was not shared throughout the advisory system, or why the Vietnamese did not demand an immediate investigation. One possible explanation lies in the basic assumptions behind the advisory system itself—that American military men and civilians can work closely and harmoniously with Vietnamese on an equal basis. In Quang Ngai, at least, the system did not work.

There were actually two advisory teams in Quang Ngai Province as of April, 1968. A mixed group of military officers and civilians—most of them from the State Department—served as overall advisers for all the civilian problems in the province, including pacification and security. James May, a State Department foreign service officer, was the senior province adviser. Perhaps a dozen American officers were also separately assigned as direct advisers to the 2nd ARVN Division, headquartered in the area. The efficacy of the system depended on the relationship between each senior adviser and his Vietnamese counterpart.* Thus,

* To a lesser extent, the relationship between the American military men and the State Department province advisers also affected the overall operation. In early 1968 this was a poor relationship in Quang Ngai; behind the dispute was a difference over how to handle the Viet Cong sympathizers in the province. Hugh Manke spent much of 1968 in Quang Ngai Province as a field worker for the International Voluntary Service (IVS), a volunteer American organization that provided aid to the civilian population of Vietnam, including refugees. He recalled the stand-off between May and the military in a mid-1971 interview: "May used to fight with

James May's counterpart, the province chief, was Lieutenant Colonel Ton That Khien. The counterpart for the senior Vietnamese intelligence officer in the 2nd ARVN Division would be the senior American adviser assigned to intelligence. Theoretically, the counterparts were to establish close personal and working relationships with each other.

On occasion, the civilian and military American advisory teams worked closely together. The American officers assigned to the province advisory team planned and coordinated military operations for the civilian Vietnamese defense forces, often in conjunction with American combat units or the 2nd ARVN Division.

Serving as an adviser—either to the ARVN Division or on the province advisory team—was not a prime assignment for an ambitious young American officer in 1968. The way to get ahead in the Army then was to lead American troops in combat, not to plan small-scale, and usually ineffective, combat operations with local Vietnamese forces, or to worry about refugee camps and their problems.*

those guys tooth and nail. He thought they were all stupid jerks. They [the military] had absolutely no sense of the guerrilla war. They were thinking in terms of how many helicopters and how much artillery. May tried to get them to carry out small operations in support of the popular forces." Adding to the problems, said Manke, who later became director of all IVS services in Vietnam, was the fact that "the military situation in Quang Ngai was always bad . . . You would see the refugees straggling into the city every night. There was tremendous frustration in that province." In midsummer, 1971, the South Vietnamese government ordered all of the field workers in the IVS, including Manke, out of the country.

* In what amounted to tacit recognition of this fact, Stanley R. Resor, then Secretary of the Army, told Congress early in 1970 he had ordered that Vietnamese advisers "be of equal quality" with men assigned as troop commanders in Vietnam. "During the years of troops build-up in Vietnam the prestige attached to command or service with American units tended to attract many of your best people at the expense of our ad-

Complicating the counterpart relationships was the fact
that the Americans were not advisers at all, but the domi-
nant force in the province. In addition, the American advisers generally had little respect for the Vietnamese. James
May, for example, could and almost did demand the dismissal of Khien. May told the Peers Panel that he and Lieutenant Colonel Guinn, his deputy, discussed Khien's replacement after the Tet offensive in February, 1968: "It was
several weeks before the colonel [Khien] got a grip on himself, and ten days later . . . he was still in very dubious
shape. We suspended judgment for many weeks as to
whether we would recommend that he would be removed
and replaced or whether we would recommend that they
forget it." Khien was finally allowed to stay on, but May remained skeptical of him: "Colonel Khien was known as
'PX' [post-exchange] Khien when he was chief of staff of the
ARVN 2nd Division, so I knew him pretty well by reputation before he became province chief, and it was not a very
impressive reputation . . . He [had] spent a great deal of his
time gambling for very large stakes and conning people out
of things at the PX, which he then sold, and so on . . . He
didn't look like a winner. The fact is he was a big crook, and
he knew it, and we knew it, and he knew we knew it, and
he'd also copped out as a coward besides [at Tet] . . ."

Khien eventually developed rapport with the American
military. He and the Army senior men—particularly Lieutenant Colonel Guinn, the deputy province adviser—discovered that they had one thing in common: they believed

viser program," Resor added. Some advisers eventually were given pay
boosts and the option of serving longer tours in Southeast Asia—up to
eighteen months—along with their wives and families. Resor's action was
reported by the *Army Times,* May 13, 1970.

that the only way to win the war was to kill all Viet Cong and Viet Cong sympathizers.*

Most Vietnamese military officers, however, found themselves in a frustrating situation: their careers and promotions depended to some degree on how well they got along with their counterparts, yet they also were aware of the Americans' negative feeling toward them. Many officers apparently decided to solve the problem by hiding their feelings—and disturbing information—from their counterparts. Most of the American officers testified that they had not heard of the atrocity allegations, and then expressed amazement when told that their counterparts had written memorandums on the subject.†

---

* Guinn was much more tolerant of Khien's defects than was May. Guinn explained his reasoning: "He [Khien] had a family in Hue. He didn't know what had happened to his family. He had property and didn't know what happened to his property. He was afraid they were going to make another Hue out of Quang Ngai . . . But as soon as we had some order restored in the province . . . as soon as the security situation started to clear up a little bit, Khien started to get back to his old self. I think he had a good administrative head on his shoulders. Other than that one incident, I felt he was a pretty sound character; had a good sense of reasoning about him . . . And I think he was honest, which was something to say for him. You couldn't say that for all of them . . . In fact, by the time I left I thought he was doing a good job."

† By mid-April the Vietnamese at Quang Ngai had received reports indicating that Viet Cong soldiers in various districts throughout the province were wearing arm bands with a slogan avowing vengeance for the Son My massacres. Lieutenant Colonel Khien told the Peers Panel that one defector reported that the Viet Cong were given indoctrination, or propaganda, lectures about the atrocities. In addition, an undetermined number of civilians from Son My staged a march on Quang Ngai City, apparently in late March, to protest the murders. Some Americans knew of the march, but were never told its purpose. The only officer to testify about any of the post My Lai 4 and My Khe 4 propaganda activities was Lieutenant Colonel Blackledge, the 11th Brigade intelligence officer, who said that he had seen an intelligence report saying that the Viet Cong were wearing red arm bands saying "determine to avenge the atrocities at Son My" or words to that effect. He downgraded the report, he said.

On April 11 Lieutenant Tan sent a third written report to Lieutenant Colonel Khien, the province district chief, that came closer to describing what actually happened at My Lai 4 and My Khe 4. "On March 16," the document, which was given the highest Vietnamese classification, began, "an American unit conducted a mopping-up operation at Tu Cung and Co Luy hamlets of Son [My] village. At about ten o'clock on the above day, the American unit encountered a VC mine and received fire from Tu Cung hamlet. One American soldier was killed and a number of others wounded. In response, the operational forces attacked the village, assembled the people and shot and killed more than four hundred people at Tu Cung hamlet and ninety more people in Co Luy hamlet. While the VC were withdrawing from the hamlet, forty-eight VC and more than fifty-two guerrillas and self-defense soldiers were wounded by helicopter gunships.

"Tu Cung and Co Luy are two areas of Son My village that have long been held by the VC. The district forces lack the capability of entering the area. Therefore, allied units frequently conduct mop-up operations and bombing attacks freely in the area. But the basic position of the report of the Son My village committee is that although the VC cannot be held blameless for their actions in the 16 March 1968 operation, the Americans in anger killed too many civilians. Only one American was killed by the VC; however, the allies killed nearly five hundred civilians in retaliation."

Lieutenant Tan added this comment: "Really an atrocious attitude if it cannot be called an act of insane violence. Request you intervene on behalf of the people."

Tan's outspoken accusation, an exceptionally harsh criticism for a Vietnamese to make about an American unit, was included on copies of the report he sent to the 2nd ARVN Division, and to Lieutenant Colonel Guinn's office.

Tan told the Panel that he also gave a copy of the report to Major Gavin. Subsequently, Gavin denied this, but Captain Rodriguez and Lieutenant Clarence J. Dawkins, the two other American advisers in Son Tinh District, separately testified that they had discussed the allegations in detail with Gavin, and agreed with him that they were enemy propaganda.

Lieutenant Colonel Khien also took no immediate action after receiving Tan's report, except to take the matter up with Guinn, who was, by then, becoming a confidant. Khien told about Guinn's reaction: "He said something about the problem, he had casualties [during the Task Force Barker operation]. He didn't think there were many killed, especially civilians. They killed maybe some VC." Khien obviously was taking his cue from the Army officer; the province chief was anxious to write off the allegations as Viet Cong propaganda. In November, 1969, he told André C. R. Feher, a C.I.D. investigator, that—as Feher reported —"He did not want the incident to be publicized, since this would adversely affect the [South Vietnam's] national policy."

Colonel Nguyen Van Toan, the 2nd ARVN Division commander, was similarly reluctant to pursue an investigation, but was confronted with a staff memorandum and compelled to take some action. Lieutenant Tan's report had initially been delivered to Major Pham Van Pho, the division intelligence officer, who forwarded it—along with a copy of the Viet Cong propaganda leaflets—to Toan. Pho's covering memorandum to Toan somehow was even more accurate than Tan's report about what happened at My Lai 4: "On 16 March 68 U.S. unit conducted an operation at Son My . . . At 1000 hours the U.S. unit received fire from Tu Cung hamlet and also hit a mine. One U.S. was killed and a number wounded. After that the U.S. unit assaulted the hamlet, assembled the people, then shot and killed over four hundred people in Tu Cung hamlet and ninety people in Co Luy hamlet."

Toan responded to his staff report by passing the buck to Lieutenant Colonel Khien, whose attitude toward such reports was well known. Toan suggested that the province chief himself conduct an investigation, and along the bottom of his copy of Tan's report, scrawled: "If this is true, link-up with the Americal Division to have this stopped." But, predictably, the issue was simply left there. Khien did not begin his investigation until mid-June, two months later. Toan also was subsequently interviewed by André Feher about his attitude as of April, 1968. The agent reported that Toan "was interested [in the allegation] and willing to cooperate, but not overly eager to commit his own people to any further investigation. He further stated that all the people in the area at that time were either Viet Cong or Viet Cong sympathizers, and he did not express too much concern about their fate."

There was a further reaction to Tan's third report, involving the Americans. A day or two after the report was filed, Captain Rodriguez—temporarily in charge of the Son Tinh district headquarters because Major Gavin had taken a week's leave—was ordered to look into the complaint and file a report on it. Rodriguez at first thought the request came directly from James May, or William Guinn, but later said he couldn't remember: "This information came from province in the regular mail . . . It seemed that it was handled in a routine manner." Rodriguez said he initiated his inquiry by discussing the allegations with Tan: "If I recall he didn't pay much attention to this, because of the fact that he said this was just plain propaganda . . . In my mind, I never actually figured that an American soldier, the way we are trained, would do something like this . . . It never came into my mind." He assumed, he said, that his subsequent report was received by Lieutenant Colonel Guinn.

Rodriguez began his report, dated April 14, by writing that it was "in reference to letter from the Son Tinh district chief to the Quang Ngai province chief, subject: Allied force gathered people of Son My village for killing, dated 11 April 1968." Rodriguez then fully summarized Tan's third report and added the following comment: "The letter was not given much importance by the district chief but it was sent to the Quang Ngai province chief . . . The district chief is not certain of the information received and he has to depend on the word of the village chief and other people living in the area." The statement concluded with Rodriguez' comment that "the two hamlets where the incident is alleged to happen are in a VC-controlled area since 1964." *

Lieutenant Tan, during his appearance in Vietnam before the Peers Panel, acknowledged that he considered the incident of little importance—as Rodriguez wrote—but for a far different reason than that which was suggested: "I didn't see it very high on my list of priorities. At that time I was really concerned about saving outposts and keeping the VC from coming in our front door . . . His [Rodriguez'] observation undoubtedly came from the fact that it [the allega-

---

* Some witnesses before the Panel cast doubt on Rodriguez' authorship of the statement, indicating that one of the senior province officials may have helped Rodriguez prepare it. Lieutenant Colonel John Green, an administrative aide at province headquarters, was shown the Rodriguez April 14 statement during his testimony. "I don't think Rodriguez could have written this," the officer said. "He doesn't write this good. He's the world's worst writer. This one's too well-written, as though it has been proofed by somebody, somebody had helped him get it together . . . This is too well-written for Rodriguez to have written it. He's had help with this thing." Rodriguez, who resigned his commission while in Vietnam, refused to testify more than once, and the mystery of how and why the April 14 statement was prepared was never cleared up.

tion] was a low priority, and not that I did not believe it was a correct report."

Within the next seven days the Rodriguez evaluation of April 14, denigrating Lieutenant Tan's report, plus a copy of the Viet Cong propaganda leaflet about the atrocities, somehow ended up together in the hands of Colonel Oran Henderson and Major General Samuel Koster instead of being forwarded—as it properly should have been—to Charles T. Cross, the deputy ambassador for pacification in the I Corps region, which included Quang Ngai Province. The Peers Panel was unable to determine how the documents got to the Americal Divison officers, although once again the key role may have been played by Lieutenant Colonel Guinn.

The panel eventually suspected that Guinn's hopes of becoming a battalion commander led him to hinder the My Lai 4 investigation.

There was another clue concerning the smuggling of the information that was not made available to the Panel. Charles Anistranski told me during a lengthy interview that he had privately transmitted a letter from Guinn to Koster sometime in April. "Guinn put it in an envelope and sealed it," Anistranski, by then retired, said. "He told me to 'make sure the general gets this letter.'" After cover-up charges against Guinn were announced by the Peers Panel in March, 1970, Guinn telephoned Anistranski to ask if he had happened to open and read the letters. Anistranski said he told him no. Yet there was evidence presented that would indicate otherwise.

Captain Donald Keshel, civil affairs officer for the 11th Brigade, testified about a visit he made to Anistranski, then his superior, at the division headquarters at Chu Lai: "I went in and the G5 was alone in his office . . . I saluted and I said, 'Good afternoon,' or 'Good morning,' I don't remember the time of day, and he pointed a finger . . . and he said that 'Task Force Barker is in big trouble, in fact, the entire 11th Infantry Brigade might be in big trouble.' And I really didn't know what he was talking about and I said, 'Well, what do you mean, sir?' . . . And he said, 'Because of what was going on down in the Barker area.' And I asked him if there was anything that I ought to know, or do . . . and he said, 'Don't worry about it; it is all being taken care of.' And he had a white folder on his desk . . . and he tapped it with his finger and said, 'Don't worry about it. I've got it all in here.' " Anistranski refused to clear up the mystery by testifying before the Panel again, nor would he explain anything further to me.

By mid-April descriptions of the Son My massacres were being broadcast by Radio Hanoi and reprinted, after translation, in the daily Foreign Broadcast Information Summary (FBIS), a compilation of world-wide radio broadcasts published by the Central Intelligence Agency, and made available to government agencies and newspapers in Washington and around the world. Hanoi charged that more than five hundred persons, mostly aged people, women, and children, had been slaughtered. The broadcasts were ignored in the United States.

15

Ending the
Inquiry

The first official contact between a Vietnamese officer and the Americal Division was made by Colonel Nguyen Van Toan, commander of the 2nd ARVN Division, who decided to talk to his counterpart—one of the few Vietnamese to do so—about the allegations. Toan told the Peers Panel that he telephoned Major General Samuel Koster shortly after receiving the third report, dated April 11, from Lieutenant Tan, to "let him know about some rumor. We didn't exactly know what happened, so I just let him know." Toan also testified that he told Koster about his order to Khien for an investigation.

What was considered by Toan to be mere propaganda at best, or—at worst—something to cover up, was taken far more seriously by the career-minded Americal Division commander, who perhaps had thought Henderson's oral report of March 20 had closed the incident. Shortly after the telephone call from Toan, Koster undoubtedly received a copy—perhaps purloined—of Tan's third report from an American on the province advisory team. Koster flew almost immediately to Quang Ngai City to see Toan, although the general would confusedly insist later that he thought his visit took place in mid-May. But before going into Toan's office, Koster said, he paid a visit to the province chief, Lieutenant Colonel Khien, and was assured that the Vietnamese official considered Lieutenant Tan's reports from Son Tinh District to be Viet Cong propaganda. Also at that meeting, the general testified, was Lieutenant Colonel William Guinn, soon to be a battalion commander in the Americal Division. Koster could not remember, under questioning, specifically whether Lieutenant Tan's third report was discussed during the meeting with Khien.

Koster then walked over to Toan's office: "I really went there to see if he felt there was anything to this, if he was concerned about it, if he had a Vietnamese source that had been able to uncover anything that we hadn't or that U.S. investigators hadn't been able to check out. I don't think he took the figures that had been put in the propaganda as being accurate, and I think I left with the idea . . . and gave him the idea—if he did uncover anything further, he should send it on to me." Koster and Toan agreed in their testimony that no documents were provided to the American commander during their meeting; Koster was allowed, however, to examine one of 2nd ARVN Division's files dealing with the allegations.

Over the next few weeks, there was unusually heavy traffic between the Americal Division headquarters and the Quang Ngai province advisory team. The division was then coordinating a series of military operations with the 2nd ARVN Division in the western half of the province, but even that didn't explain the many telephone calls and per-

sonal visits between Chief of Staff Nels Parson, Province
Adviser James May, and Lieutenant Colonel William
Guinn. James Ritchie, who served as administrative sergeant in the headquarters, was one of many headquarters
clerks who reported that "I knew something was up. There
were far more people moving and going than usual during
the next few weeks."

It was during this time, Koster said, that he and his deputy, Brigadier General George Young, had "numerous discussions" about the Vietnamese accusations. General
Young similarly testified that he had discussed Tan's third
report with Guinn during a routine meeting at province
headquarters: "I don't recall any names or the number of
people involved, and I don't recall if I informed General
Koster of any numbers involved, or the names of the villages, other than it was located north and east of Quang
Ngai City." Young said he did not ask for a copy of the report, and said, to the amazement of the Panel, that he did
not connect the new allegations with the Task Force Barker
operation of March 16 "because, if I recall properly, this information was [provided] sometime after the incident,
which allegedly occurred on the 16th of March . . . I never
tied these two factors together." Questioned sharply about
that failure, Young acknowledged that "looking back on it,
I can see it was strange, and we should very possibly have
dug into it deeper than we did."

General Koster said that he at no time thought that he
was investigating a war crime, despite the receipt of specific
allegations accusing American troops of the slaughter of
nearly five hundred Vietnamese civilians: "I considered
those [allegations to be] emanating from a Viet Cong source
and a propaganda-type document." The general's testimony
about his view of the new evidence contrasted sharply with

his next move; he sent directly to Colonel Henderson a private, "eyes only," letter demanding that he investigate the Vietnamese allegations. Enclosed was a copy of Lieutenant Tan's third report.

The existence of the letter was revealed to the Panel by Robert Gerberding, the intelligence sergeant for the 11th Brigade. Gerberding said that the letter, which arrived about April 20,* was written on American Division stationery and specifically called on Henderson to complete an indepth investigation. The sergeant was shown a copy of Tan's report and identified it as the one that was enclosed with the general's letter.†

But General Koster did not recall sending the letter. He initially testified: "It seems to me that I directed him [Henderson] to do something about it [the Vietnamese allegations] . . . but I don't specifically remember it being in writing or how it went or the sequence of it." Later he suggested that "I was not inclined to write personal notes like that. If one had been sent, I would have said that it could have been prepared by either General Young or Colonel Parson." Those officers, however, separately denied sending the letter. The major general went so far as to insist, after being confronted with Gerberding's testimony, that he had never seen Tan's third report—one of a few direct contradictions

* On that day, ironically, General Westmoreland visited the 11th Brigade headquarters at Duc Pho for a routine briefing, one in which the seemingly successful Task Force Barker operations may have been described.
† Gerberding also told the Panel that most of the Task Force Barker personnel he talked with considered Tan to be a Viet Cong sympathizer, apparently as a result of his assiduous reporting of the My Lai 4 and My Khe 4 massacres. "I guess it was felt by our people working up there [that] . . . he was reluctant and hesitant and it was felt that he just did not want to fully cooperate with the Americans. He knew on which side his bread was buttered."

that emerged from his statements to the Panel. (A few days before Koster's appearance, Colonel Parson had testified that he saw a Vietnamese letter or report about My Lai 4 on Koster's desk in Chu Lai.) Koster further claimed, however, that he did not obtain any information from the Vietnamese "until, on my own instigation, I went around and talked to them."

Koster, Toan and Khien all agreed in their testimony that there were no documents exchanged in their meetings, raising an obvious and important question. If, as Gerberding testified, Koster did in fact send a letter to Henderson with a copy of Tan's report enclosed, where did he get it? One possible answer, based on my own interviews, was that Tan's report was transmitted to Koster by Anistranski, who had been told by Lieutenant Colonel Guinn to deliver an "eyes only" envelope to the general from Quang Ngai province headquarters. Asked specifically by General Peers if Guinn could have given him a copy of the Tan report, Koster, again speaking vaguely, indicated he did not think so: "I can't say how all this first came to our attention, but I wouldn't have put myself in the channel of communication for Colonel Guinn to go through." The general added, however, "I think he would have kept us informed of what was going on in the province."

Colonel Henderson also denied any knowledge of Koster's letter ordering him to file a report, saying that "I am positive that I received no letter from General Koster." He also denied ever seeing Tan's third report, despite Gerberding's testimony. But he did begin asking questions again. Why? Henderson explained it was not because of a letter from Koster but because of the receipt of a mysterious and unsigned statement referring to an allegation that American troops had slaughtered more than four hundred civilians. Henderson said that the statement also indicated that Lieutenant Tan, the Son Tinh district chief, did not give the allegations much importance. The colonel attached the document, without comment or explanation, to his resulting report to Koster.

The origin of the statement became a major concern of the Peers Panel; it was finally determined that the unsigned document was nothing more than a copy of the refutation prepared earlier by Captain Angel Rodriguez of Son Tinh district headquarters. Henderson steadfastly maintained that he had never seen the initial Rodriguez document, but received his statement—the one eventually given to Koster —from his staff. Both the statement and a copy of a Viet Cong propaganda leaflet about Son My, Henderson claimed at one point, were delivered to his intelligence officer, Lieutenant Colonel Richard Blackledge. "I do not know how he got the report," Henderson said. He added that copies of both documents were sent by his staff to division headquarters for its perusal.

Within two days of the mysterious receipt of the statement and the propaganda leaflet, the colonel said he decided to visit Colonel Toan—just as Koster earlier had—at the 2nd ARVN headquarters. As Henderson recounted it, he showed Toan the leaflet and told the Vietnamese officer that "I was very much interested in this thing and that when he looked into this I would make available to him a battalion or any number of troops to go into this area . . ." Toan assured him that the leaflet was simply propaganda and said, according to Henderson, "There is no truth to this, absolutely no truth to this." Henderson continued, "When I finished discussing this with . . . Toan, I immediately went over to Colonel Khien's headquarters . . . and met with Mr. May, who was a civilian adviser . . . and I believe I met for the first time Lieutenant Colonel Guinn . . . and I explained to [Khien] my regret and how disturbed I was

over this thing, and that I wanted to get to the bottom of it."
Khien also characterized the allegations as Viet Cong propaganda, Henderson said.

Two or three days after his visit, Henderson said, "General Young came down and said General Koster wants you
to—and it was not to make an investigation because I specifically asked, 'Does he want this open again and a formal
investigation?' and General Young said, 'No, this paper you
sent up, this VC propaganda message, has tripped his memory here a little bit, and he just wants some back-up in the
files here if anything further should develop on the matter.
So provide him with a written report.' " At this point, Henderson said, he sat down and wrote a report, relying on
notes taken during his interviews the month before—when
only the Thompson confrontation with ground troops and
the allegations of wild shootings were being investigated.

Many other witnesses contradicted some aspects of Henderson's testimony. General Young testified he had no recollection of a conversation in late April with Henderson
about a written report. Lieutenant Colonel Blackledge testified that his office relayed to Colonel Henderson not the
statement nor a Viet Cong propaganda leaflet, but only
some incomplete allegations of an atrocity which were
being disseminated by the Viet Cong.* Blackledge added

---

* Blackledge told the Peers Panel that he received a fragmentary intelligence report indicating the Viet Cong were claiming that up to five hundred civilians had been slain by American soldiers. "It did not name people who had been killed nor did it cover a three-day period, as far as I
can recall," the intelligence officer said. The document, however, did list
the date of the alleged massacre, and Blackledge concluded that "it had
to be our people that were there at the time." Blackledge said he mentioned the allegation to Henderson, who told him that "division is aware
of it and looking into it." A few days later a propaganda leaflet was
handed to a guard on duty outside the brigade headquarters by two Vietnamese children; this, too, Blackledge said, described the Son My massa-

that he knew nothing about the origin of the statement attached to the Henderson investigation. And Henderson himself eventually gave two different reasons to the Peers Panel to explain how he obtained the Rodriguez statement. Initially, he testified that the statement—Tan's third report plus Rodriguez' skeptical evaluation—had been supplied to Blackledge's office by the 52nd Military Intelligence Detachment stationed at Duc Pho, which had a liaison officer at Quang Ngai. Henderson next testified that Tan's third report was read to him by Colonel Khien, who then evaluated it in terms similar to that which appeared in the statement. Finally, Henderson acknowledged that he really did not know how or from where he received the information.

The Panel proposed a third possible source. "We have had it suggested that it came to you from an individual at province on the U.S. advisory team," one of the panelists told Henderson, referring to William Guinn.

cre. "I . . . thought it was propaganda the whole time," Blackledge said of the two pieces of information. "I never thought otherwise, except that it was a little different kind of propaganda." He was shown a copy of the Viet Cong propaganda leaflet submitted by Henderson in his April 24 report; Blackledge claimed that he had never seen it before. There was a bizarre footnote. Captain Richard J. Holbrook, the assistant intelligence officer for the 11th Brigade, told the Panel that he, too, had seen the propaganda leaflet describing the Son My massacre. Asked if he knew how Lieutenant Colonel Blackledge, his superior, obtained the document, Holbrook replied, "I recall it exactly and specifically. On that day I had been working and I was sleeping during the day. I was living in a tent and we had a Vietnamese girl that came in to clean up and do things like that. I had told her that she could use my radio, to turn it on while she was shining shoes or while she was working. She picked up the radio and said, 'It's VC! It's VC!' . . . Of course I don't understand Vietnamese and the broadcast was in Vietnamese. I called down to the 2 [intelligence] shop, got the driver to come and bring this girl with the radio still tuned to that station over to the 52nd MI [military intelligence] Detachment to one of their interpreters, and that's where that came from, sir." Holbrook explained that the interpreter instantaneously translated the broadcast—a claim that the Peers Panel found difficult to believe.

Henderson's subsequent report to General Koster, dated
April 24, included two enclosures: the Viet Cong propaganda leaflet and the Rodriguez material, which was shorn
of its signature bank but inadvertently retained its April 14
date. The fourteenth, of course, was the day that Rodriguez
forwarded it to the Quang Ngai province headquarters. The
document was attached to Henderson's report under the
simple heading, "Statement." Henderson's classified report,
addressed to the commanding general, Americal Division,
said:

1. An investigation has been conducted of allegations cited in inclosure 1 [the Rodriguez statement]. The following are the results
of this investigation.
2. On the day in question, 16 March 1968 . . . Task Force
Barker, 11th Inf Bge, conducted a combat air assault in the vicinity of My Lai hamlet (Son My village) in eastern Son Tinh District. This area has long been an enemy stronghold and Task
Force Barker had met heavy enemy opposition in this area on 12
and 23 February 1968. All persons living in this area are considered to be VC or VC sympathizers by the district chief. Artillery
and gunship preparatory fires were placed on the landing zones
used by the two companies. Upon landing and during their advance on the enemy positions, the attacking forces were supported by gunships . . . By 1500 all enemy resistance had ceased
and the remaining enemy forces had withdrawn. The results of
this operations were 128 VC KIA. During preparatory fires and
the ground action by the attacking companies 20 noncombatants
caught in the battle were killed. U.S. forces suffered 2 KHA
[killed by hostile action] and 10 WHA [wounded by hostile ac-
tion] by booby traps and 1 man slightly wounded in the foot by
small arms fire . . . Interviews [here Henderson listed only Lieutenant Colonel Barker, Major Calhoun, Captains Medina and
Michles] revealed that at no time were there any civilians gathered together and killed by U.S. soldiers. The civilian habitants in
the area began withdrawing to the southwest as soon as the operation began and within the first hour and a half all visible civilians
had cleared the area of operation.

3. The Son Tinh district chief does not give the allegations any importance and he pointed out that the two hamlets where the incident is alleged to have happened are in an area controlled by the VC since 1964. Col. Toan . . . reported that the making of such allegations against U.S. forces is a common technique of the VC propaganda machine. Inclosure 2 is a translation of an actual VC propaganda message targeted at the ARVN soldier and urging him to shoot Americans. This message was given to this headquarters by the CO, 2nd ARVN Division [Toan], on about 17 April 1968 . . . It makes the same allegation as made by the Son My village chief in addition to other claims of atrocities by American soldiers.

4. It is concluded that 20 noncombatants were inadvertently killed when caught in the area of preparatory fires and in the crossfires of the U.S. and VC forces on 16 March 1968. It is further concluded that no civilians were gathered together and shot by U.S. soldiers. The allegation that U.S. forces shot and killed 450–500 civilians is obviously a Viet Cong propaganda move to discredit the United States in the eyes of the Vietnamese people in general and the ARVN soldier in particular.

5. It is recommended that a counter-propaganda campaign be waged against the VC in eastern Son Tinh District.

The report, signed by Henderson, obviously relied heavily on Lieutenant Colonel Frank Barker's after-action report. The original typed copy was placed in a double-sealed envelope marked "For CG [Commanding General] Eyes Only" and sent by courier to division headquarters at Chu Lai. Only one copy was kept in brigade headquarters, according to Sergeant Gerberding, who was in charge of filing it, and it was handled on a "close-hold" basis. "I kept this [the copy] in what I called my personal or confidential file," the sergeant explained. "And it was not filed with the normal correspondence." Gerberding's personal file was in his desk, where, he said, "I kept things I didn't want anybody else to see."

The Army later found the carbon file copy in Gerberding's safe, where someone had moved it; it was the only existing record of any investigation in connection with My Lai
4.

The file copy was initialed RKB, for Richard K. Blackledge, and its existence enabled the Peers Panel to confront
a witness with documented evidence that contradicted his
testimony (the lack of records prevented the investigators
from directly challenging the many witnesses who simply
could not recall a fact, or said they were not sure what had
happened). Blackledge was asked if he had ever seen the
Henderson report prior to his testimony in 1970. "Negative,
absolutely negative," the former intelligence officer replied.
"I never saw this until I came here . . ." After being shown
his initialed file copy, Blackledge made this statement: "I
now retract what I said because those are my initials and I
recognize the way I write my initials. But I don't recall the
document . . . I had nothing to do with the preparation. In
fact—well, you caught me with my pants down. That's my
initials right on there, so I must have seen it, but I just don't
recall. I know damn well I didn't have anything to do with
preparing it."

The Peers Panel found it amazing that Koster did not
challenge Henderson's inclusion of an unidentified statement in his report; a statement, moreover, that referred to
two letters alleging American atrocities—an undated one
from Do Dinh Luyen, the Son My village chief, to Lieutenant Tan, and Tan's subsequent April 11 report to Quang
Ngai—neither of which was attached.

"General Koster," one of the panelists said, "I believe I
know you as a senior officer. I don't think you'd let Colonel
Henderson get away with submitting a paper like this dated
14 April without having a copy of that 11 April [Tan's] re-

port available, or without knowing whose statement this was, or where it came from. I just don't think that that would have happened. I believe the first question you would have asked is, 'Where did you get this statement? Whose is it? Where is that letter of 11 April? What does it say?'" Koster's answer again was foggy: "I would have to agree with you, but I don't recall this portion of it . . . I do not recall the 11 April letter was ever shown to me. The first time I really remember seeing this statement as such was when I saw the [Henderson report]. This is the only time I recall . . ." Told that Captain Rodriguez had written the statement, Koster said, "I wondered whose statement that was. I have never really known."

Henderson similarly was unable to give a satisfactory answer when asked, "How can you include in your report of investigation a statement—one, you don't know where you got it; two, you don't know who the author is; and I would say three, in the opening paragraph of this statement it refers to a letter from the village chief to the district chief. How can you possibly include a statement like this without knowing where you got it, who the author of it was, or having never seen the back-up materials?" Henderson simply replied, "Sir, I just can't remember . . ."

The panelists found it difficult to believe that there wasn't some collusion between Koster, Henderson, and perhaps Lieutenant Colonel William Guinn. "It is absolutely inconceivable to me," one of them told Henderson, "that you as a senior commander would, unless there is more that is known between yourself and General Koster than has been brought forward to the present time, that you could have sent a paper forward to General Koster that you didn't know the origin of."

Although Henderson's report was sent as a high-priority "eyes only" message, Koster testified that he did not recall seeing it until he returned from a brief vacation to Hawaii in early May. As usual, his recollection was imprecise. At another point, Koster testified that even if he had seen the report before departing on his vacation, he would not have taken any action on it, "but turned it over to General Young for his consideration."

Henderson, however, testified that "two or three days after I delivered the letter to Division, General Young visited me and informed me that General Koster had seen the report and had passed it to him, and he felt that General Koster was satisfied with the report." Henderson added that Young told him, "This issue was now dropped and that the thing had been put to bed and there was no evidence supporting allegations. I recall telling Colonel Barker, 'I hope we heard the last of this thing now.'"

By the time Koster returned from his vacation, however, he had decided that the written report of April 24 was inadequate. "As best I recall," Koster said, "it was not my intent that this [the report] should be limited to only some discussion of some VC propaganda." The division commander further said he and his staff "discussed the adequacy of the report" and decided to request Henderson to submit a full analysis, covering not only the new Vietnamese allegations but Hugh Thompson's claims of indiscriminate shooting. Koster wasn't sure how or when the decision was relayed to Henderson: "I would have said it would have been either General Young or Colonel Parson or perhaps by direct communication. I would have said one of those two . . . I know General Young was in agreement that what we had here wasn't what we had in mind when we asked for a written report of investigation."

Henderson confirmed Koster's account. He told the Panel that Young made another trip to the Duc Pho headquarters area in early May and informed him that Koster now wanted a formal investigation of the incident to embrace all of the allegations—both from the Vietnamese and the pilots. General Young "had no knowledge of any additional data which the division commander—which I didn't have," Henderson said. "I discussed with him who the logical individual was to perform the investigation and told him that if he had no objections, I would assign Colonel Barker to it. And General Young . . . indicated to me that this was certainly satisfactory."

Henderson then had this incredible exchange with a member of the Peers Panel:

Q. Doesn't it seem unusual, however, to have somebody investigating himself?

A. At no point at this time had I been led to believe or had any information that Colonel Barker was personally involved in this.

Q. No, his unit. When I say himself I am referring to something which took place in units under his command.

A. No, frankly, it did not enter my mind.

No orders were issued by division or brigade headquarters officially naming Barker as the investigating officer, a step that is a prime requirement of Army military regulations governing such official inquiries. Henderson testified that he simply went to Barker and "told him that General Koster, the division commander, wanted a formal investigation and that he was to take statements from anybody and everybody who was directly or indirectly related to this incident and that I wanted these statements taken in adequate detail to prove or disprove that anything had taken place." The date was about May 10, Henderson recalled, and Barker completed his report the next week. "To the best of my knowledge," the colonel testified, "the report included statements from certainly all of the company commanders, from various pilots . . . from enlisted personnel, both Charlie and Bravo Companies, it included statements from personnel working in the battalion TOC [operations center]."

Barker's formal report concluded once again that twenty civilians had been killed by artillery and gunships, Henderson said. He added, "There was no term of atrocity used, or massacre or anything of this nature. There was no evidence to support that any soldier had willfully or negligently wounded or killed civilians during this operation." Henderson estimated that Barker attached fifteen to twenty single-page signed statements to his three-page covering report. The colonel said he submitted Barker's work with a written endorsement saying that "I had reviewed the investigation . . . that the facts and circumstances cited throughout the investigation agreed generally with my own personal inquiry into the matter . . . and I recommended that the report be accepted."

General Young continually maintained that he could recall no conversations with Henderson about the April 24 written report to Koster and also denied any knowledge at all of the subsequent Barker report. But Henderson testified that Young came to visit him in mid-May "and told me that he had read the [Barker] report, had discussed it with General Koster again and that he recommended that General Koster buy [the] report, that he thought it had all the pertinent details in it, and this is the last that I have heard of that report. I received no further comeback from General Koster or anyone else."

The Peers Panel was subsequently unable to find any copies of the formal Barker report, either in the headquarters of the Americal Division or the 11th Brigade. In addition, only two of the nearly four hundred witnesses who appeared before the Panel claimed to have any knowledge of it—Colonel Henderson and Major General Koster. Even in the face of hostile questioning, Koster maintained that such a report did come into his headquarters. "I am positive that there was a stack of statements," he testified with assurance. "These were written statements by a number of the people who had been interrogated verbally prior to that time, and I know there was a sheaf of papers . . . that included these reports."

If such a report was indeed prepared by Frank Barker, the evidence was overwhelming that it was a complete fraud. None of the principals in the My Lai 4 investigation, including Captain Medina, Hugh Thompson, Major Watke, and Lieutenant Colonel Holladay, had knowledge of any further inquiries. For them, the investigation had ended a few days after it began in March.

Koster further testified that he did give a copy of the formal report to Colonel Nels Parson, for filing. "I thought it was the report with all the statements as being the last thing of the case," Koster explained. "Certainly, when we compiled them [the My Lai 4 documents], we would have filed them for any future reference there might have been."

During the weeks following My Lai 4, Thompson and many other pilots and crewmen in the 123rd had remained angered and demoralized by the Americal Division's failure to investigate the massacre and punish the offending participants. Thompson was personally convinced that his two crewmen deserved medals for helping him rescue the threatened civilians at My Lai 4, even though there were no enemy troops opposing them. He put both in for citations. By so doing, he made it easy for one of his superiors, fully aware of Thompson's bitterness over My Lai 4, to reward him in turn for keeping his peace and continuing to be one of the boys.*

On April 23 the American Division awarded a Bronze Star to Glenn U. Andreotta, a two-year veteran of Vietnam who had flown with Hugh Thompson as a door gunner on March 16. The award was made posthumously; Andreotta died before its final approval. He was honored for his heroism "in connection with military operations against a hostile force" at My Lai 4. Andreotta was credited with saving the lives of civilians hiding in a bunker "located between friendly forces and hostile forces engaged in a heavy fire fight." Major Frederic Watke signed the falsified recommendation; an eyewitness statement was submitted by Thompson. A few weeks later Specialist Four Lawrence Colburn, the other door gunner, also got a Bronze Star. A medal was sought for Thompson, too, and he eventually received the Distinguished Flying Cross. The citation that came with the pilot's medal noted that Thompson had rescued fifteen young Vietnamese children who were "caught

---

* Thompson's action in accepting a patently false reward and also signing a falsified witness statement came under heavy censure by a special subcommittee of the House Armed Services Committee that conducted its own investigation in 1970 of the My Lai 4 massacre. The subcommittee devoted eleven pages in its subsequent fifty-three-page published report to Thompson's action in opposing Calley at My Lai 4 and his receipt of the Distinguished Flying Cross. The report of the Congressional group, published July 15, 1970, suggested that the medal for Thompson and his crew "might have been part of an effort to cast the best light upon an operation of American Division which had resulted in serious criticism of the action of its troops." There were more persuasive reasons. Captain Thelmar Moe, a section leader for the 123rd Aviation Battalion, told the Peers Panel that "it seemed highly improbable that they [the crew members] would receive an award and he [Thompson] didn't. So I believe we solicited someone to provide a statement as to Thompson's merits on that particular day." Moe added that he wasn't sure which officer initiated the award.

in the intense cross fire" at My Lai 4. "Officer Thompson's heroic actions saved several innocent lives while his sound judgment greatly enhanced Vietnamese–American relations in the operational area," the citation, written by the 123rd Aviation Battalion, said. The Peers Panel discovered the original typewritten file copy of the citation and noted that the phrase "caught in the intense cross fire" had been scratched in between two typed lines with a pen, apparently at the last moment.

There's no question that Thompson felt guilty about his award, which he did accept—in the Army, one just doesn't refuse such honors. Father Carl Creswell described Thompson's attitude to the Panel: "He came in that day [after getting the medal], and he had the box and the citation . . . He read it and then threw it in his footlocker."

In June, Lieutenant Colonel Khien, the Quang Ngai province chief, finally decided to make his on-the-spot investigation of the atrocity allegations contained in Lieutenant Tan's third report in April. He personally led two groups of rural forces into Son My village. A dispute during the Peers Panel testimony arose over the extent of the resistance in Son My and what Khien learned about My Lai 4 there from the survivors.* In any case, as Khien later told

---

* Khien explained to General Peers that as his men started to enter the My Lai 4 area, there was sporadic firing by Viet Cong units and some shelling. Robert T. Burke, a young Foreign Service officer who had just replaced James May as senior province adviser, accompanied Khien into the field that day. He said that he was impressed by the fact that Khien "spent a lot of time talking to the villagers. They were kind of taking cover, I guess. There was a little bit of firing going on." Lieutenant Colonel John Green, who was still attached to the advisory team, described the engagement as more intense: "No sooner than we got out of there they [the Viet Cong] did start firing mortars right in there where we were standing." In his C.I.D. statement, Khien said he and his men "met heavy resistance from the enemy" that limited his ability to interview the

an investigator for the C.I.D., he never filed a formal report and considered his operation a failure.

There was a tragic aftermath. On the second day of Khien's operation, an Air Force observation plane collided near My Lai 4 with a helicopter carrying Lieutenant Colonel Frank Barker, by then promoted to a battalion commander in the 11th Brigade. With Barker was one of his former company commanders, Captain Earl Michles, late of Bravo Company, who was then serving as battalion intelligence officer. Both men were killed.

That day, too, Major William Ford, a local forces adviser who also was on the mission, became the first American to enter My Lai 4 since Charlie Company's assault. He described the area to the Panel: "The houses were demolished. There were quite a few VC entrenchments there . . . This was a VC village and dug in to be defended . . . this was a typical VC village." There were fewer than twenty old men, old women, and children living in the area, Ford said. "They were scared to death," he added. "I saw the women and children myself. They were scared. They were frightened."

Son My residents. The few survivors of the Task Force Barker assault who were interviewed told him, Khien testified, that about one hundred civilians were killed during a fire fight between American and Viet Cong forces. Only about twenty or thirty of the victims were women and children, Khien claimed, and fifty or sixty of the dead were guerrillas, Viet Cong, or troops.

16

The Missing Files

*B*y March, 1969, Task Force Barker's assault on Son My village was just another forgotten military victory. Barker and Michles were dead; Koster was superintendent of West Point; Henderson and Young were assigned to new duties out of Vietnam; and most of the GIs from Bravo and Charlie Companies were either out of the service or counting their days left in.

Ronald Ridenhour also was out of the service, and at the end of the month he mailed his letter describing the "dark and bloody" assault on My Lai 4 to thirty members of Congress and government officials. The carefully worded letter was a bombshell; nothing like it had crossed the desks of three- and four-star generals before. "Quite frankly, my initial reaction to these charges was one of disbelief," General William Westmoreland, then serving as the Army's Chief of Staff, told a House Armed Services Subcommittee during later closed briefings on My Lai 4. "Group conduct of the sort described in the letter was so out of character for American forces in Vietnam that I was quite skeptical."

Ridenhour's mass mailing posed an immediate public relations threat to the military, then in the process of helping to sell President Nixon's "Vietnamization" program to the nation, and within days, the military command in Saigon was ordered to investigate the charges. The task fell to Colonel Howard K. Whitaker, a senior officer in the inspector general's office in Saigon; he was dispatched north to the Americal Division headquarters at Chu Lai. "I was directed by the inspector general to . . . see what I could dig up, see what I could find out, and if possible talk to any of these witnesses or participants that were listed in the . . . message," Whitaker told the Panel. The names of witnesses and participants had been provided by the now closely held Ridenhour letter—which was never seen by Colonel Whitaker—and most of the GIs mentioned in it were back in the United States. The only participant still serving in Vietnam was Calley, who was by then serving in a reconnaissance unit in the Americal Division, but Ridenhour misspelled his name in the letter and the lieutenant was not immediately traced.

Whitaker's subsequent investigation was similar in concept to the earlier My Lai 4 investigations. The colonel spent less than two days at the Americal Division, where he accepted at face value every document he could find. Thus, he could write after reading Frank Barker's after-action report for March 16: "A review of the combat after-action report . . . revealed that an estimated enemy Local Force BN [battalion] was in the vicinity of the My Lai area . . . Enemy losses during this action were heavy . . . The civilian population supporting the VC in the area numbered approximately two hundred. This created a problem in population control and medical care of those civilians caught in fires of opposing forces." Whitaker did not, however, mention that only three enemy weapons were captured, nor did he express any concern over the fact that a check of the files in the Americal Division and 11th Brigade produced no evidence of an investigation. Ridenhour's letter had suggested that one did take place.

The colonel's attempt to "dig out" the truth apparently stopped with a series of discussions he had with the top-ranking officers of the Americal Division, including Major General Charles M. Gettys, the commanding general, and Colonel John W. Donaldson, the chief of staff. Whitaker's report noted: "Both stated they knew of no investigation ever having been conducted concerning the alleged incident." The colonel's final conclusion was skeptical: "An examination of all available documents concerning the alleged incident reveals that the complainant [Ridenhour] has grossly exaggerated the military action in question. No evidence could be uncovered which would substantiate the allegations." The officer did suggest, however, that interviews be conducted with some of the pertinent witnesses to "determine if the allegations have substance." None of the participants had been questioned about My Lai 4 since March, 1968.

In mid-April the Inspector General's office in the Pentagon was ordered to conduct a full-scale investigation; officials there, in turn, assigned Colonel William V. Wilson to the case in late April. With that decision, the Army set in motion the subsequent inevitable events. The basic sources Ridenhour had were the men of Charlie Company, some of whom had done the shootings, and they became Wilson's sources, too. In the early stages of the investigation, there were no colonels or majors to contrive false reports, just guilt-ridden ex-GIs anxious to tell what they knew, and why they did what they did. By late May, Wilson personally had tracked down at least six members of Charlie Company and had accumulated enough solid evidence to order Lieutenant Calley brought back from Vietnam for questioning. Although no word of the pending atrocity case was hinted to the public, the officers at work in the Pentagon knew something was up. One man who was serving then as a lieutenant colonel on the Joint Chiefs of Staff recalled in an interview with me that everyone knew "there was something going on in Vietnam; that the IG [Inspector General] had gone out to do an investigation; that there was big trouble; some kind of a flap. But nobody knew what it was—it was really closely held stuff. I figured some troops had refused to fight, or there was some kind of a mutiny."

The word also reached the headquarters of the Americal Division at Chu Lai and—as the Peers Panel later established—all but two of the reports relating to the Henderson investigations had vanished. Files pertaining to March 16 and thereafter were found to be missing at the Americal Division headquarters, 11th Brigade headquarters (where one copy of Henderson's April 24 report was located), Quang Ngai province headquarters, and Son Tinh district headquarters. All of the records for the artillery battalion commanded by Lieutenant Colonel Robert Luper of the 11th Brigade also were missing for March 16. Detailed interrogations by the Panel of dozens of brigade and division officers, sergeants, and clerks who were serving in 1969 produced only two witnesses who could recall handling a file on the My Lai 4 investigations—Robert Gerberding, the intelligence sergeant for the 11th Brigade, and his replacement, Kenneth E. Camell, who took over the job early in the year. Gerberding explained how he had taken Camell in hand and "showed him this file which I said . . . was a strictly confidential piece of correspondence. I told him that I kept it confidential the time I was here, and that he should treat it the same way, not put it in the normal file." The file contained many of the reports dealing with My Lai 4, Gerberding recalled, including Koster's April, 1968, letter to Henderson, and similar documents.

Colonel Whitaker's early investigation failed to uncover the secret file; no one knew it existed. In late May, 1969, however, Colonel Wilson, who was now in charge of the Inspector General's inquiry, contacted Henderson and ordered him to report to Washington for interrogation in connection with the massacre. Henderson, then on duty in Hawaii, promptly telephoned Chief of Staff Donaldson at American Division headquarters. He told Donaldson that a copy of his investigation had been filed either in the intelligence or operations office of the 11th Brigade. Henderson added, "I asked him if he would call down to the 11th Brigade and have somebody look in the S2 or the S3 safe to see if there was an envelope in there with a report of investigation in it." Henderson later testified that he was requesting the May, 1968, formal Barker investigation, with its attached multitude of statements.

By that time, however, the official files had disappeared and Donaldson sent Henderson a message stating that "a thorough search of division headquarters files and 11th Infantry Brigade files has failed to produce the *informal investigation* you requested [emphasis added]." It is not known why Donaldson's message referred to the informal report, one which usually is filed on an interim basis. A few days later, however, Donaldson telephoned Henderson with the news that a continuing check of the files had produced only the two-page April 24 interim report, which was subsequently mailed to Henderson, who in turn gave it to Colonel Wilson.

The copy Donaldson forwarded had been given him by Sergeant Camell's office in the 11th Brigade. Before it was sent to Division, other typed copies were made and at least one of them was filed in the brigade intelligence office (where an investigator for the Peers Panel found it on January 7, 1970). The other retyped copies—including copies of the Viet Cong propaganda reports and the material in Gerberding's original secret file—were never located. Camell testified that his material disappeared in two separate stages. That spring a senior officer of the 11th Brigade came to him for the complete file. "He had to make a report to someone else on it," Camell said of the officer, whose identity was never determined. When the folder was returned to him a day or two later, he said, he noticed that some of the papers were missing: "As to what they were, I cannot tell you. I just recalled . . . the sensation I had when I received it back, that there was something missing . . . I didn't pay any attention to it." In September, 1969, Camell said, he was again asked for the file by a senior staff officer. He never saw the folder again. On the fifth of that month the Army announced that murder charges had been filed against Lieutenant William Calley.

Camell was an informative but reluctant witness who repeatedly claimed that he could not recall who took either file from him. The one officer he did name, after some prodding from the Panel, had left the 11th Brigade even before the initial inspector general's inquiry in April, 1969.

The Peers Panel concluded its investigation in March, 1970, without being able to discover how the My Lai 4 files had disappeared. General Peers himself suspected that some of the key officers involved at the time were responsible. For example, he closely interrogated all of Major General Koster's personal aides and clerks to determine such things as how much and what kind of luggage he took with him when he left Vietnam for West Point in June, 1968. The truth was more damaging to the Army's system than even Peers could imagine—that subsequent senior officers of the Americal Division who had no direct involvement with My Lai 4 and its investigations destroyed evidence to protect their fellow officers who preceded them.

The first evidence that some My Lai 4 reports, including Barker's formal investigation, were on file at the Americal Division headquarters as late as May, 1969—fourteen months after the massacre—became known to the Army in the spring of 1970. The evidence was supplied by Lieutenant Colonel Barney L. Brannen, Jr., who had served with the Americal Division in the spring of 1969 as staff judge advocate, its senior legal officer. Brannen later told a military pre-trial hearing into the cover-up charges against Major General Koster—charges that had been filed by the Peers Panel—that he had seen the original copy of Frank Barker's May, 1968, investigation while in Vietnam. "It was sometime in May of 1969," he explained. "I received a phone call from the division chief of staff, who at the time was Colonel John Donaldson [who] asked me if I could come over to his office. So I did . . . When I arrived at the headquarters . . . in Colonel Donaldson's office was the division G1 [the officer in charge of administration and personnel] . . . a Lieutenant Colonel Henry [I.] Lowder. I don't recall anyone else being present at that time." Donaldson gave Brannen a copy of the Ridenhour letter to read and then ordered him to search his office for files for any information on the alleged incident. It's not known who in the Pentagon made a copy of Ridenhour's letter available to Donaldson. The only official link at that point between the letter and the Americal Division had been Colonel Whitaker, who testified that he was never given a copy of it.

Brannen found no trace of the investigation. "So," he testified, "I left my office and went down to the G1's office, which was about one hundred yards away . . . and I entered Colonel Lowder's section, his own personal office, and . . . he had a file in his hand at the time I walked in and he said, 'Well, we found this,' and handed me this file . . . perhaps one-half inch thick." The file was Barker's May, 1968, report complete with the letter of endorsement from Henderson. Brannen recalled that there were perhaps a dozen or more statements attached to the report "which appeared to have been written by the same individual in ink, probably ball point, but the ink was the same color throughout all the statements and appeared to be the same handwriting. And there again," the lieutenant colonel added, "I didn't consider anything unusual about that because quite often the investigating officer himself [Barker, in the case of the My Lai 4 investigation] will write out questions and answers or the summarization of the statement he's taken from the witness . . ."

Brannen went on: "I said to Colonel Lowder, 'This appears to be the document we're looking for. Do you want me to go with you back to the chief of staff's office?' He said, 'No, I'll take it over and talk to him about it'. . . . And [that] then and there ended my connection with this investigative file."

Brannen left the Americal Division that summer and returned to the United States to take the year-long course at the Army's Command and General Staff College at Fort Leavenworth. He was in school when the My Lai 4 story first broke in newspapers that November. Brannen read many of the newspaper and magazine stories about the atrocity, and became particularly offended at one *Newsweek* magazine account. "They [the magazine] went through the My Lai incident and they pretty well concluded that the

Army had a big cover-up and that there had never been any sort of investigation and so forth," the lawyer complained. "Well . . . during the [Christmas] holidays . . . we were out of school for two weeks. I had a cocktail party . . . and there were some other judge advocate officers who attended it . . . The discussion of My Lai came up in the course of the evening because they knew I had been in the American. And one of them referred to the article . . . and I told them in no uncertain terms that I didn't think the article was accurate, but that was not unusual because I felt that a lot of news reporting was inaccurate anyway, and a lot of editorializing when they reported to be facts. [I told them] that I had seen . . . a formal investigative report that related to the My Lai incident. In fact, it did not appear to me that the American Division had in any way attempted to cover anything up, but had in fact investigated it."

Brannen's story traveled the Army's legal circles, and three months later, in March, 1970, he was asked to make a formal statement about the file he had seen in Colonel Lowder's office by one of the attorneys for Major General Koster. Brannen gave another statement in June to agents for the C.I.D. A few days later he passed a lie detector test at the Pentagon. The test was urged upon the officer because Donaldson, by then promoted to general and assigned to a key position on the Joint Chiefs of Staff, and Lowder were vigorously denying Brannen's account. By midsummer, 1970, both Donaldson and Lowder were under secret investigation themselves by the C.I.D. for their part in the cover-up of the My Lai 4 tragedy.

Brannen told the Koster pre-trial hearing in September that Lowder had telephoned him shortly after he submitted his first formal statement to the Koster defense team. Their conversation was cited in full by Brannen: "He [Lowder] said, 'Hey, I just got a call from so-and-so . . . I don't re-

member anything about that report.' And he said, 'It must
not have been me. It must have been the other G1 [who
served after Lowder].' And I said, 'Well, Henry, if you don't
remember, tell them you don't remember. I'm telling them
what I remember and that's all I can do and that's all you
can do.' And he said 'Okay.' " Lowder subsequently failed a
Pentagon lie detector test he volunteered to take in an attempt to prove that he had never seen the Barker investigation.

General Donaldson testified at the Koster hearing on
September 14, 1970, five days after Brannen. He again denied any knowledge of the Brannen encounter, and further
claimed that he did not see the Ridenhour letter while in
Vietnam. Donaldson also testified that he sent a copy of the
informal Henderson report, once it was discovered by Sergeant Camell, to higher Army headquarters in Saigon. But
the Peers Panel had already checked the files there and
found no evidence of the report.*

After Brannen's allegations became known inside the

---

* Donaldson also maintained that he first heard of the Brannen statements during a home leave in November–December, 1969. Yet Donaldson never mentioned it when he returned to Vietnam at the end of the
year, as a deputy commanding general of the Americal Division, in time
to help General Peers and his staff conduct their on-the-spot investigation of the My Lai massacre. Donaldson knew that Peers was looking for
documents; he even testified that he and Robert MacCrate, a civilian attorney who joined the Panel, had a conversation over breakfast just before the Peers team returned to Washington, in which MacCrate commented on the fact that they were unable to find any traces of the formal
investigation. Donaldson was asked during the Koster hearing why—if
he did, in fact, hear of the Brannen statement in late 1969—he did not
then volunteer the information he had. The general responded, "The
Peers committee had their program well laid out. The first things they
wanted to do was to go, actually go, into My Lai, to reconstruct the entire alleged incident. And they seemed more interested in the interrogation of local Vietnamese, any Americans who might still be in the area
. . . They never questioned me, for example, about the incident."

Army in mid-1970, government sources told me, there was some high-level thought given to reconvening the Peers Panel. This step was ruled out, sources said, because "it would have been too embarrassing." The subsequent C.I.D. investigation of Donaldson and Lowder was unable to develop any direct testimony linking either of the men with the actual destruction of files. "They never found anybody who could say they saw the files destroyed," a source said. "All Brannen could establish is that Lowder had possession of the files."

But the C.I.D. never talked to Bruce Brown of Hays, Kansas, an enlisted man who was in charge of the Americal Division's top-secret and "Specat" (Special Category) files in the division's message center. Brown told me in mid-1971 he was convinced that the Task Force Barker investigation was kept under wraps in the highly secure "Specat" safe. "Most of the other files were a form letter or a message, but this was special," Brown related. "It was maybe one-half-inch thick and had many pieces of paper. They wanted to be sure that it was controlled properly. Nobody ever called for it but the chief of staff [Donaldson]." The message center files were under the control of the G1 office (headed by Lowder) and no other officer, not even the commanding general, could keep top-secret or "Specat" material out overnight.

The Peers Panel spent hours interrogating file clerks who worked in the division headquarters to determine where the Henderson investigations would have been filed, but no one talked to the message center personnel. Koster testified that he gave the final Barker report to Colonel Parson, his chief of staff, for safekeeping; the document was to be held close. Parson and subsequent division chiefs of staff often deposited such material with the message center.

Within a year, nonetheless, General Donaldson's promising career was badly marred. Late in 1970 an Army prosecutor, checking out a tip that Colonel Henderson had engaged in "gook-hunting" while serving as brigade commander in 1968, interviewed a number of helicopter pilots who had flown in Vietnam. The investigator discovered that his tipster had been mistaken in the identity of the "gook-hunter"; it was not Henderson but Donaldson who allegedly spent dozens of hours circling in helicopters looking for targets of opportunity. An investigation was initiated, and in June, 1971, Donaldson was formally charged with the murder of six Vietnamese civilians and the assault with intent to kill of two more. He was abruptly transferred from a key position with the Joint Chiefs of Staff at the Pentagon. In December, after a four-month closed hearing, the Army exonerated Donaldson of all the charges, permitting him to resume his career.

17

The Pentagon Investigates

Secretary of Defense Melvin A. Laird and other high Pentagon officials monitored the Associated Press and United Press International newspaper wires with trepidation on the evening of September 5, 1969. Earlier that day the public information office at Fort Benning, Georgia, had issued its first press release about the mass-murder charges filed against one of its young lieutenants, William Calley. The official concern wasn't necessary; the military news release—such announcements were routinely issued in connection with serious crimes —gave no hint of the scope of the My Lai 4 massacre. Calley was charged with murder, it said, "for offenses allegedly committed against civilians while serving in Vietnam in March, 1968." There was no press outcry, and the military continued its investigation in secrecy. Ronald Ridenhour, who by then was making increasingly impatient telephone calls to the Pentagon demanding action,

was informed by the Inspector General's office of the
charges against Calley but was urged to "avoid any public
discussion which could prejudice the continuing investigation or the rights of Lieutenant Calley." The chairmen of
the House and Senate Armed Services Committees, Representative L. Mendel Rivers of South Carolina and Senator
John C. Stennis of Mississippi, were briefed on the impending scandal and also urged not to talk.

By early fall the full scope of the My Lai 4 tragedy was
becoming clear to the Army, and the investigation of Charlie Company GIs was transferred from the inspector general
and put in the hands of a newly organized office of the
Criminal Investigation Division, headed by Colonel Henry
H. Tufts, an experienced agent. At the same time the Army
broadened the scope of its inquiry, assigning many agents
to Tufts' office. Dozens of Charlie Company officers and
men were being interrogated. But in those months none of
the senior officers in the 11th Brigade and American Division was thought to be involved in a cover-up. "Nobody
could believe that senior officers could know about it and
not say anything," one military source told me during an interview in mid-1971. "The early emphasis was on Medina
and Calley and Mitchell. But when your story broke [a
reference to my article of November 13, 1969, revealing
that Calley had been charged with the deaths of 109 Vietnamese civilians],* we realized that this aspect [the pos-

---

* The first stories also prompted Major General Koster to telephone
Colonel Henderson, then attending the Armed Forces Staff College at
Norfolk, Virginia. Henderson told the Peers Panel that he and Koster
had about five telephone conversations over the next few months, all but
one initiated by the general, who was then at West Point. Henderson
claimed, however, that he remembered little about the conversations,
other than that they dealt with the reports and investigations of My Lai 4.
Koster subsequently gave General Peers a memorandum in which he acknowledged initiating three telephone calls to the colonel. The first call,

sible cover-up] had not been emphasized enough."

Within days, as the furor over the Calley story grew, a crisis atmosphere developed in the Pentagon. A series of meetings was held among high officials to discuss ways of abating the growing criticism from the press and the public over what seemed to be an obvious case of cover-up. Incredibly, that possibility had never been formally discussed within the Pentagon until then. A working group that included Secretary of the Army Stanley R. Resor, General Counsel Robert E. Jordan, III, Vice Chief of Staff Bruce Palmer, and Daniel Z. Henkin, Assistant Secretary of Defense for Public Affairs, determined that, as one official close to the process said, "some kind of inquiry was needed. The idea [for an Army investigation] originated between Resor and Palmer. But the basic structure of the group; what kind of independent organization; who's to be on it? All those questions were discussed."

Before any decision was reached in mid-November, a number of officers attached to the Americal Division and to the Quang Ngai province advisory team were brought in for a series of private discussions inside the Pentagon. Among those interviewed were Major Frederic Watke of the 123rd Aviation Battalion, Lieutenant Colonel William Guinn of the Quang Ngai advisory team, and Lieutenant Colonel Jesmond Balmer, the former chief of staff under Koster. "Our personal feeling [after the interviews] was, 'Yeah, something's rotten in Denmark,'" the military source told me.

It was decided not to entrust the inquiry to Colonel Tufts' newly established C.I.D. office; his investigators would be

Koster said, took place sometime around November 20, just as the newspaper revelations began appearing. "I discussed at some length with Colonel Henderson," Koster wrote, "what appeared to be the exaggerations and inaccuracies of reported accounts of the combat action in the press . . ."

outranked by the men they were interrogating. Because of Koster's high rank, a two- or three-star general would be needed to head the investigating panel. "We wanted a military man with experience in Vietnam, and someone who was senior to Koster. General Peers met those criteria" the source said, with an added bonus: "He was not West Point and we were afraid of the WPPA [West Point Protective Association]." The West Point Protective Association is a nonexistent organization, but the belief that West Point graduates take care of their own is widely held. Many military men—particularly those who are not graduates of the Academy—are convinced that young West Point generals get the choice assignments. "WPPA is a two-edged sword," my source said. "The West Pointer who goes down is trampled on harder, but it usually takes a higher standard of proof."

Another advantage of the Peers appointment was his Pentagon position as director of the Army Reserves, a three-star position that is not usually considered a stepping stone to more important positions in the Army. "Peers' job was one in which he could be missed," the source said. "Let's face it: you don't charge a member of the club and tear up the system the way he did and expect to get ahead."* The gruff, cigar-smoking general was given carte blanche in picking his staff, and eventually amassed a group of bright, young officers, who had served as commanders in Vietnam, to serve on his interrogation teams. (By the end of the inquiry, the Army had assigned thirty-four officers,

---

* In August, 1971, seventeen months after the Panel finished its work, Lieutenant General Peers was named deputy commanding general of the 8th Army in South Korea. Army sources told me that Peers would spend one year in Korea and then be assigned as deputy commanding general of Army forces in the Pacific (USARPAC), with quarters in Hawaii. After that two-year post, considered a plush assignment, Peers would probably retire.

forty-eight enlisted men, and eleven civilians to the Panel.)
On November 24 the Pentagon formally announced that
General Peers had been chosen to head an all-military inquiry into the "nature and scope" of the initial investigations into My Lai 4.

Most members of the military establishment had already
independently and almost spontaneously arrived at the
same attitude toward the killing and cover-up of My Lai 4,
as reflected publicly by Army Secretary Resor on November 26. "I have reviewed what we know of the incident at
My Lai with a number of officers who have served in Vietnam," Resor told the Senate Armed Services Committee.
"It is their judgment—a judgment which I personally en-
dorse and share—that what apparently occurred at My Lai
is wholly unrepresentative of the manner in which our
forces conduct military operations in Vietnam."

On the same day the White House made its initial re-
sponse to the growing clamor over the incident by depicting
My Lai not only as isolated, but also a responsibility of the
Johnson Administration, which was in office at the time of
My Lai. On December 8 President Nixon declared at a
news conference, "I believe that it is an isolated incident.
Certainly within this Administration we are doing everything possible to find out whether it was isolated . . ." But
on December 8, the day of the news conference, Henry
Kissinger, Nixon's chief adviser on national security affairs,
sent a private memorandum to Secretary of Defense Laird
in connection with My Lai 4. The memorandum took note
of a published account of atrocities by Terry Reid, who had
served with Bravo Company, Task Force Barker. Kissinger
wrote that "Reid claimed to have witnessed a number of
atrocities in the Chu Lai area of South Vietnam, including
the shooting of sixty children, women, and old men and the

murder of raped women." Kissinger then asked: "The President has asked if there is any factual basis to Reid's story and if you expect similar stories to surface which have some veracity." At that stage the White House seemed more concerned with the public relations aspects of My Lai 4 than with the dimensions of human tragedy or with the probability that there were far-reaching institutional problems in the Army itself.

By early December, Peers was beginning to realize that he had badly underestimated the scope of his inquiry. In a memorandum written November 30—before he began hearings—to Resor and Chief of Staff Westmoreland, the general had outlined a six-week investigation involving a trip to Vietnam and the interrogation of thirty to forty witnesses in the Pentagon. By Christmas, however, he and his staff had already interrogated more than fifty witnesses, some of them twice. Two prominent New York attorneys, Robert MacCrate, a Harvard Law School graduate who had once served as a special assistant to Governor Nelson A. Rockefeller of New York, and Jerome K. Walsh, Jr., joined the investigating team early that month. The civilian attorneys were added, my source told me, because "at one stage of the game, Bob Jordan [the Army general counsel] and Resor became aware of the credibility problem."

With these steps, the military blunted the demand, from liberals and conservatives alike, that an outside panel be established to investigate the cover-up. Such proposals had been made by such disparate men as Hubert H. Humphrey, the former vice-president; John C. Stennis of Mississippi, the conservative chairman of the Senate Armed Services Committee; and Arthur J. Goldberg, the former Supreme Court Justice. Still the Army's announcement November 24 of the Peers inquiry triggered some Senate and House criticism. Two senators, Stephen M. Young of Ohio and Charles

H. Percy of Illinois, immediately called for Senate investigations into My Lai 4. Young, perhaps anticipating the long military delay in making an uncensored version of the Peers Panel report public, told the Senate that "Americans must know—and the sooner the better—the long-suppressed facts about what certainly has been one of our nation's most ignoble hours." In the House, Chairman Rivers of the Armed Services Committee announced that he had ordered his investigating subcommittee, headed by Representative F. Edward Hébert of Louisiana, to investigate the massacre in closed hearings. That group's report, like the Army's, was released in heavily edited form eight months later. Perhaps most disturbing to the Pentagon was a proposal by a group of House liberals that a fifteen-member commission, none of them military, be set up to study American troop conduct at My Lai 4. As envisioned by the congressmen, the commission would be comprised of five House members, five senators, and five private citizens, who would be obligated to report their findings within six months of establishment.

The political furor over the cover-up died as My Lai 4 receded from the front pages. No serious critic questioned the integrity of General Peers, who made it clear he did not intend to whitewash any findings. In December, Peers assured a closed meeting of the Hébert subcommittee that "I intend to investigate all aspects of the incident and its subsequent investigations and in sufficient depth to arrive at valid conclusions and recommendations. As far as I am concerned, the chips will fall where they may irrespective of the grade or position of the individual involved."

The Peers Panel investigation was a model of integrity and industry; at one time the general had four separate interview teams at work, compiling massive volumes of testimony. Complicating the group's problems was a question of time; under military law, the statute of limitations for some criminal offenses—but not murder—was two years. Thus, all charges would have to be prepared by March 16, 1971.

Yet, in the final analysis, General Peers and his staff failed to explore fully, not the individual actions of a few generals, colonels and lesser officers, but an institution that made it almost inevitable that the investigations of My Lai 4 would be covered up. The Panel members, perhaps unconsciously, were convinced that My Lai 4 and Task Force Barker were both aberrations. The witnesses, particularly field-grade officers of the task force or 11th Brigade were considered to be individuals who were somehow unlike all of the others in the Army.

Major Watke, for example, had appeared to be an ambitious officer more concerned about his career than about reporting the My Lai 4 atrocity. At one point Watke was accused by Colonel Franklin of giving an impression, "whether intended or not, [of] an officer greatly concerned over making waves in his own career, whose judgment or information of a possible horrible war crime . . . has been filtered, or clouded, or even almost diverted by the negative impact it could have on his career." Watke responded by telling the officer an important truth about the military: "If it had been my career at stake, I wouldn't have done anything. I think the fact that I carried this to my commander and to Colonel Barker . . . If I had been worried about my career . . . I would have just let it just stop right there when it came to me." Peers simply couldn't accept Watke's comment. "Major Watke," he said, "let's be reasonable. You couldn't, and even if you had been thinking about your career the worst thing that could have ever happened to you—and look at it very realistically—was for [Thompson's complaints] to get up the line without having gone through you. You wouldn't have had to worry about a career." Yet the overall testimony taken by the Peers Panel suggested that if Watke had said nothing, there would have been no immediate investigation at all.

There was evidence that General Peers considered himself morally and professionally superior to the officers involved in the My Lai 4 cover-up. Often when a key witness stood on his constitutional right not to testify, Peers berated him for avoiding his responsibility to the Army. Thus when William Guinn, on his attorney's advice, decided to stop answering questions after being warned that he was suspected of a number of offenses, Peers told him, "I'd like to talk to you for just a few minutes . . . because I'm not sure that you really recognize the gravity of this situation and the enormity of the incident that took place and the responsibility that has been placed upon this investigating team . . . The purpose of this investigation . . . goes way beyond you and me and your . . . counsel . . . It's not just the people of Task Force Barker that are on trial in the eyes of the American public; it's the Army; it's you and me and it's everyone and everything that we know, that we think of. And it even goes beyond that, because it includes the entire Defense Department . . . You see, in my view and the view of the American public, we've got a senior U.S. Army officer sitting here [Guinn] who does have responsibilities . . . You also, when you came into the Army, swore certain things as far as the defense and protection of this country. And your appointment was approved by Congress to the effect that you were going to be an officer and a gentleman. So I don't think it would be fair to put you in the same light as some ordinary civilian citizen . . ." Similar speeches were made to the few key witnesses who chose to stop testifying.

Peers' attitude was reflected by the other investigators, including MacCrate and Walsh. When Major Robert

McKnight, the 11th Brigade operations officer, refused to testify after being warned of the Peers Panel's suspicions of him, he and his military attorney, Captain Kenneth Griffiths, were badgered by both Peers and Walsh, who kept on asking questions and even submitted a series of written statements for McKnight to identify. Griffiths protested: "I don't know why we were asked to be counsel if we are going to have our advice disregarded by the members of the committee . . . I think that he [McKnight] has a right under the Constitution not to listen to the questions, and certainly not to answer them." Walsh's persistence led him to make a ridiculous, if factual, assertion: "Captain, the Constitution says nothing about not answering questions, and I'm not aware that the Uniform Code of Military Justice has anything about not listening to questions." McKnight eventually was permitted to stop testifying.

These are extreme examples, of course, but are indicative of the attitude of the Panel. As the testimony proceeded, it should have become clear to General Peers and the others that there were many underlying problems that were exemplified by the officers testifying before them. Yet My Lai 4 was always discussed in terms of which officer failed to fulfill his military duty by not reporting a war crime; never in terms of the system that prevented literally hundreds of men and officers from telling their superiors about My Lai 4.

Ronald Ridenhour, asked by General Peers why he didn't report his information about the massacre to his military superiors in Vietnam rather than writing his letter responded, "I didn't have a whole lot of trust in the Army, especially after some of these things happened. And I was told bluntly from time to time that if accidents occurred, don't worry about it, because we'll cover you . . . I couldn't help feel that this was a policy that was all-pervading within the [Americal] division, and everybody was covering everybody's ass. That's the first thing that you learn when you go in the Army now. We didn't learn 'Don't volunteer,' we learned 'Cover your ass.' "

Peers' reaction to Ridenhour's frank opinion of what he saw as a Vietnam reality was unsurprising: "As a bit of background for you, Mr. Ridenhour, so that you'll understand how I feel on this thing, and not I only feel, but how I know General Westmoreland felt about it, I'd like to acquaint you with just a couple of documents which we have already had entered into our record." The general then read excerpts from current regulations against war crimes to the unbelieving ex-GI. Earlier, Peers had acknowledged to Ridenhour that he hadn't known what the term "dink" referred to until he began interviewing some of the Charlie Company GIs. "I think it's a very unfortunate term to use," the general said to Ridenhour's amazement. "As a matter of fact, I will be very frank with you. It wasn't until I joined this investigation . . . that I really realized that people used the term 'dinks'—because in the First Field Force [which Peers commanded in Vietnam], we had not used it." Ridenhour later told me that he found the general's statement wholly implausible.

The Peers Panel also was reluctant to permit known critics of the Vietnam war to testify. None of the civilians, for example, who worked with relief and volunteer agencies in Quang Ngai Province were called upon to appear, although they would have been freer to describe the workings of the province advisory team. In one case, the Army deliberately by-passed a potentially important witness who was deemed to be anti-war. Dr. Alje Vennema, a Canadian, worked in early 1968 at a Quaker hospital in Quang Ngai City. He told newsmen in London, after the massacre of Vietnamese civilians became known, that he had been told, in Quang

Ngai, of My Lai 4 within days of its occurrence. None of the military or State Department officials who were in Quang Ngai at the time said as much during their testimony. But Vennema was not asked to testify after an Army intelligence check determined that the doctor "manifested a strong anti-U.S. attitude."*

On the other hand, those who approved of the Army seemed to win quick acceptance from General Peers. He and Robert MacCrate worked together smoothly during the fifteen-week investigation; one reason for the cooperation became clear during the testimony of Father Carl Creswell. The Episcopalian priest, asked by MacCrate why he did not report Thompson's charges to the staff judge advocate, replied, "Well, sir, let me tell you something at this point. I'm not a complete stranger with the JAG [advocate general's] office. I went over there from time to time. And from time to time I saw charges filed against American troops in cases of out-and-out first-degree murder which, nine times out of ten, were reduced to manslaughter. And I became absolutely convinced that as far as the United States Army was concerned, there was no such thing as murder of a Vietnamese civilian."

MacCrate was quick to defend the military code of justice: "You're talking about technical charges, and simply the fact that something is reduced from murder to man-

* A February 20, 1970, memorandum to the Panel from Colonel Werner E. Michel, chief of Army Intelligence's Counterintelligence Division, reported that a Defense Intelligence Agency (DIA) attaché at Ottawa, Canada, had learned that Vennema "had made several speeches in Canada condemning U.S. presence in Vietnam, alleged atrocities committed by U.S. in Vietnam, and the U.S. military in general. The attaché further indicated," the memorandum said, "that his sources have lead him to believe that Dr. Vennema would make a biased witness in any hearing concerning the U.S. military." Vennema was never personally contacted by the American intelligence agent.

slaughter doesn't mean that it isn't taken seriously and the prosecution continued . . . in my mind, there is a substantial difference between sweeping everything under the rug and saying that a particular charge would be the most serious crime or a less serious crime." But the problem was far more substantial than MacCrate seemed willing to acknowledge. Many ex-GIs have told me and others of cases in which a soldier, after being convicted of killing or assaulting a Vietnamese civilian, was merely reduced in rank and sent back to his unit.*

Thus MacCrate's vision of the problems facing the Army was on occasion just as narrow and restrictive—although he is a highly reputed Wall Street lawyer—as that of the Colonel J. Ross Franklin, the most moralistic military member of the Peers Panel. Franklin often bluntly criticized many

---

* Even those convicted of premeditated murder rarely serve their full sentences. The most prominent recent example was Lieutenant William Calley, whose conviction March 31, 1970, of first-degree murder and subsequent life sentence to prison was reduced to twenty years' imprisonment five months later by an Army review board. Further reductions could follow. Twenty-one other Army men and officers have been convicted of premeditated murder involving a Vietnamese since 1964; each defendant was automatically sentenced to life imprisonment. All of those sentences were quickly reduced by military review boards. One 1971 study by a Navy lawyer of six cases involving premeditated murder of Vietnamese civilians by Marines revealed that the men were ordered to serve, after all reviews and appeals, a total of thirty-five years at hard labor. The men were convicted of a total of thirty-one murders, one rape, and one attempted rape; each crime, therefore, earned its perpetrator an average of slightly more than one year's imprisonment.

In addition, there have been many newspaper and magazine accounts of what has become known as the "MGR"—Mere Gook Rule. In Vietnam, "MGR" was a short-hand explanation for a battlefield crime that was investigated but not brought to trial or for a case that the Army prosecuted, but which resulted in an acquittal. Thus, the planners of the My Lai 4 assault could reason that anyone in the hamlet must be a Viet Cong or Viet Cong sympathizer and, therefore—by applying the "MGR"—the area could be shelled and bombed at will.

witnesses and suggested that they were lying; as such, he seemed to be playing the role of de facto spokesman for General Peers, making comments with which the general obviously agreed but would not say himself. Sergeant Michael Bernhardt's appearance before the Panel particularly upset Franklin. Bernhardt, one of the first men to talk to newsmen about My Lai 4, calmly testified about the many Charlie Company rapes and murders that he had witnessed or been told about.

Asked by Franklin to give a specific example, Bernhardt told of a woman carrying baskets who was shot after ignoring a request to stop running. Franklin didn't find the action disturbing: "Well . . . can you think of a better way to stop people that are running than doing that? I mean, are you comparing that woman carrying baskets that was shouted at to stop with the lining up and the gunning down of men, women, and children in My Lai 4? . . . The only point I want to make to you is if you are going to make damning accusations like this, and these very general statements, you had better have something to back it up. You're still wearing the uniform and you're portraying people that wear the uniform as really animals."

Franklin then offered the young sergeant some advice: ". . . in the future when you are called before any kind of an official body, and also in your conversations, what you saw you saw, and what you heard you heard. You don't want to confuse the two, Sergeant Bernhardt."

Other witnesses, however, were constantly urged to give hearsay evidence, as long as the investigators thought that such information might help them build another case against another GI or officer in connection with the My Lai 4 massacre.

General Peers obviously thought very highly of Franklin. During a private briefing in December, 1969, to the Hébert subcommittee, Peers said he selected Franklin for his team "because of his operational experience in Binh Dinh Province as the deputy commander of the 173rd Airborne Brigade. The situation there and the operations which are conducted are quite similar to the My Lai area of Quang Ngai Province. His knowledge will be invaluable in the providing of the operational input to the interrogation."

During the hearings, Franklin was often cited as an example of the proper and responsible commander. Yet, one year later Colonel Franklin was himself charged by a fellow officer with seven counts of dereliction of duty and failure to comply with written directives in connection with the murder in 1969—before the Peers Panel was convened —of at least five Vietnamese prisoners and electric torture of a sixth. The charges were formally filed March 15, 1971, by Lieutenant Colonel Anthony B. Herbert, the holder of four Silver Stars, who served in early 1969 as inspector general and a battalion commander for the 173rd Brigade under Franklin and his superior, Major General John W. Barnes.* Barnes also was charged by Herbert with three counts of dereliction of duty.

---

* Franklin was serving in a prestige position in November, 1970, as a brigade commander with the First Cavalry Division (Airmobile), when Herbert initially reported the allegations to the C.I.D. Herbert testified that he began relaying instances of mistreatment and murder of prisoners to Franklin soon after taking over his battalion. The lieutenant colonel described to the C.I.D. one typical incident, which involved a murder committed by Vietnamese police in front of an American officer: "One Vietnamese had a young woman by the hair with his hand around her throat and a knife dug into her neck. I brushed past the [American] lieutenant and hollered for the Vietnamese to stop. There was a child holding onto the woman's pants leg and crying. There was another child face down into the sand screaming and a Vietnamese soldier had his feet in the upper part of the child's back and was pushing the child into the sand. The Vietnamese soldier looked me directly in the eye, cut the woman's throat, and dropped her to the sand. I went to talk with the lieutenant.

General Peers may have spoken from limited knowledge about Colonel Franklin when he told Ronald Ridenhour during the ex-GI's testimony, "I'm very distressed to do what I am doing because I've been very proud of our Army and what it stands for and what I stand for within the Army. I'm sure that this is what Colonel Franklin was alluding to [referring to an earlier conversation about rigorous training], because we do have these extremely high standards. I just can't understand anything that deviates from it."

There is some reason to believe that General Peers himself was conditioned by the Army system, and found it impossible to meet his own expressed views on the responsibility of reporting atrocities; as he explained to Jay Roberts, the combat correspondent for the 11th Brigade: "The regu-

He explained that these Vietnamese were not under his command; he was just their adviser. I explained that he was an American officer and should have and could have stopped the killing of the detainees. I told him . . . that I did not want [the Vietnamese soldiers] or him with me any longer nor for any future operations." Herbert testified that he immediately reported the incident to Franklin, but was accused by Franklin of either exaggerating or lying. "Franklin told me that he would take care of it and that it was no longer any of my concern," Herbert claimed. Nevertheless, Herbert, the most highly decorated Army veteran of the Korean War, continued to insist that his men stop murdering and torturing Vietnamese suspects. After another complaint over the use of water torture by American officers on Vietnamese suspects, Herbert said he was told by Franklin "that interrogation methods conducted by brigade personnel were none of my concern." Herbert continued to file protests until he was abruptly relieved of command and sent back to the United States. On July 21, 1971, the Army officially dismissed Herbert's charges against Franklin, and his similar complaint against General Barnes was dropped on October 15, 1971. (Barnes was routinely promoted to major general four months after Herbert initiated his charges). But by July, Franklin's career coincidentally had suffered a serious setback that had nothing to do with Herbert's charges. He was relieved of his command with the First Cavalry Division after an incident involving a dead Vietnamese civilian and became an adviser to an ARVN unit in the Mekong Delta; a transfer that, in effect, dimmed his chances for a bright career.

lations indicate very clearly that whenever an atrocity is committed, irrespective of by what side, whether it involves one individual or might be termed a 'massacre' such as this, people are obligated to report it, and this is every atrocity, irrespective of whether it is an atrocity in fact or only an alleged atrocity."*

Yet Peers, who was primarily responsible for the investigation of the Bravo Company, apparently failed to do all that he could to ensure that those men and officers who were involved at My Khe 4 were properly punished or reprimanded. The first hint of Bravo Company's actions was given by Nguyen Dhi Bay, the resident of My Khe 4 who was raped and forced to serve as a human mine detector during the March 16–18 Bravo Company operation. Mrs. Bay was interviewed on December 17, 1969, at the Quang Ngai hospital by André Feher of the C.I.D. Peers, MacCrate, and a few other members of the investigating team arrived at the American Division headquarters a few weeks later to begin interviewing witnesses and survey My Lai 4. Almost immediately, Peers sent the following "eyes only" message to Resor and Westmoreland:

---

* Not surprisingly, Peers' personal view of his reporting obligations was similar to the official position on such incidents expressed by the Department of the Army in a fact sheet made public April 2, 1971, during the outcry over the conviction of Lieutenant Calley: "The Department of the Army had a moral and legal obligation to adopt a continuing policy of investigating fully all substantive allegations of violations of the laws of war involving American personnel. Every allegation of misconduct on the battlefield—regardless of the rank or position of the person purportedly responsible—must be thoroughly explored." In addition, the Peers Panel specifically had been ordered by Secretary of Defense Melvin A. Laird, through the Secretary of the Army, to "investigate expeditiously each allegation" of an atrocity. In a memorandum dated December 11, 1969, and relayed to the Panel on December 17, 1969, Laird gave two reasons for his request: "In order to ascertain the facts and also to prevent endless repetition of false allegations [in the press]."

You will recall that you had asked me to include Co Luy in our investigation. Two of the female detainees taken in the operations of the . . . 1st Cav on 13 Dec 69 south of My Lai 1 were recently interrogated by the C.I.D. in the Quang Ngai civil hospital. Both of them indicated that on the day of the 16th, possibly the 17th, of Mar 68 approximately 90–100 women and children in [My Khe 4] were removed from bunkers and shot in the immediate locality . . . A few instances of rapes were also reported. This would have been the operation of B Co . . . in that general area.

The two women have since been released from the hospital, but we will try to locate them and have them reinterrogated by members of this team. Additionally, we will continue pressing for information concerning any unusual activity in that area on the 16–17th of Mar 68. You should also know that Mr. West [Bland West, an attorney on the investigating team] and the other members . . . in Washington are developing a list of individuals from B Co . . . to be interrogated in the CONUS [Continental United States] when we return.

The two Vietnamese women were not found, but by mid-January the Peers Panel had set up a separate team to interrogate the former GIs of Bravo Company. Peers officially changed the scope of his inquiry on January 21, when he told Resor and Westmoreland in a memorandum that "there is evidence to show that other atrocities and/or violations of military regulations were committed in the other three hamlets of Son My village . . . In light of the above, it is recommended that the geographic scope of the final report be extended to include the entire Son My village." The approval came routinely. More than thirty members of Bravo Company were interrogated by February 5, and soon after the Panel had at least four GIs and one officer, Lieutenant Thomas Willingham, under suspicion of murder.

The heavy questioning of Bravo Company stimulated press interest at the Pentagon, where military spokesmen had a standing rule against discussing any details of the Peers inquiry, but did provide a daily list of witnesses and their units. A few newspaper stories were published in early February pointing out that the Panel had broadened its probe of My Lai 4 to embrace the activities of Bravo Company, but no reporter was able to learn what had happened at My Khe 4. Spokesmen simply told the reporters that the Panel was investigating the entire Son My area, and not limiting itself to My Lai 4.

On February 10 the Army formally charged Captain Thomas Willingham, the Bravo Company platoon leader, with the unpremeditated murder of about twenty Vietnamese civilians. Willingham had been scheduled to leave active duty on that day, after three years of service. The charges were preferred against him at the last minute—as they were against Lieutenant Calley—in order to assure the military of jurisdiction. Few details of the case against Willingham were made public, although Pentagon officials did link the Willingham incident to the My Lai 4 operation. Willingham had earlier refused to testify during a brief appearance before the Panel. On February 18 the National Broadcasting Company interviewed two survivors of the My Khe 4 assault, who told how nearly a hundred villagers were killed there during the Task Force Barker operation. This time, however, the American press—still focused on My Lai 4— paid little attention to the story; an accurate UPI dispatch about the NBC report, for example, was published in eight paragraphs on page 24 of the *Washington Post*. Pentagon spokesmen told the *Post* separately that they were not discounting the possibility that NBC was accurate in its report, but added that they had not heard of any casualty estimates indicating that up to one hundred civilians were slain. No reporter in Vietnam or the United States chose to follow up on the story.

On February 21, 1970, Peers sent Resor and Westmoreland another memorandum advising them that twenty to twenty-five persons were suspected of offenses "which could be made the subject of court-martial charges." Some of those under suspicion had been members of Bravo Company. Under military law, the Peers Panel could not directly prefer charges on the cover-up offenses, but before the statute of limitations for such violations ran out March 16, had to submit its recommendations to a group of officers from the Judge Advocate General's Corps, who would determine if there was sufficient evidence against each suspect. "The bulk of these offenses," the memorandum said, "are affected by the statute of limitations." The other offenses—presumably the pending murder charges against members of Bravo Company—were not affected by the two-year rule.

Peers eventually presented a list of nineteen suspects who were still on active duty, only one of them from Bravo Company. Fourteen officers were charged, although many lawyers were convinced that the evidence was meager in some cases. One law officer defiantly refused to file charges against three of the suspects, but the three-star general solved that crisis by ordering one of his investigators, not a lawyer, to file the charges.*

---

* The five officers who were not charged were Lieutenant Calley and Captain Kotouc of the task force, both of whom were facing criminal charges; Colonel Dean E. Hutter, the senior military adviser to the 2nd ARVN Division in Quang Ngai City, accused of dereliction of duty and possible false swearing; and Lieutenant Colonels John Holladay and Francis Lewis, the chaplain, both accused of dereliction of duty for not ensuring that a proper investigation was conducted. The accusations in the cases of Hutter, Holladay, and Lewis were not pressed because of lack of evidence. The final Peers report also cited seven former military

The last few days were hectic. A special team of attorneys representing the Army's General Counsel's office also decided to review the evidence, and determined that it was sufficient. Peers had meetings with a number of top aides, including a three-hour session with Daniel Henkin, the Pentagon's chief spokesman, and others, to prepare for his news conference, scheduled for March 17. Meanwhile, another group of officers was reviewing the final one-volume summary report of the investigating team to decide how much material should be released to the press; fifty of the two hundred and sixty pages in the report were eventually published. The sections cleared for release dealt with the background of Quang Ngai Province, the training and make-up of the 11th Brigade and Task Force Barker, and the appropriate rules of regulations and command directives that were in effect on March 16, 1968. Withheld were sections summarizing the March 16 operations by Task Force Barker and the subsequent cover-up of the investigation. A section dealing with the investigators' conclusions and recommendations also was deleted.

The summary report, known as Volume I of the Peers Inquiry, analyzed Bravo Company's assault on My Khe 4 in great detail, revealing that the number of civilians killed there "may have been as high as ninety." Its final chapter, dealing with "Findings and Recommendations," listed as its first finding the fact that "during the period 16–19 March, 1968, U.S. Army troops of TF [Task Force] Barker, 11th Brigade, Americal Division, massacred a large number of noncombatants in two hamlets of Son My village, Quang Ngai Province, Republic of Vietnam." The thirty-two books of individual testimony that comprised Volume II of the

officers as suspects, although the Defense Department had no possible jurisdiction over the men.

Peers report included nearly three thousand pages of testimony taken from the Bravo Company officers and men. In addition, the Army's C.I.D. agency was then in the midst of an extensive investigation of the new allegations of the second Task Force Barker massacre. None of this information was hinted at during the Peers news conference at the Pentagon.

So, on March 17, 1970, the general announced that charges had been filed against the following officers:

—Major General Samuel Koster, accused of failure to obey lawful regulations and dereliction of duty.

—Brigadier General George Young, similarly accused of failing to obey regulations and dereliction.

—Colonel Oran Henderson, accused of dereliction, failure to obey regulations, making a false official statement, and false swearing.

—Colonel [then Lieutenant Colonel] Robert Luper, accused of failing to obey a lawful order.

—Colonel Nels Parson, failure to obey regulations and dereliction of duty.

—Lieutenant Colonel William Guinn, failure to obey regulations, dereliction, and false swearing.

—Lieutenant Colonel [then Major] David Gavin, failure to obey regulations, dereliction, and false swearing.

—Major Charles Calhoun, charged with dereliction and failure to report possible misconduct. (An earlier accusation that he helped plan a mission whose sole target was a civilian population was withdrawn.)

—Major Robert McKnight, accused of false swearing.

—Major Frederic Watke, accused of failing to obey regulations and dereliction.

—Captain [then Lieutenant] Kenneth Boatman, who was serving as an artillery observer with Bravo Company, was accused of failing to report possible misconduct. His connection with Bravo Company was not spelled out in the Army's press releases.

—Captain [then Lieutenant] Dennis Johnson, the intelligence officer for Charlie Company, was charged with failing to obey lawful regulations.

—Captain [then Lieutenant] Thomas Willingham, already facing unpremeditated murder charges, was accused of making false official statements and misprison [failing to report] of a felony.

—Captain Ernest Medina, also charged with murder, was accused of misprison of a felony.

The press properly focused attention on the charges against Koster, the West Point superintendent. He and Young were the first Army generals in eighteen years to face a possible court-martial. At the news conference, reporters were told that much of the Peers material, including the transcripts of interviews, "cannot be made public at this time because of the possible prejudice to the military justice against the fourteen officers who have been charged this past weekend."

Despite that statement, there seemed to be little legal justification for withholding from the public information about the second massacre at My Khe 4. Peers did announce to the press: "Our inquiry clearly established that a tragedy of major proportions occurred there [in Son My village] on that day." One lawyer, who worked with the Peers Panel in drawing up the press release, asked during an interview with me why word of My Khe 4 was omitted, said, "It's a good question. I can't help you because I don't remember anything about it." There was no mention of the tragedy one and a half miles away from My Lai 4, he said, during the last few days when the first volume of the Peers report was being edited, and final charges were being drawn up. One senior Pentagon official, who also was involved with the report, downgraded the significance of Bravo Company's action during an interview with me in mid-1971. "One of the problems with that action [Bravo Company's] was that, although we had some information, it was really a fringe benefit of the Peers investigation," the official said. Peers was prepared to answer questions at his news conference about the second massacre, the source said, but it was agreed to try to keep the case quiet: "We were very much afraid of scaring off some of the B Company witnesses." A similar concern for the rights of potential defendants was expressed in the Peers' summary Volume I report, which noted that "the full story must await the completion of ongoing criminal investigations and any resulting prosecutions." The concern about frightening off potential witnesses with pre-trial publicity may have been legally sound, but the C.I.D. never did complete its investigation of My Khe 4 after the Peers Panel disbanded, although even a cursory examination of the Bravo Company testimony accumulated by Peers demonstrated that a significant atrocity had taken place. No further charges were filed in connection with My Khe 4.

At his news conference, Peers was asked: ". . . Is there any evidence that the type of behavior that the charges [against the officers] are based on was more widespread than what happened at My Lai on March 16? In other

words, other days or other places?" The general's answer
was unequivocal: "If there is, I have no knowledge of it. It
was not brought out to me in the evidence and I, personally,
from my roughly thirty months in South Vietnam, I had no
knowledge of anything that would approximate this." The
next question dealt with Bravo Company: "What about in
the Son My area in that day? You have charges placed
against a member of Company B [Willingham] who was not
in My Lai village." Peers' answer was a classic example of
obfuscation: "This is the reason why, if you will read that
[the censored version of Volume I of his report] very carefully, it was expanded to include Son My village, as compared to My Lai 4 actually, because when we got to South
Vietnam, we found that My Lai 4, when we say My Lai 4,
they [the Vietnamese] didn't know what we were talking
about . . . What really is involved, what you might say in
My Lai 4, encompassed several of the subhamlets, of which
My Lai 4 is one of them . . . But Bravo Company was not
in that area, they were in another area further to the east.
But it's all encompassed within the greater area of Son My
village, and that is why we refer to it now as Son My village
rather than try to delineate it to that one piece of terrain,
My Lai 4." None of the reporters pressed the issue despite
Peers' failure to answer the question. After the news conference, a source said, Peers stopped by a colleague's office
and exclaimed, "Three hours of hell [referring to the
briefings before the news conference], and there were no
tough questions asked."

No attempt was made in the final Volume I report to deal
with the continuing and more substantial issues raised by
My Lai 4 and My Khe 4: the military attitudes; the caliber
of officers; the training techniques; the promotion system—

these and other factors basic to the Army itself.* Instead, the summary volume limited itself to three comments about the adequacy of the Army's policies, directives, and training as revealed by the two massacres. First, it said that the existing policies "expressed a clear intent" regarding the proper treatment of noncombatants and prisoners. Second, it noted with comment that the regulations failed to provide procedures for the reporting of a war crime to superior officers when the officers participated in or sanctioned the crime in question. Third, the personnel in the 11th Brigade were described as not being adequately trained in the provisions of the Geneva Convention, nor were they aware of their responsibilities for the reporting of war crimes. (Elsewhere in Volume I, specifics were cited: "Evidence of scattered incidents involving the mistreatment, rape, and possibly the murder of Vietnamese by 11th Brigade soldiers prior to the Son My operation indicates that a permissive attitude existed and was not uncovered and corrected under BG [Brigadier General] Lipscomb's command."—Lipscomb preceded Henderson as brigade commander.) The sole recommendation provided by the final Peers Report, made after a 250-page review of the atrocities at My Lai 4 and My Khe 4, was the following: "Consideration [should] be given to the modification of applicable policies, directives, and

---

* During a conversation in November, 1971, with one of the senior officials of the Peers Panel, I mentioned my complaint about the narrow scope of the inquiry. Without hesitation, the official noted that the directive issued to General Peers in November, 1969, by General Westmoreland and Army Secretary Resor clearly indicated that Peers was only to involve himself in a study of the "nature and scope" of the early Army investigations into My Lai 4. With that limitation, the official suggested, it was impossible to attempt an analysis of the Army as an institution. In effect, the official was saying that Peers and others on the Panel were merely following orders, a position similar to that invoked by Lieutenant Calley and other My Lai defendants during their courts-martial.

training standards in order to correct the apparent deficiencies noted . . . above."

A few hours after Peers' news conference, the military began reacting predictably: Major General Winant Sidle, chief of Army public information, told a newsman that measures to speed up the reporting of alleged war crimes already were under study by the Department of the Army. Yet there was nothing in the next few months to indicate that any recommendations of the Peers Panel were being implemented; there was no sign that the system would change; no such demand had been made by the Army's investigation. In fact, it became increasingly clear after March 17, 1970, that Peers and his investigating team had served as a palliative for the Army, faced with serious public relations and morale problems.

18

The System Prevails

*I*n the days and weeks immediately after Lieutenant General Peers' report, some high-ranking Pentagon officials and Army men with access to it began to rationalize how a group of GIs could massacre 347 Vietnamese civilians and not get immediately detected. It was agreed that the four men directly in positions of command responsibility at My Lai 4 were misfits: all men who were borderline officer material. All were "mustangs," men who enlisted in the service and later went through Officer Candidate School. Calley, so the reasoning went, was a junior college dropout; Medina was an overaged mustang; Barker, who never finished college, enlisted in the Army through the National Guard; and Henderson was described as a man who had enlisted in the Army in 1939 and then waited four years—in the midst of World War II—to receive a commission. If one of those men had been a graduate of West Point or the Citadel, many Army men seriously told me, the massacre would have been reported.

The theory was said to be shared by Peers and others on his investigating team. One high former defense official, queried by me about the "mustang" theory, explained, "I think it would be very hard anywhere and any time in Vietnam to find a situation where you had four echelons of command with this kind of background."

Even if true, that coincidence could not account for the conduct of Major General Koster and Brigadier General Young; nor could it explain General John Donaldson's possible involvement in the destruction of documents after My Lai 4.

On April 1, 1970, two weeks after the Panel announced its findings, the cover-up charges against Captain Ernest Medina were withdrawn by legal officers at Third Army headquarters, Fort McPherson, Georgia, where Medina and other Charlie Company defendants accused of murder at My Lai 4 were assigned.* An Army statement explained that the accusation of misprison of a felony was dropped

---

* Twelve officers and enlisted men—including Medina—eventually were charged by the Army with murder or assault with intent to commit murder at My Lai 4. Only one of them—Lieutenant Calley—was convicted after his trial in 1971 at Fort Benning, Georgia. (Calley and Sergeant David Mitchell were both charged before the Army's 1970 decision to consolidate the criminal cases at Fort McPherson; thus each was tried at his duty post—Calley at Benning, and Mitchell at Fort Hood, Texas.) Murder charges were dismissed before trial at Fort McPherson against Sergeant Esequiel Torres, Corporal Kenneth Schiel, Specialist Fours William F. Doherty and Robert W. T'Souvas, and Privates Max D. Hutson and Gerald A. Smith. An assault charge was dismissed against Sergeant Kenneth L. Hodges. Four men were acquitted after trials. Captain Eugene Kotouc was acquitted of a maiming charge at Fort McPherson (earlier assault charges were dropped), and Sergeants Charles E. Hutto and David Mitchell were acquitted of assault with intent to kill charges. Mitchell's trial was the first to begin in connection with the My Lai 4 investigation. Captain Ernest Medina was found not guilty on September 22, 1971, of premeditated murder, involuntary manslaughter, and two counts of assault after his trial in August, 1971, at Fort McPherson.

"because it is not common practice to charge an individual
with the commission of an offense and its concealment."
Medina was instead accused of being responsible for all the
My Lai 4 murders committed by the men under his command.

The dismissal of Medina's cover-up charges was reasonable. But two months later the Third Army announced it
had dismissed both the murder and cover-up charges
against Captain Willingham of Bravo Company. A
statement explained that commanding officers there had
"determined that based on available evidence, no further action should be taken in the prosecution of these
charges."

The other accused officers, including Generals Koster
and Young, were administratively transferred to the First
Army headquarters at Fort Meade, Maryland, pending a
review of the charges against them. Under military law, the
commanding general of the First Army, Lieutenant General
Jonathan O. Seaman, first had to review the charges to determine if they were sufficient to convene an Article 32
hearing, the Army's equivalent of a grand jury, or pre-trial,
proceeding. The investigating officer of an Article 32 has
the power, after taking testimony, to order the defendant to
stand court-martial. One high-ranking official, looking back
on the decision to assign the defendants to the First Army
headquarters, described it as one of the biggest mistakes of
the My Lai 4 probe. "We didn't investigate Seaman that
carefully," the source said during a mid-1971 interview. "He
was just sort of the best man who was available." Within a
year the charges against eleven of the twelve officers at Fort
Meade who had been named by the Peers Panel were dismissed.

Seaman, a West Point graduate and former Vietnam division commander nearing mandatory retirement age, dismissed all cover-up charges on June 23, 1970, against General Young, Colonel Parson and Major McKnight. A statement issued at Fort Meade said Seaman acted after "his evaluation that the charges were unsupported by the evidence." In Young's case, Seaman acted one day after he received a dismissal recommendation from Colonel John P. Stafford, Jr., the staff judge advocate for the First Army. Stafford obviously took General Young's defense at face value, and argued the very narrow questions of what Major Watke or Lieutenant Colonel Holladay may have told the general and what Koster may or may not have ordered him to investigate. Stafford's discussion of the case against Young took up two paragraphs—one each to discuss what Young had been told and what his obligations to investigate were—in a two-and-one-half-page recommendation to General Seaman:

Although LTC [Lieutenant Colonel] Holladay says BG [Brigadier General] Young was informed of facts which would constitute a war crime, both Major Watke and BG Young corroborate the fact that BG Young was aware of only the confrontation and the indiscriminate fire. This view is also corroborated by the fact that Col. Parson and Col. Henderson claim to have received only that limited information from the same source. The preponderance of the evidence further supports that BG Young reported the lesser amount of information to MG [Major General] Koster, which is apparently all the information he knew of.

The evidence pertaining to BG Young's requirement to supervise Col. Henderson's investigation is tenuous at best, being based not on specific directive but only on implication. Assuming the duty existed, however, Col. Henderson's activity of reporting directly to MG Koster and the fact that MG Koster accepted this report, weakens the theory of BG Young's dereliction . . .

Using the same set of facts one year later, Secretary of Army Stanley Resor concluded that Young "did not meet the required standards" of a general. Resor's brief was prepared in defense of his subsequent decision to censure the general administratively and to strip him of his Distinguished Service Medal. Resor's statement said:

General Young was informed by officers in the aviation unit the day following the incident at My Lai that a serious confrontation had occurred between American ground and helicopter personnel. There has been some dispute as to whether General Young was also given information concerning the killing of civilians and the presence of a number of bodies in a ditch. General Young discussed the matter with General Koster and was instructed to have a subordinate commander [Henderson] initiate an investigation. Subsequently, General Young made inquiries of the commander concerning the progress of the investigation.

Prior to the time General Young received the report from the aviation officers, he was aware of and had commented to Koster on the unusual nature of the operation at My Lai on March 16, 1968. He also knew that a very high number of enemy killed had been claimed, with a disproportionately low number of weapons captured and very low American casualties, in an action purportedly against a unit which General Young knew to be a combat-experienced VC battalion.

General Young therefore knew as of the 17th or 18th of March 1968 not only that the operation on March 16 had produced results of an unusual nature, but also that during the operation an almost unheard of confrontation had occurred between American ground troops and a helicopter pilot . . .

Despite the fact that he possessed this information, and that General Koster had utilized him as the officer responsible for seeing that the subordinate commander initiated an investigation, General Young appears to have disassociated himself from the substance of the subsequent investigation. He made no effort to review or discuss with General Koster either the verbal report which General Koster had received from the commander or a subsequent written report which General Koster instructed the commander to prepare. It is General Young's position that he was unaware that the allegations being investigated included the actual deaths of noncombatant civilians. Assuming that to be the case, it indicates the inadequate degree to which General Young involved himself in the investigation, for it is clear that General Koster and the subordinate commander, as well as various others involved in the investigation, understood that a central issue in the investigation was that of civilian casualties. General Young did not seek to assure himself that a satisfactory resolution had been made respecting the confrontation, a confrontation which had serious implications concerning cooperation between infantry and helicopter units in future operations. He did not review the matter either with the aviation commanders who had originally brought the matter to him or with the commander of the infantry task force conducting the My Lai operation.

I have concluded that General Young did not exercise the degree of initiative and assume the responsibility which is expected with respect to a general officer serving as an assistant division commander.

Young, after losing a legal battle to avoid censure (although he did fight off an attempt to reduce him in rank to colonel), retired from the Army on June 30, 1971.

On July 28, 1970, General Seaman announced that he had decided that seven of the twelve officers under his jurisdiction—including Koster—were to be held for Article 32 hearings. The officers were, besides Koster, Colonel Henderson, Lieutenant Colonels William Guinn and David Gavin, Majors Charles Calhoun and Frederic Watke, and Captain Dennis Johnson. But cover-up charges against two other officers, Colonel Robert Luper, the artillery battalion commander at My Lai 4, and Captain Kenneth Boatman, who served as Bravo Company's forward artillery officer, were dismissed. The Article 32 sessions began at Fort Meade in August and were closed to the public.

On January 6, 1971, after the hearings, General Seaman dismissed charges "because of insufficient evidence" against four officers. Those freed were Guinn, Gavin, Calhoun and Watke.

Twenty-two days later General Seaman also dismissed the charges against General Koster "in the interest of justice." A Pentagon statement said that Seaman had found "some evidence" that Koster had heard about the deaths of the twenty civilians, but determined that the major general was not guilty of any "intentional abrogation of responsibilities." Seaman's action was based on a four-page memorandum that was submitted to him October 27, 1970, by Major General B. F. Evans, Jr., the investigating officer for Koster's Article 32 hearing. It is not known why Seaman waited nearly three months before announcing the findings, which he accepted in full. The general, however, did issue a statement acknowledging that there was some evidence that Koster did not properly report the deaths of twenty civilians to higher headquarters, and also did not thoroughly investigate the matter. But Seaman added that he considered "the long and honorable career of General Koster" and the fact that Koster did not intentionally lapse in deciding to dismiss all the charges. Evans' confidential memorandum—as did Colonel Stafford's in General Young's case—conceded every point of dispute to Koster, who was accused of violating seven Army regulations.

Specification 1 dealt with Koster's alleged failure to report the twenty known civilian casualties to higher headquarters, as prescribed by Army regulations. Evans managed to say, after agreeing that such a report should have been filed, "However, I do not consider General Koster personally responsible for submitting the report. A commander would normally expect this to be accomplished by a member of his staff."

Specification 2 alleged that Koster violated the regulations because his command did not report to higher headquarters that civilians were killed by artillery fire. Evans' analysis simply ignored the important point—brought out during the hearings—that the artillery fire was directed right at the hamlet of My Lai 4, in violation of international law. Evans also said nothing about civilian casualties, limiting his comments to the accuracy of the artillery fire: "There was no evidence presented which indicated that the artillery fire placed on My Lai on March 16, 1968, was misdirected. It was a preparatory fire mission which was executed as planned."

Specification 3 related to Koster's alleged failure to report a serious criminal offense to higher headquarters: "There has been no evidence presented which would indicate that the accused was aware that there had been criminal acts committed or that the deaths of foreign nationals had occurred other than by combat operations. Logically, then, General Koster cannot be charged with reporting something that he did not have knowledge of."

Specifications 4 and 5 alleged that Koster knew or had reason to believe that a war crime had been committed. Evans based his rejection of those complaints on the low credibility of the Vietnamese documents that were floating around headquarters: "In my opinion one could not reasonably expect General Koster to accept the VC document [the propaganda leaflet] or the village chief's report [to Lieutenant Tan of Son Tinh District] as bona-fide allegations of a war crime."

Specifications 6 and 7 dealt with Koster's dereliction of duty in not challenging the initial oral reports from Colonel Henderson and General Young and the subsequent written reports. Evans concluded: "There appears to be no reason why General Koster should not have expected a complete and truthful and accurate report from two of his senior officers. It is my opinion that General Koster, in accepting the oral report of investigation, did what one could reasonably expect of a division commander under like circumstances." Evans similarly concluded that Koster was acting reasonably in accepting the later written reports. The investigating officer did concede, however, that "examining it now after more than two and one half years, it is obvious that General Koster should have challenged every element of the report. If he had challenged the report of investigation, a subsequent investigation might have brought to light the true facts." At this point, General Evans went so far as to indicate there may have been nothing that Koster could have done after My Lai 4 to get at the truth: "However, there is no assurance that this would be the case, for if there were a conspiracy to keep the facts from General Koster, a second investigation may have been just as unrevealing."

Evans concluded that Koster's "testimony was completely truthful. It is also my belief," Evans added in summary, "that there was no attempt by General Koster to hinder the investigation of the My Lai incident . . . The [testimonial] letters included with [the] thirty-two investigation attesting to General Koster's character coupled with his past record of outstanding service would render it highly unlikely that General Koster would be a party to any subterfuge or dishonesty." Evans' reverence for Koster's truthfulness was based, in large measure, on the testimony indicating that the May, 1968, final report did exist, as the general had claimed during the hearings. The thornier question of how much Koster knew about that May, 1968, report was dismissed by Evans: "If this were a 'manufactured' report, I am convinced that General Koster had no knowledge of it."

The dismissal of the Koster charges brought an immediate outcry from Robert MacCrate. He told *The New York Times,* in his first public comment on My Lai in ten months, that "I am shocked by the action of the commanding general [Seaman] in dismissing at this time the charges against General Koster." MacCrate's criticisms were not directed toward the substance of Seaman's actions, however, but its timing. "Charges are still pending against men who were within his [Koster's] command" at the time of the incident, the attorney said, referring to the officers under investigation at Fort Meade. He accused Seaman of cutting off "the orderly progress of the inquiry of the chain of command."

Aside from MacCrate, there was little indignation over the Army's decision to drop charges against the senior officer involved in the My Lai 4 massacre; most newspapers—whose information was limited to what they had been told by the Army—treated the dismissal as a routine one-day story. And only one Congressman, Samuel S. Stratton, a New York Republican who served on the Son My investigating subcommittee, challenged the decision. Stratton, a former Navy officer, called Koster's dismissal "a grave miscarriage of military justice. To drop the charges against the top officer responsible in this situation," the congressman, usually a military booster, added, "raises once again the whole question of a military whitewash." Stratton then made the kind of threat the Army understood: "If the Army system is either unwilling or unable to produce the facts and to publish the guilty in this case, then I am inclined to feel that we do need some independent tribunal which will be higher and separate from the ordinary military-controlled court-martial proceeding to make a final determination in this case."

Within a day an Army spokesman revealed that General Seaman had indeed issued a letter of censure to Koster—along with throwing out the charges—for "his failure to report civilian casualties and [his failure] to insure that the circumstances of these casualties were investigated promptly and thoroughly." There was no attempt to explain why the letter of censure had not been made public the day before.

A few days later, Stratton gave his fellow House members a lengthy dossier on Koster's alleged derelictions, as culled from the censored Son My subcommittee's report that had been published the previous July. Once again few newspapers paid attention to the congressman's charges. "I am afraid," Stratton told the House, "that this is a case where the ground rules of the mythical WPPA, the West Point Protective Association, have taken precedence over the welfare of the nation and the fundamental right of the American people to know the facts: never mind what happens to the Army or to the country, just make sure we keep our paid-up members out of embarrassment and hot water." The congressman also questioned the timing of the Pentagon's revelation that a letter of censure had been given to Koster. "One cannot help wondering why this censure action was not made public at the time the original announcement was made that charges were being dropped?" Stratton said. "Why was the impression given that General Koster was being let off completely free and clear? Was the Army perhaps waiting to test public reaction to their decision to sweep the Koster case under the rug?"

Koster was subsequently demoted by administrative fiat to a brigadier general and stripped of a Distinguished Service Medal, an action he unsuccessfully fought. On August 1, 1971, he began a new assignment in what amounted to a retirement position—as deputy commander of the Army's

Test and Evaluation Command at the Aberdeen Proving Grounds in Maryland. Secretary Resor's statement justifying the administrative action against Koster contrasted sharply—especially in his view of the responsibility of a commander—with Major General Evans' argument for dismissing the case. Resor wrote:

A great deal of information suggesting that a possible tragedy of serious proportions had occurred at My Lai was either known directly to General Koster, or was readily available in the operational logs and other records of the division. He did not utilize the investigative staff resources available in the division either to conduct an investigation, or to review the investigations which were conducted. In so doing, he took upon himself a much greater personal burden than would otherwise have been the case.

As the division commander, General Koster clearly must be held responsible for ascertaining the accuracy of the information which he had about My Lai, as that information indicated that his troops might have been guilty of serious misconduct. Any other conclusions would render essentially meaningless the concept of command responsibility accompanying senior positions of authority.

On February 26, 1971, the First Army completed its review of the year-old charges by announcing that Colonel Oran Henderson would be tried by a general court-martial for his role in the cover-up of My Lai 4. At the same time Lieutenant General Seaman dismissed all charges against Captain Dennis Johnson, the intelligence officer, on grounds of insufficient evidence. Thus Henderson became the only officer out of fourteen initially charged to be required to face a court-martial.*

---

* In August, 1971, Army Secretary Robert F. Froehlke, who replaced Resor the month before, initiated administrative punishment against five of the accused officers. Pending appeals, Colonels Nels Parson and Rob-

The colonel's military attorneys depicted their client as a
scapegoat, and claimed that he would not have been
charged if Congressman Stratton hadn't begun objecting to
the Koster dismissal. (One source told me that more than
seven thousand pages of testimony were taken during Henderson's five-month Article 32 hearing at Fort Meade.)* At
the conclusion of the hearing in January—just before the
Stratton attacks in the House—the investigating officer dismissed two of the four specifications against Henderson,
but found some evidence to support the complaints of dereliction of duty and false swearing. The officer did not recommend a court-martial, sources said, instead suggesting
that Henderson be given a form of nonjudicial Article 15
punishment.

General Seaman's decision to proceed with the court-
martial, however, was announced shortly after Army Secre-

---

ert Luper were stripped of their Legions of Merit and given letters of reprimand; Major Charles Calhoun was removed from the list of eligible
majors for promotion to lieutenant colonel; Captain Dennis Johnson was
given a letter of reprimand. The identity of the fifth officer was not
known. Four enlisted men who served with Charlie Company and were
cleared—as were the officers—of criminal charges, also were handed administrative punishments by Froehlke. The four—Sergeants Kenneth
Hodges and Esequiel Torres, Corporal Kenneth Schiel, and Private Max
Hutson—were told that they would be honorably discharged from the
Army at the convenience of the government. Details of Froehlke's actions were leaked to the Associated Press and published on August 18,
1971. The AP, however, was not told the identity of the punished officers,
although the names and hometowns of the enlisted men were provided
and published.
* More than 100,000 pages of testimony resulted from the Peers Panel
hearings; Article 32 hearings; and courts-martial in connection with the
My Lai 4 and My Khe 4 investigations. Some of the published Peers
Panel material included expensive reproductions of color photographs.
Despite all the evidence, the net result, as of fall, 1971, was one conviction and a few administrative slaps on the wrist. The cost of all this has
never been made public.

tary Resor began his administrative proceedings to censure
Koster and Young. But Stratton, then the Army's chief
critic over its handling of the cover-up prosecutions, wasn't
pacified either by the administrative action or the filing of
charges against Henderson. Still unable to attract wide
press coverage, Stratton wrote an article for the editorial-
page section of *The New York Times* on March 8, 1971,
caustically pointing out that a letter of censure "has one
clear advantage over a court-martial; it keeps the general's
[Koster's] case out of the papers."

Yet Stratton's public criticisms of the Army over its handling of the Koster charges, as important as they were, still
did not bear on the crucial issue of the Army as an institution which was capable of covering up a My Lai 4 and ignoring a My Khe 4.

Neither did Colonel Henderson's subsequent court-martial, which began August 23, 1971, at Fort Meade, and
quickly became mired in technical disputes over, among
other things, the validity of the colonel's testimony before
the Peers Panel. Henderson's attorneys also spent weeks attempting to establish the existence of the May, 1968, Barker
investigation, although the evidence before the Panel made
it clear that the document was a fraud. The trial, which
dragged on through the fall, was marked by much self-serving and less than candid testimony. At least two key witnesses changed testimony. Warrant Officer Hugh Thompson, a captain by late 1971, testified that he was no longer
positive that he had made a statement about My Lai 4 to
Colonel Henderson two days after the massacre. (Before the
Peers Panel, Henderson, among others, had identified the
pilot as the man to whom he had spoken.) Warrant Officer
Jerry Culverhouse, who also had been promoted to captain,
told the court-martial that he no longer could say whether

Henderson "was or was not" the man to whom he reported on March 18, 1968. Lawrence Colburn, the third aviator who told Henderson about My Lai 4, wasn't permitted to make a courtroom identification by the military judge, who ruled that Army investigators had marred his recollection by showing him photographs of the colonel. On December 17, 1971, Henderson was found not guilty of the cover-up charges.

In the end, only legal technicalities and personalities were being debated.

It's unlikely that any other atrocities of the magnitude and character of My Lai 4 have taken place in South Vietnam, but how many My Khe 4's have there been?

By the fall of 1971 the massacre by Bravo Company was forgotten, although in that slaughter lay an important truth about the American Army. Bravo Company killed between forty and a hundred innocent Vietnamese civilians with impunity on the morning of March 16, 1968. There was no Lieutenant Calley ordering other men to "waste them." There was no confrontation with a helicopter pilot, and no protesting and screaming over a radio network.

My Lai 4 was out of the ordinary, but it was not isolated. My Khe 4, however, was just another atrocity; and that atrocity was covered up—after its uncovering in the midst of the My Lai 4 investigation—by a lieutenant general and a Secretary of the Army unwilling or unable to face up to its meaning. Even the best generals in the Army and its highest civilian officials have a point at which they, like the Vietnamese at My Lai 4 and My Khe 4, become victims.

Chapter Notes

1. Three Hundred Forty-Seven

For full accounts of the My Lai 4 massacre from the point of view of the GIs who participated in it, see my earlier book, *My Lai 4: A Report on the Massacre and Its Aftermath* (New York, Random House, 1970), and Richard Hammer's detailed account, *One Morning in the War* (New York, Coward, McCann & Geoghegan, Inc., 1970). The Ridenhour letter is reprinted in full in *My Lai 4* and also in Richard Hammer's subsequent book on Calley, *The Court-Martial of Lt. Calley* (New York, Coward, McCann & Geoghegan, Inc., 1971). Also see *Calley,* written by three Associated Press reporters, Arthur Everett, Kathryn Johnson, and Harry F. Rosenthal (Dell paperbacks, New York, 1971).

The news release extolling Task Force Barker's victory was made a part of the Peers report, as Exhibit M-61 in one of the books containing supplemental reports, documents, etc. The news release, numbered 76–68, was published by the Office of Information of the United States Military Command; it noted that: "Thus far, 128 enemy have been killed in an engagement between elements of the Americal Division's 11th Light Infantry Brigade and an enemy force of unknown strength. . . . This morning at 0750, a company from the brigade made contact with the enemy force when the company entered an area that had been subjected to artillery preparatory fires. Another company from the brigade . . . was inserted into the area at 0910 approximately . . . [two miles] east-northeast of the point of original contact. As the companies moved toward each other sweeping the area, they engaged the enemy in sporadic contacts throughout the day. . . . At last report the contact was continuing." Most of the subsequent news stories were based on the information in the release. For details on the author's role in making My Lai 4 public, see "How I Broke the My Lai Story," *Saturday Review,* July 11, 1970, and "The Story Everyone Ignored," *Columbia Journalism Review,* Winter, 1969–1970.

Since the Peers report findings were first made public in March, 1970, the Army has given every newsman who asks about its public release more or less the same answer, such as this one on October 7, 1970: "Public release of most of the Peers–MacCrate inquiry must be deferred at this time because of its prejudicial relationship to pending military justice proceedings. Some portions of the report were released on March 17, 1970 [a reference to the heavily censored version of Volume I of the Peers report that was handed out] . . . and it anticipated that the remainder of the report, except for portions classified for national security reasons, can be released later." The official Army census of civilian casualties at My Lai 4 was completed on February 17, 1970, and signed by Colonel W. H. Brandenburg, then acting as the provost marshal for the Army. It was Exhibit M-124 before the Peers Panel. Volume I, which was still classified as of December, 1971, is entitled "The Report of the Investigation." It is dated March 14, 1970.

2. The Other Massacre

Lawrence L. Congleton testified before the Peers Panel on January 29, 1970; I interviewed him in Evansville, Indiana, on May 27, 1971. Donald R. Hooton appeared before the Panel on February 17, 1970; I interviewed him in Jackson, Michigan, on May 3, 1971. Lieutenant Kenneth W. Boatman testified on January 19, 1970. Larry G. Holmes testified on January 23, 1971. Mario Fernandez appeared on February 3, 1971. Barry P. Marshall testified two days later. Ronald J. Esterling's testimony was given on January 29, 1970. Terry Reid refused to appear before the Army investigating team, but permitted me to interview him on May 26, 1971, at the home of his brother in Baraboo, Wisconsin. Mrs. Nguyen Dhi Bay was interrogated by André C. R. Feher of the Criminal Investigation Division (C.I.D.) on December 17, 1969, at her hospital bedside in Chu Lai. Two other survivors of the My Khe 4 massacre were interviewed by C.I.D. agents on March 15, 1970, just as the Peers Panel was completing its work. The survivors, Le Thi Hien and Nguyen Thi Hai, both estimated that ninety-seven persons were killed by the American soldiers. Marvin G. B. Jones testified on February 7, 1970. Task Force Barker's log for March 16, 1968, was Exhibit M-14 before the Peers Panel. Richard F. Silva testified on February 19, 1970. Morris G. Michener's appearance was on January 22, 1970; James L. Sweeney testified on February 18.

3. A Division at War

Koster's assignments are listed in his official Army biography, available from the Department of the Army at the

Pentagon. Lieutenant General Bruce Palmer testified on February 25, 1970; he was the highest-ranking officer to appear before the Peers Panel. The appearance of Lieutenant Colonel Cecil E. Granger, Jr., took place on February 14, 1970. Lieutenant Colonel Jesmond D. Balmer appeared two times, on December 18, 1969, and on February 13, 1970. Lieutenant Colonel (Retired) Charles Anistranski testified on January 12, 1970. He later refused to testify again, but did allow me to interview him in his Wilkes-Barre, Pennsylvania, office on March 24, 1971. James R. Ritchie III was interviewed in his Hyattsville, Maryland, home on June 4, 1971; he testified on February 12, 1970. Colonel Nels A. Parson Jr., appeared three times before the Panel, on December 12, 1969, and February 14 and 17, 1970. Major John D. Beasley III also testified on three occasions, December 22, 1969, and February 14 and 16, 1970. The information about Cushman's praise for Koster's high kill ratio came from an Army source. The Americal Division's poor showing (footnote) during the battle for the Special Forces camp was the subject of a special inquiry by one of the Peers investigators. Koster's attitude toward reporting the loss was described to the Panel by Colonel Jack L. Treadwell on January 30, 1970. A specially prepared fact sheet on the operation and the heavy losses was prepared in early February, 1970, and became Exhibit M-115 in the Peers report. Among the reported allied equipment losses were ten aircraft, seven cannons, fifteen mortars, fifteen trucks, and twenty-eight radios. Total American casualties were 183 men, including 33 Marines. Vietnamese losses were placed at 508. Although Koster allegedly acted improperly, the matter was eventually dropped.

Lieutenant Colonel Warren J. Lucas' testimony came on January 15, 1970. Lieutenant Colonel Anthony B. Herbert compared reporting a war crime in South Vietnam with a Mafia confession during a brief interview June 2, 1971, with Robert Goralski on the NBC "Nightly News" television program. Father Carl E. Creswell, formerly a captain, testified on January 12, 1970; his interview with me took place on May 12, 1971. Lieutenant General Robert E. Cushman, who later became deputy director of the Central Intelligence Agency, testified on December 22, 1969. Lieutenant Colonel Stanley E. Holton's appearance was on January 24, 1970. Marine Brigadier General Carl W. Hoffman testified on January 15, 1970.

For information on the allegations regarding prisoner abuses, contact the Vietnam Veterans Against the War (VVAW), 25 West 26th Street, New York, N.Y. 10010, which held forty-seven public hearings into war crimes between February, 1970, and September, 1971. The testimony of its "Winter Soldiers" hearings, held in January, 1971, in Detroit, Michigan, received scant newspaper attention at the time, although much of the proceedings were published in the *Congressional Record* on April 6 and 7, 1971. A series of similar hearings has been sponsored by the Citizens Commission of Inquiry (CCI), 156 Fifth Ave., room 1005, New York, N.Y., 10010, another veterans' anti-war group which was organized in November, 1969, following the first public disclosures of the My Lai 4 massacre. CCI sponsored more than a dozen hearings across the nation by December, 1970, culminating with its "National Veterans' Inquiry into War Crimes," held December 1–3, 1970, in a Washington, D.C., hotel. The hearings received somewhat better press coverage (see " 'We can't sleep, man,' " by Lucian K. Truscott IV, *The Village Voice,* December 10, 1970), but not as much as at least one leading journalist thought they should: see "New Vietnam Atrocity Charges Little Noticed," by

Jules Witcover, *Los Angeles Times,* December 8, 1970. The full transcript of the CCI hearings was published, however, in the *Congressional Record* on March 1, 1971, and much of the material later appeared as part of *Standard Operation Procedure,* by James S. Kunen (Avon paperback, New York, 1971). On April 26–29, 1971, a number of former GIs and officers testified about war crimes before an ad hoc Congressional committee chaired by Representative Ronald V. Dellum, California Democrat, and endorsed by twenty-two Congressmen. Newspaper coverage of those sessions was good. For example, see "Ex-intelligence Agents Tell of Torturing Viets," by Robert Gruenberg, *Chicago Daily News* service, in the *Washington Evening Star* for April 28, 1971. An excellent compilation of alleged American violations of international law in South Vietnam—as reported by newspapers—is *In the Name of America,* a study published in January, 1968, by the Clergy and Laymen Concerned about Vietnam and distributed by E. P. Dutton & Co., Inc., 201 Park Ave. So., New York, N.Y. 10003. Also see *Crimes of War,* edited by Richard A. Falk, Gabriel Kolko, and Robert Jay Lifton (New York, Random House, 1971).

General Samuel W. Koster's initial appearances before the Peers Panel were on December 15 and 16, 1969; he was recalled on February 18, 1970. Lieutenant Colonel Patrick H. Dionne, who later served as Koster's information officer at West Point, appeared on January 16, 1970. General Palmer's June 15, 1968, letter to Chief of Staff Harold K. Johnson was Exhibit M-123 in the Peers report.

4. The 11th Brigade

General Andy A. Lipscomb testified on January 23, 1970. Colonel Oran K. Henderson spent more hours before the

Peers Panel than any other witness, beginning December 2, 1969. He returned on December 11, December 19, and his final appearance was on February 13, 1970. Henderson's transcribed testimony filled more than 400 pages. Lieutenant Colonel Richard K. Blackledge testified two times, on December 3, 1969, and February 12, 1970. He also permitted me to interview him briefly by telephone from an Atlanta, Georgia, motel room (he had just testified in a court-martial case at Fort McPherson) on April 29, 1971. Joseph W. Walsh testified on February 3, 1970. Captain Donald J. Keshel testified on January 19, 1970. Michael C. Adcock appeared on January 29, 1970; I interviewed him at his Roanoke, Alabama, home on May 25, 1971. John Waldeck of Grand Rapids, Michigan, was interviewed by telephone on June 24, 1971, in Edgerton, Wisconsin, where he was teaching at a private school. William Bezanson of Detroit, Michigan, now a member of the Vietnam Veterans Against the War, was interviewed April 18, 1971, at his home. "Operation Body Snatch" was described to me by an Army source. Sergeant Major Robert K. Gerberding testified on January 27, 1970. Dr. Brian Schoolfield testified on January 13, 1970; I interviewed him at his home in Flint, Michigan, on April 18, 1971. The 11th Brigade's official history was Exhibit R-18 before the Peers Panel. James E. Ford's testimony came on January 24, 1970.

Lieutenant Colonel William O. Glaff's footnoted comment about serving as a civil affairs and pacification adviser was made to the Panel on March 6, 1970. Major John L. Pittman testified on January 20, 1970. Ronald L. Ridenhour's testimony was taken on January 29, 1970; he subsequently gave me many interviews on his role in developing the massacre investigation. Arthur J. Dunn's testimony took place on December 22, 1969; he was then living in Forest

Park, Illinois. Jay A. Roberts, then living in Alexandria, Virginia, appeared before the Peers Panel on December 17, 1969; I interviewed him for this book (we had talked earlier when I was researching *My Lai 4*) on April 26, 1971. Frank D. Beardslee testified on January 31, 1970; I interviewed him at his home in Fenton, Michigan, on April 18, 1971. Many GIs who served with the 11th Brigade headquarters confirmed details of General Lipscomb's use of flares to bring his house trailer to brigade headquarters. Ronald L. Haeberle, then living in Rocky River, Ohio, testified on January 17, 1970, and subsequently told me about the interrogation during a later conversation.

5. Task Force Barker

The statistics about Task Force Barker's casualties were compiled by the Peers Panel and published in the censored version of Volume I of the "Report of the Department of the Army Review of the Preliminary Investigation into the My Lai Incident," which was distributed to the press on March 17, 1970. The disparity between the high total of enemy body count and the few captured weapons during Task Force Barker's two February operations also can be confirmed by statistics in the published Peers report.

Staff Sergeant Lones R. Warren, who was in charge of the task force's military police unit, testified before the Panel on January 21, 1970. He, like many others, would not discuss My Lai 4 with me during a subsequent telephone interview, nor would he agree to see me. Major Charles C. Calhoun testified on four days: December 5, 6 and 10, 1969, and February 10, 1970. He refused to answer questions during the February appearance. Captain Ernest L. Medina testified on December 4, 1969; he was accompanied by his attorney, F. Lee Bailey. Major Patrick M. Trinkle's testimony came on December 10, 1969, surprisingly early for someone who was not in Charlie Company or even in Task Force Barker at the time of My Lai 4. Donald R. Coker testified on February 18, 1970; he later permitted me to interview him briefly by telephone at his home in Dickinson, Texas, on September 10, 1971. See pages 4–11 and 4–12 of the censored Peers report for the Panel's description of the two February task force operations into Pinkville. Colonel Carl C. Ulsaker's testimony was given on January 14, 1970. Lieutenant Colonel Barker's March 24 after-action report dealing with the February operations was Exhibit R-12 before the Peers Panel.

6. Planning the Mission

Sergeant Cecil D. Hall testified on January 8, 1970, and was interviewed by me on November 1, 1971, by telephone from his home near Fort Leonard Wood, Missouri. Captain Eugene M. Kotouc testified on December 6, 1969; he was recalled on February 9, 1970, but refused to testify after being warned that he was suspected of offenses in connection with the My Lai 4 cover-up. Lieutenant Colonel William D. Guinn originally testified on December 17, 1969; he also refused to testify after his recall on February 11, 1970. Lieutenant Colonel Tommy P. Trexler testified on December 19, 1969. Captain Charles K. Wyndham's brief appearance before the Panel took place on January 29, 1970. Former Lieutenant Clarence E. Dukes, now living in Alma, Georgia, testified on January 23, 1970. Lieutenant Colonel Robert B. Luper's initial appearance before the Panel was on December 10, 1969; he was recalled on February 11–12, 1970. Captain Wayne E. Johnson testified on February 16, 1960.

The 1969 relocation drive that produced more than twice

the expected number of refugees in Son My was described
to the Panel by a number of witnesses who served on the
Quang Ngai province advisory team. The similarly short-
sighted operation in 1971 (footnote) was revealed in "New
Drive Begins in Area of My Lai," by Henry Kamm, *New
York Times,* April 1, 1971. The article also alluded to the
1969 relocation.

Captain Stephen J. Gamble told about the March 15
meeting at Landing Zone Dotti during his appearance before the Panel on December 16, 1969. Major Frederic W.
Watke appeared five times before the Peers Panel, on December 8, 10, 12, 19, 1969, and on February 10, 1970. Sergeant Nguyen Dinh Phu's testimony was taken in South
Vietnam on January 1–2, 1970.

7. The Intelligence.

Major David C. Gavin testified on two occasions, December 6, 1969, and February 11, 1970.

There are a number of excellent unclassified reference
sources on the Phoenix program in South Vietnam. The
most comprehensive, however, is *Vietnam: Policy and Pros-
pects, 1970,* the title for a series of published hearings before
the Committee on Foreign Relations, United States Senate,
into the "Civil Operations and Rural Development Support
Program" in South Vietnam, February 17, 18, 19, and 20,
and March 3, 14, 17, and 19, 1970 (U.S. Government Printing Office, Washington, 1970). Especially note testimony by
William E. Colby, deputy to the Military Assistance Command—Vietnam (MACV), for Civil Operations and Rural
Development (CORDS). A number of policy statements by
Colby regarding the Phoenix program are printed in full,
beginning on page 716 in the hearings. The specific statistics
on the number of neutralizations and yearly quotas can be

found on pages 726–7 of the volume. Other valuable references include "New Intelligence Push Attempts to Wipe Out Vietcong Underground," by Peter R. Kann, *Wall Street Journal*, September 5, 1968; "Elite 'Phoenix' Forces Hunt Vietcong Chiefs in an Isolated Village," also by Kann, *Wall Street Journal*, March 25, 1969; "The Controversial Operation Phoenix: How It Roots Out Vietcong Suspects," by James P. Sterba, *New York Times*, February 18, 1970; "U.S. Aides in Vietnam Scorn Phoenix Project," by Robert G. Kaiser, Jr., *Washington Post*, February 17, 1970; and "Political Liberty a Dispensable Saigon Luxury," by Richard Dudman, *St. Louis Post-Dispatch*, July 10, 1969. Also see a speech by Representative Jerome R. Waldie, California Republican, on Phoenix and the Province Interrogation Centers (PIC) as reprinted in the *Congressional Record*, April 22, 1971, p. E3329. Waldie's speech received no press attention, although it was an excellently documented exposé of the Phoenix interrogation techniques. The material on SOP-3 and the MACV directives about the Phoenix operation cited herein were taken from Waldie's speech. For a general description of the interrogation centers, see "The New Tiger Cages of Con Son," a statement by Representative William R. Anderson, Tennessee Democrat, in the *Congressional Record*, April 29, 1971, p. H3285.

The CIA's involvement in the My Lai 4 operations became one of the little publicized themes of the Calley court-martial. See "Calley Defense Asks Disclosure of Top-Secret Data on Songmy," United Press International, *New York Times*, August 25, 1970. Charles Weltner, the former Congressman and Atlanta attorney, also raised the issue a number of times during his defense of one of the My Lai 4 defendants, but never received any serious national attention. For the footnoted quote from Colby, see "U.S. Aide Defends Pacification Program in Vietnam Despite Killing of Civilians," by Felix Belair, Jr., *New York Times*, July 2, 1971, page 2. Patrick J. McGarvey, of suburban Washington, D.C., was interviewed by me on March 31, 1971, and many times thereafter.

Robert B. Ramsdell's secret testimony before the Peers Panel came on January 13, 1970; his offer then to join the Peers team as an investigator was not accepted. My interview with him took place on May 19, 1971, in his Orlando, Florida, office. Gerald Stout of Syracuse, New York, was interviewed by me on May 13 at the University of Syracuse law school; he did not testify before the Panel. Randolph L. Lane, who retired from the Army in 1970, was interviewed by me on May 19, 1971, in a restaurant near his Atlanta home; he had testified on February 20, 1970. Former Lieutenant Norman Freemyre, now a law student at the University of Colorado, was interviewed by telephone from his home in Boulder on May 21, 1971. Dr. Margaret Nelson's testimony about the Province Interrogation Center at Quang Ngai came during hearings July 17, 1970, before the Foreign Operations and Government Information Subcommittee of the Committee of Government Operations. The hearings, into "Conditions at Con Son Prison," were not published as of September, 1971, but Dr. Nelson's testimony is available from the subcommittee office.

Marine Captain Jon Fasnacht, by then retired, was interviewed by me in Orlando, Florida, on May 19, 1971. He did not appear before the Peers Panel. Jesse Frank Frosch's disguised assessment of Ramsdell was made in "Anatomy of a Massacre," *Playboy*, July, 1970. The cited province report for Quang Ngai appears as Exhibit R-14 in the Peers report. The footnoted account of the Quang Ngai City battle during Tet came from the classified "After-Action Report of the Attack on the Quang Ngai City Area," submitted to higher headquarters by the Quang Ngai intelligence team in February, 1968, and made available privately to me.

8. The Operation

Captain Brian W. Livingston testified on January 12, 1970; Scott A. Baker, then a resident of Carmichael, California, appeared five days later. Lieutenant James T. Cooney testified on January 9, 1970. Warrant Officer Robert W. Witham's appearance was on February 16, 1970. Warrant Officer (later Captain) Jerry R. Culverhouse gave his version of the My Lai 4 activities on January 10, 1970. Daniel R. Millians testified on December 11, 1969. Warrant Officer (later Captain) Hugh C. Thompson testified on three occasions before the Panel: December 3, 1969; January 6, 1970, and February 10. Major Robert W. McKnight initially testified on December 3, 1969; he chose to stop answering questions during his second appearance, February 12, 1970. Air Force Lieutenant Colonel William I. MacLachlan testified on January 31, 1970; he was ordered to reveal no details of his interrogation to Air Force officials. Specialist 5 Lawrence J. Kubert testified on January 15 and 16, 1970. Captain Thelmar A. Moe (footnote) testified on January 14, 1970; former Captain Randolph E. Sabre, then a patient at the Veterans Hospital in Denver, Colorado, appeared on January 16, 1970. The task force operations sergeant, William J. Johnson, now retired and living in Columbus, Georgia, testified twice before Peers, on December 18, 1969, and on February 9, 1970, without acknowledging that he ever had any clue that anything was amiss during the operation. Captain Charles L. Lewellen's testimony before the Peers Panel on December 23, 1969, included a detailed explanation of how and why he made his tape recording of the

radio traffic over My Lai 4. The tape eventually supplied by
Lewellen to the Panel had been edited and spliced onto a
larger reel. Peers and his team made two transcripts of the
tape, Exhibits M-20 and M-20A, the second of which was
annotated and revised by Lewellen to include sequence
numbers and estimated times. The 11th Brigade staff journal for March 16, 1968, was included in the Peers report as
Exhibit M-46. Former Captain Dennis R. Vazquez, then
living in Williamsburg, Virginia, testified two times before
Peers, on December 20, 1969, and February 9, 1970.
Former Lieutenant Roger L. Alaux, Jr., then living in
Tempe, Arizona, testified on January 6 and February 10,
1970. Colonel Mason J. Young, whose exchange with General Peers is footnoted, testified on January 16, 1970. The
footnoted discussion of radio transmissions over Charlie
Company's frequency was commented upon in an analysis
of the operation that appeared in Volume I of the Peers report, on page 10-7. The quote from Sergeant Lawrence C.
LaCroix appeared therein. Sergeant Thomas J. Kinch testified before Peers on January 21, 1970. Sergeant William E.
Watson, also of the mortar platoon, testified on January 21,
1970. The pilots of the 123rd Aviation Battalion told of
their refusal to fly in support of Task Force Barker during
the court-martial of Colonel Henderson: see "Pilot Cites
Threat to Halt Mylai Flight," by Douglas Robinson, *New
York Times*, September 18, 1971; and "Pilot Says He
Balked at Mylai," by Peter Braestrup, *Washington Post*,
September 18, 1971.

9. The Cover-Up Begins

Roy Kirkpatrick, the brigade operations sergeant, testified on January 30, 1970. Captain James A. Logan's appearances came on January 27 and 28, 1970. Sergeant Du

Thanh Hien's testimony was on January 2, 1970, and was taken in South Vietnam. Captain Gerald S. Walker gave his testimony on February 3, 1970. Lieutenant Colonel Francis Lewis testified on January 12, 1970, about his role in attempting to report the massacre. Captain Daniel A. Roberts testified about what he overheard on January 27 and 28, 1970. Captain James H. Henderson's recall of the cocktail conversation at Duc Pho after My Lai 4 was related to the Peers Panel on January 26, 1970. Former Captain Barry C. Lloyd, now living in Concord, California, gave his testimony on January 12, 1970. Lieutenant Colonel John L. Holladay testified about his key role in reporting the massacre on four occasions: December 9, 12, 22, and on February 10, 1970. He and Watke testified jointly on December 12 in an attempt to fix the chronology of the first reports. Captain Brian Livingston's letters to his wife were extracted and received in evidence by the Peers Panel as Exhibits M-21 and M-22.

10. The Day After

Brigadier General George H. Young testified on December 13, 1969, and February 17, 1970. A serious discrepancy over whether Koster talked with or personally visited Barker on the afternoon of March 17 was unresolved. In his testimony before the Panel, Koster mentioned that he questioned Barker about the report. Volume I of the Peers report said, without listing any additional evidence, that Koster visited with Barker. Task Force Barker's operations log for March 14 through 18, 1968, showing the day-by-day movement of Charlie and Bravo companies, was Exhibit M-16 in the Peers report. Warrant Officer Charles H. Mansell's testimony about his flight the day after My Lai 4 was made on January 9, 1971. There was no attempt by anyone on the Peers Panel to determine who ordered the flight. The specific weather conditions for March 17, 1968, were cited in the intelligence summary for the Americal Division for that day (number 76-68). The document was Exhibit R-22 in the Peers report. Former Captain Donald T. White, then living in Newport News, Virginia, testified on January 27, 1970. Henry E. Riddle, then living in Windsor, Missouri, testified on March 14, just two days before the close of the hearings. Former Sergeant Gregory Olsen's interview with me took place in November, 1969, when I was researching the *My Lai 4* book. The 11th Brigade intelligence summary for March 16, 1968, was Exhibit M-87 before the Peers Panel.

11. A Day of Denial

Major Watke's letter to his wife, then living in Columbus, Georgia, was Exhibit M-12 before the Peers Panel. It was dated March 18, 1968. Lieutenant John P. Newell's testimony about General Young's state of mind was given to the Peers Panel on February 19, 1971. Former door gunner Lawrence M. Colburn, of Mount Vernon, Washington, testified on December 20, 1969. Sergeant Jay A. Buchanon's recollection of the post-My Lai 4 interrogation of Charlie Company by Colonel Henderson was provided to the Peers Panel on January 8 and 9, 1970. David F. Meyer's statement to the C.I.D. was taken October 17, 1970, at Meyer's Manhattan Beach, California, home by agent Thomas J. Porter. Meyer has since moved. Sergeant Michael A. Bernhardt testified two times before the Peers Panel: December 29, 1969, and January 27, 1970. Major Glenn D. Gibson testified on December 10, 1969.

12. The First Reports

General William C. Westmoreland's telegram of congratulations to the Americal Division and Task Force Barker in the aftermath of My Lai 4, and General Koster's subsequent endorsement of the telegram appear many times in the Peers Exhibits—as M-7, M-89 and M-90. Koster's March 24 letter regarding "The Safeguarding of Noncombatants" is Exhibit M-9. Colonel Nels Parson's memorandum regarding the term "search and destroy" was dated April 13, 1968, and can be found on pages 79–80 in *Calley,* by Everett, Johnson and Rosenthal, cited earlier. Colonel Henderson's letter of commendation to Medina, which was not seriously discussed during the hearings, was dated March 27, 1968, and appears as Exhibit M-90. The subsequent awards to Medina were found in Americal Division records by the Army investigators. Barker's after-action report for My Lai 4 is Exhibit R-2 in the Peers report.

13. Those Who Knew

Lieutenant Colonel William D. Kelley, who was Calley's superior officer (footnote) after My Lai 4, testified on December 23, 1969. Lieutenant Colonel Edwin D. Beers testified twice, on December 23, 1969, and February 9, 1970. Captain Jerry W. Swenson (footnote) was interviewed May 20, 1971, at St. John's University in Collegeville, Minnesota, where he was a ROTC instructor. The quoted diary extract, dated May 3, 1968, appears as Exhibit M-86 in the Peers report. Major Harry P. Kissinger III told his anecdotes about Captain Medina to the Peers Panel on January 19, 1970. The unnamed lawyer's letter telling of his attempts to investigate the My Lai 4 massacre after a complaint by one of the Charlie Company GIs was privately made available to me by an Army source in Europe. Major Robert F. Comeau's denial of any knowledge of My Lai 4 came during his testimony February 19, 1969. Sergeant Clinton P. Stephens testified two times, on January 7 and February 9, 1970. The cited Army report on My Lai 4, "TF Barker Crushes Enemy Stronghold," appeared in the March 22, 1968, edition of *Trident*, the newspaper published by the 11th Infantry Brigade's public information office. Livingston's March 19, 1968, letter to his wife was excerpted by the Peers Panel and appears as Exhibit M-22. Captain Winston Gouzoules told the Panel on January 26, 1970, of his problems with the increasingly sensitive officers of Task Force Barker (footnote).

14. The Vietnamese

Do Dinh Luyen's testimony came on December 31, 1969, in South Vietnam. His oral report, as relayed by Lieutenant Tran Ngoc Tan, chief of Son Tinh District, was dated March 22, 1968, and appears as Exhibit M-49 in the Peers report. (Most of the Vietnamese documents cited herein were translated by Lieutenant Colonel Billy M. Stanberry of the U.S. Army, who aided the investigating team.) The March 18, 1968, census grievance report appears as Exhibit M-31. Major Donald R. Keating (footnote), who was known to most officials in Quang Ngai Province as an agent of the Central Intelligence Agency, testified on January 21, 1970; he was officially described as an assistant province aide for rural development. Maurice M. Prew (footnote), another employee of the CIA, testified on January 13, 1970, described as an employee of the Agency for International Development (AID). Lieutenant Colonel William D. Guinn testified on December 17, 1969; during his second appearance on February 11, 1970, he refused to answer questions.

Lieutenant Tan's March 28 report appears as Exhibit M-5 and again as M-28 (the document apparently was found in two offices in Vietnam by Peers researchers during their Christmas, 1969, visit). Former Captain Angel B. Rodriguez, then teaching school in Rio Piedras, Puerto Rico, testified on January 24, 1970. Rodriguez subsequently discussed by telephone some of the conflicting aspects of his testimony with Major H. L. Coop of the Peers Panel. He was not recalled as a witness. A copy of the National Liberation Front's propaganda leaflet appears as Exhibit M-34A; the document is entitled: "Concerning the Crimes Committed by U.S. Imperialists and Their Lackeys Who Killed More than 500 Civilians of Tinh Khe, Son Tinh [Tinh Khe is apparently the Viet Cong name for My Lai 4]." Two translations of the intercepted broadcasts were made for the Peers team and appear as Exhibits M-33 and M-36; the script is entitled "The American Devils Show Their True Form."

James A. May testified candidly and at length about his mixed feelings as the senior American province official; his appearances were on January 12 and February 17, 1970. Hugh Manke's footnoted comments were made to me during an interview on May 4, 1971, while Manke was in Washington conferring with officials of the International Voluntary Services. More information concerning the footnote dealing with Secretary of the Army Stanley R. Resor's decision to increase the importance of military advisers can be found in "Extra Pay for Viet Advisers Proposed," by Gene Famiglietti, *Army Times*, May 13, 1970.

Lieutenant Tan's third report, dated April 11, 1968, was found in at least two Quang Ngai files by Army investigators, and appears in the Peers report as Exhibits M-29 and M-34. Lieutenant Clarence J. Dawkins, the intelligence officer for Son Tinh District, testified on January 23, 1970. Lieutenant Colonel Ton That Khien testified on December 30, 1969, in Vietnam. He gave his subsequent statement to André C. R. Feher of the C.I.D. on November 15, 1969. Colonel Nguyen Van Toan testified on December 30, 1969, also in Vietnam. Major Pham Van Pho's memorandum to Colonel Toan was dated April 12, 1968, and appears as Exhibit M-36. Toan's answering message is scrawled on the document. Toan's subsequent interview with André Feher also took place on November 15, 1969. Captain Angel Rodriguez' controversial April 14, 1968, report to the Quang Ngai province advisory team—which later became attached to Colonel Henderson's official report—appears as Exhibit M-30. Lieutenant Colonel John Green (footnote) testified on January 14, 1970, about his doubts on the authenticity of the Rodriguez report. The Radio Hanoi broadcasts concerning the atrocities at My Lai 4 and My Khe 4, as translated and extracted by the CIA's Foreign Broadcast Information Service (FBIS), appear as Exhibit M-132. The broadcasts were made on April 16, April 23, June 2, 1968, and November 24, 1969, according to a military analysis. The initial broadcast April 16 was based on a commentary that was published in *Nhan Dan*, the Hanoi daily newspaper, describing a massacre "at Son My village in Son Tinh District, Quang Ngai Province, during which 501 persons, mostly aged people, women, and children, were slaughtered."

15. Ending the Inquiry

General Westmoreland's April 20 visit to the Duc Pho headquarters of the 11th Brigade was confirmed by the Pentagon on April 17, 1971: "Army Admits '68 Trip by Gen.

Westmoreland," *Washington Post.* Former Captain Richard J. Holbrook (footnote), then living in Orlando, Florida, told the Peers Panel how his cleaning woman overheard the Viet Cong propaganda broadcast during his testimony on January 31, 1970. Henderson's April 24, 1968, report of investigation was Exhibit R-1 before the Peers Panel. The carbon file copy of the report, found in Sergeant Gerberding's safe, became Exhibit R-5. General Koster's vacation in Hawaii lasted from April 28 until May 7, 1968; he reported for duty the next morning. The general's chronology was carefully charted by the Peers Panel and appears as Exhibit M-119 in the report. All of the American Division documents pertaining to the awards for Warrant Officer Hugh Thompson and his two crewmen were found by Peers investigators, and appear as Exhibit M-42 in the report. The House document cited in the footnote is the "Investigation of the My Lai Incident," a report of the Armed Services Investigating Subcommittee of the Committee on Armed Services, House of Representatives, July 15, 1970 (U.S. Government Printing Office, Washington, D.C., 1970). Thompson is criticized by the Congressmen for allegedly ordering his guns trained on Calley's troops, beginning on page 15, and also criticized, beginning on page 40, for his role in awarding the medals to his crew and accepting one for himself.

Robert T. Burke, the foreign service officer quoted in the footnote telling of Khien's June, 1968, investigation, testified on January 21, 1970. Colonel Khien's cited C.I.D. statements were those made November 15, 1969, to André Feher. A copy of a report on his investigations that was submitted by Khien on November 30, 1969, after the outcry over the massacre had begun in the United States, is attached to the Peers report as Exhibit R-33. Former Major

William Ford, then living in College Park, Maryland, testified on January 22, 1970.

16. The Missing Files

A copy of General Westmoreland's statement before the House Armed Services Investigating Subcommittee was made available privately to me. Colonel Howard K. Whitaker's testimony took place on January 26, 1970; his earlier report to the inspector general, dated April 17, 1969, became Exhibit M-98 in the Peers report. See my previous book, *My Lai 4*, for an account of Colonel William V. Wilson's early investigation into the massacre. The Peers Panel spent weeks searching through all of the Americal Division records and materials on file or stored in the United States or Southeastern Asia in a vain attempt to locate the missing reports.

Sergeant Kenneth E. Camell's testimony was provided on January 30 and 31, 1970. Colonel John W. Donaldson's back-channel message to Colonel Henderson advising him that the My Lai 4 report could not be found was dated May 23, 1969, and became Exhibit M-101 in the Peers report. Henderson's letter to Colonel Wilson, with the subsequently discovered report, was dated June 2, 1969; a copy of it also was made available to the Peers Panel. A transcript of Lieutenant Colonel Barney L. Brannen, Jr.'s, testimony September 9, 1970, before General Koster's closed Article 32 hearing at Fort Meade, Maryland, was privately made available to me. Two other witnesses during the pre-trial hearing confirmed some aspects of Brannen's story. Michael DeFilipo, Jr., of Johnston, Rhode Island, told the hearing on September 22, 1970, that he had typed the May, 1968, formal investigation of My Lai 4—the one prepared by Lieutenant Colonel Frank Barker—while serving as a clerk in the 11th Brigade headquarters at Duc Pho. DeFilipo had never been contacted by the Peers Panel. Another witness, described only as Chief Warrant Officer Battig, identified himself as Brannen's chief administrative aide during his testimony September 9, 1970, and confirmed that he had carefully and unsuccessfully searched the judge advocate's office to seek the formal investigation, as Brannen claimed. Donaldson's testimony was given on September 14, 1970; that transcript also was made available to me. Bruce Brown was interviewed by me on May 12, 1971, at his home in Hay, Kansas. Formal murder charges were filed against General Donaldson on June 2, 1971. For a detailed story on Donaldson's background, see "Donaldson Was Viet Hero," by Orr Kelly, *Washington Evening Star*, June 9, 1971.

17. The Pentagon Investigates

See *My Lai 4* and *One Morning in the War* for details of the Army's first press release, the Pentagon's fears about it, and the events prior to the public disclosure of the atrocity. Information about the inner working of the Pentagon in those days came from a series of interviews with officials and Army men who requested anonymity. The Koster memorandum about his telephone calls to Colonel Henderson, cited in the footnote, became Exhibit M-129 in the Peers report. The Army's announcement on August 13, 1971, of General Peers' new assignment in Korea (footnote) rated only a few paragraphs in most newspapers: see "Mylai Prober Going to Korea," United Press International in the *Washington Post*, August 14, 1971. For some examples of Congressional hostility to the initial Peers Panel announcement, see "Army Will Review Study of '68 on Alleged Killings," by Robert M. Smith, *New York Times*, November 25, 1969. Henry A. Kissinger's classified memorandum regarding atrocity stories was numbered 6641 in the Pentagon security files and dated December 8, 1969; it was provided to me by a military source. The Pentagon's December, 1969, concern over the Congressional and other criticisms about its investigating panel was clearly spelled out in "Pentagon Shies from Whitewash in My Lai Probe," by Patrick J. Sloyan, *Baltimore News-American*, December 11, 1969. The Congressional proposal for a fifteen-member commission to study the My Lai 4 massacre was filed as House Resolution 15319 and signed by twenty-five House liberals, including Representative Robert L. Leggett, a California Democrat who is a member of the House Armed Services Committee.

For an example of Dr. Alje Vennema's public criticism of the Army, see "Atrocities Common," *London Times*, January 11, 1970. The reduction of the life sentence for Lieutenant William Calley, Jr., was announced on August 20, 1971, by Lieutenant General Albert O. Connor, commander of the Third Army: See "Army Reduces Calley's Term to 20 Years," by Peter Braestrup, *Washington Post*, August 21, 1971. The footnoted list of Vietnam cases involving premeditated murder was compiled by Commander Maitland G. Freed of the Navy's Judge Advocate General's office in the Navy Building, Washington, D.C. For an excellent discussion of the "Mere Gook Rule," see " 'Mere Gook Rule' Haunts Calley Trial," by William Greider of the *Washington Post*, March 14, 1971. Greider's day-by-day coverage of Calley's court-martial was superior. The "Mere Gook Rule" is also cited in "U.S. War Crimes: The Guilt at the Top," by Robert C. Johansen, *Progressive* magazine, June, 1971. The text of General Peers' briefing to the closed meeting of the House Armed Services investigating subcommittee was privately made available to me. Lieutenant Colonel Anthony B. Herbert's charges against two fellow officers received a great deal of publicity early in 1971: see any major newspaper for March 15 and 16, 1971. Herbert made three separate statements to the C.I.D. on November 4 and 5, 1970, seeking to provoke that agency into an investigation. The statements were given to Elmer E. Snyder, a C.I.D. investigator, and witnessed by two C.I.D. officers, Lieutenant Colonel Ferdinand Kelley and Major Carl B. Hensley (Hensley later committed suicide, an action that Herbert claimed—amid official denials—was prompted in part by his investigation into the charges). All three C.I.D. statements were made available in full to me. For the dropping of charges against Major General Barnes, see "War Crimes Coverup Case Dismissed," by Fred Farrar, *Chicago Tribune*, July 22, 1971. Barnes' promotion after the filing of charges against him was revealed by Morton Kondracke of the *Chicago Sun-Times*; see "Officer Promoted During Viet Probe," *Washington Post*, June 7, 1971, for the Associated Press version of the story. Peers' "eyes only" message regarding Bravo Company's massacre of the My Khe 4 residents was seen by only four offices in the Pentagon: those of the Chief of Staff, secretary of the general staff, Army Provost Marshal, and Peers' own investigating unit.

The Army fact sheet cited in the footnote was dated April 2, 1971, and simply titled a "Department of the Army Fact Sheet on the Son My Incident." It received much press coverage. The memorandum from Secretary of Defense Melvin A. Laird also cited in the footnote was made available privately to me. Many of the Peers Panel internal memorandums also were made available to me. Typical of the press accounts about the expanded investigation was "My Lai Panel Widens Probe to Actions of 2nd Company," by Orr Kelly, *Washington Evening Star*, February 4, 1970.

The charges against then Captain Thomas K. Willingham made the front pages: see "Murders at Songmy Charged to Officer with 2nd Company," *New York Times*, February 13,

1971. Yet the NBC interviews with survivors six days later was routinely handled: see "NBC Report Says 100 Murdered Near Mylai," United Press International in the *Washington Post*, February 19, 1970. The most thorough coverage of the Peers Panel charges against Major General Koster and the others was given by the *New York Times*: see "Army Inquiry Charges 14 Officers in Suppression of Songmy Facts; West Point's Head, Accused, Quits," by William Beecher, March 18, 1970. For the Army's predictable response to the outcry over the Peers report, see "Army Acts to Prevent 'Cover-Ups,' " by Orr Kelly, *Washington Evening Star*, March 18, 1970.

18. The System Prevails

The popular "mustang" theory espoused to explain away My Lai 4 in the upper reaches of the Pentagon may have some basis, but the suggestion that a West Point or similar service academy graduate would have behaved more suitably during or after My Lai 4 was sharply challenged by a random survey and comparison of the attitudes of ROTC officers, military academy graduates, and non-ROTC college undergraduates which was published in the Spring, 1971, issue of *Foreign Policy* magazine. Entitled "ROTC, Mylai, and the Volunteer Army: Citizen Soldiers Against Professionals," the survey reported that "service academy students were consistently more aggressive and absolutistic than either the ROTC or non-ROTC groups." Similarly, the eight authors of the paper reported, "One conclusion is that those critics of ROTC who have suggested that 'an officer trained at Princeton kills as quickly on orders as an officer trained at the Point' are probably incorrect." The article was placed into the *Congressional Record* on March 15,

1971, by Representative Donald M. Fraser, Minnesota Democrat, p. E1871.

For an explanation of the revised charges against Captain Ernest Medina, see "New Charges Blame Medina for All Deaths at My Lai," by Muriel Dobbin, *Baltimore Sun*, April 2, 1970. The dropping of charges against Captain Thomas Willingham attracted little press attention: see "One Freed in My Lai Army Case," by Fred Farrar, *Chicago Tribune*, June 10, 1970, for one of the most complete accounts. The dropping of charges against General George Young, Colonel Nels Parson, and Major Robert McKnight was a one-day front-page newspaper story: for example, see "Officers Exonerated by Army on Songmy Cover-Up Charges," *New York Times*, June 24, 1970. Colonel John P. Stafford's legal memorandum on Young's case was made available privately to me. Secretary of Army Stanley Resor's brief outlining of his reasons for stripping both Generals Young and Koster of their medals, and demoting Koster in rank to a brigadier general, were contained in a nine-page statement his office issued on May 19, 1971. Both the *New York Times* and *Washington Post* reported the censure on the front page on May 20, 1971. General Seaman's announcement dropping charges against two more officers but holding seven others for pre-trial hearings was reported in full by the press: see "7 Army Officers Face a Further Inquiry on Songmy," *New York Times*, July 29, 1970. The dropping of charges against four more officers on January 6, 1971, was similarly well-reported, although few newspapers raised any editorial objections to the move. The continuing My Lai 4 story—by then nearly two years old—flared again in late January when the dropping of charges against General Koster was announced. See "General Cleared of Mylai Charges," by Fred P. Graham, *New York Times*, January

30, 1971. Attorney Robert MacCrate's critical reaction was given to the *Times* and published in the same dispatch. Major General B. V. Evans' memorandum concerning the dismissal of charges was privately given to me.

The rationale and chronology of Representative Samuel S. Stratton's attack on the decision to release Koster can be found in his speech made to the House: "The Case Against Maj. Gen. Samuel W. Koster," published in the *Congressional Record*, February 4, 1971, pp. H445–50. For an account of the filing of charges against Colonel Henderson, see "Colonel Faces Mylai Trial Over Charges of Cover-Up," by Richard Halloran, *New York Times*, February 27, 1971. The dropping of charges against Captain Dennis H. Johnson was briefly mentioned in the story. Army Secretary Robert F. Froehlke's decision to censure nine men in connection with their activities at My Lai 4 (footnote) was initially reported by Robert Dobkin of the Associated Press: see "Army Will Punish 9 in Mylai Affair," AP in the *New York Times*, August 18, 1971.

Congressman Stratton's *New York Times* article was "The Army and General Koster," published on March 8, 1971. By then, there were only a few critics of the move, although at least one was normally a pro-military columnist. See two articles by Robert D. Heinl, Jr., a retired Marine Corps colonel and columnist for the North American Newspaper Alliance: "Army's Nonprosecution of Koster a 'Grave Judicial Miscarriage,' " *Omaha World-Herald*, February 14, 1971, and "Lieut. Calley and General Koster," *Philadelphia Bulletin,* April 4, 1971.

Warrant Officer Hugh Thompson's testimony before the Henderson court-martial came on September 21, 1971. Jerry Culverhouse testified on September 17, and Lawrence Colburn on October 6, 1971. Charles Whiteford of the *Baltimore Sun,* Peter Braestrup of the *Washington Post,* and

Douglas Robinson of the *New York Times* each provided daily coverage of the court-martial. For a good analysis of some of the deeper issues raised by the trial, see "A Lesson on Flaws in the Army's Command System," by Braestrup, *Washington Post,* October 25, 1971.

Index

SEYMOUR M. HERSH is the author of *My Lai 4: A Report on the Massacre and Its Aftermath* and *Chemical and Biological Warfare: America's Hidden Arsenal.* His reporting of the My Lai 4 massacre in 1969 earned him the 1970 Pulitzer Prize for International Reporting and many other top journalism awards, including a 1970 George Polk Memorial Award and the Distinguished Service Award of Sigma Delta Chi. He covered the Pentagon for the Associated Press and served as press secretary and speechwriter for Senator Eugene J. McCarthy during the 1968 Presidential campaign. He is thirty-four, and lives with his wife and two children in Washington, D.C.